Ernest Logan.

PASTOR E. LOGAN

**QUESTIONS
ANSWERED**

QUESTIONS ANSWERED

GATHERED FROM THE
QUESTION CORNER DEPARTMENT
OF THE "SIGNS OF THE TIMES"

By MILTON C. WILCOX

*"Stand ye in the ways, and see, and ask
for the old paths, where is the good way,
and walk therein, and ye shall find rest
for your souls."*

PACIFIC PRESS PUBLISHING ASSOCIATION
MOUNTAIN VIEW, CALIFORNIA
Omaha, Nebraska   Cristobal, Canal Zone   Portland, Oregon

TABLE OF CONTENTS

A FOREWORD

Surely we have reached a day when the imperative need is for a deeper knowledge of the Scriptures and the truths therein contained. We have tried almost every human suggestion for the betterment of mankind, and yet we find ourselves baffled at every turn by problems apparently insoluble. In such a time as this, should we not go back to God's revelation in the Bible, and make diligent search there for principles that will guide us through the turbulent and perplexing days that lie ahead before our Lord shall come?

This volume is offered to help you in your study of the Scriptures. The material first appeared in that great religious weekly, the *Signs of the Times,* when it was so ably edited by Milton C. Wilcox, recently gone to his rest.

The answers given to actual questions then sent in to the editor make no pretense to infallibility. In the search for truth sorry indeed is the man who believes he knows it all, for "the path of the righteous is as the *dawning light,* that shineth more and more unto the perfect day." Prov. 4:18, A. R. V. The answers are intended to inspire you to delve further into your own Bible, rather than to be taken as ex-cathedra, dogmatic, and inflexible assertions.

May God richly bless you as you open the pages of this book, and study your Bible with new interest and stimulation.

THE PUBLISHERS.

*Throughout this book, unless other-
wise noted, the texts used are from
the King James and the Revised
Versions of the Bible, the author using the wording which most clearly
conveys the thought in present-day
diction.*

THE BIBLE

When Was the Bible Compiled?

The Old Testament canon was compiled under the direction of Ezra and Nehemiah. Of the New Testament it may be said that from the days of the apostles the Gospels and Epistles were read in the churches, and generally received. "We possess in the Latin Fragment, published by Muratori in 1740, something like a full list of the New Testament Scriptures from a writer who describes himself as contemporary with Pius, Bishop of Rome about 150 A. D. A similar list may be made out from the Syriac Version, which can hardly be later than the second century. . . . The great Athanasius [296–373 A. D.] enumerates unhesitatingly all the Scriptures of the New Testament as we have them now; and so do the Latin 'fathers' Augustine and Jerome."—*S. S. Teacher's Combination Bible Helps, section 14, page 34.* In the Sinaitic MS. of the fourth century, the New Testament is entire. The books of the New Testament were all received as they were written, but it took some little time to bring them all together.

Is Any Part of the Bible Obsolete?

How much of the Bible is done away? Is it to be accepted in its entirety by men today?

The whole Bible is for man now. Every part has its lesson for these days, though not all its laws are binding. To illustrate: God commanded men to offer sacrifices of different kinds for different purposes. He does not now ask us to offer these sacrifices, for they have all been met in Christ Jesus. Yet from each of these sacrificial laws we may learn important lessons concerning God's requirements, our duty, God's love, and Christ's offering. The sin offering, the trespass offering, the burnt offering, the peace offering, teach precious lessons of how repulsive sin should be in our sight,

9

how utterly we should renounce it, how great and effectual are God's love and grace. The injunction to circumcise is not now binding; but the very law and the circumstances of its giving show how absolutely we should put off the domination of the body, of the flesh. Some of these laws expired by limitation; but the lessons of the laws, and the conditions which called them forth, still abide. For example, it is no one's duty to warn now of a coming deluge, but the lesson of the Deluge still remains. There are many other illustrations. But one law forever abides, God's great Constitution, Heaven's Magna Charta, summarily comprehended in the Ten Commandments; and the only Saviour from sin is Jesus Christ our Lord.

Effect of Multiplied Translations.

> Are not the different versions of the Bible, with their different renderings, likely to engender doubt as to the inspiration and reliability of any of them?

It does not so seem to us, any more than does the rendering of the Scriptures into almost one thousand languages and dialects into which they have been translated. To us it confirms the Scriptures. All the differences that there are in all the various renderings into English do not in any way change the teaching of the Bible. They may alter some texts. A better rendering may show that some text which has been used to support some doctrine does not support it; and yet if the doctrine is worthy of support, there will be other scriptures sufficient, or the general teaching of the Bible will support it.

The whole aim of the child of God ought not to be to desire a translation that is in harmony with his views; his whole soul ought to go out into the question, What does the Father say in His word? And the best translation that he could get from the earlier copies ought to be the one which would best satisfy?

The King James, or Authorized Version, was translated from what would be called late copies of the original; that is, copies of copies of copies for centuries. The American Revised Version has been compared with the very earliest original copies which have been found. This is especially true of the New Testament. These copies clearly show that they were very early copies, much nearer the time of our Lord. One was found, for instance, in a convent near Mount Sinai; another one in the Vatican in Rome; another in Alexandria, Egypt; all entirely different copies, one not copied from the other, and each confirming the other. Indeed, all the great New Testament manuscripts have been unearthed since the Authorized Version was put out in 1611.

Every additional copy of this kind, every additional good translation, confirms the Scriptures of truth, leads some to read who might not otherwise read, and tends to spread abroad the knowledge and glory of God.

It is not difficult to imagine how we would feel if we were to receive a letter from a dear relative who had left us a large fortune on certain conditions; that letter written in the Bengali language, for instance, or the Sanskrit, a language of which we are totally ignorant. That letter had been copied several times before it reached us, our copy perhaps being the fifteenth or twentieth which had been made. Naturally we would go to the best scholar we knew to get a translation. That translation furnishes us very much satisfaction and joy; but it leaves some doubts, we are not clear in regard to the meaning of some passages. We find that there are earlier copies, copies which are nearer the time of the writing of that letter. We search and find those; we take them to still other scholars. The translation of these earlier copies confirms us all the more in the blessings and bounties which came to us through that letter. We learn of still earlier copies, of still better masters of the language in which the letter was written. Again we obtain a translation. We find different rendering sometimes, very minor differences; but in all the great things of which the letter speaks, there is no difference. Would any of these translations lead us to doubt? Nay, but each would confirm all the others, and all would confirm and establish our faith that the letter was what it purported to be, and that the message which it brought to us was in every wise genuine.

The Scripture Canon.

When, by whom, and by what authority, whether by church or by state, were the original manuscripts collected and compiled and dedicated to the world as the word of God? What means were used to separate the inspired from the uninspired, and to decide concerning the various parts of our Bible?

The Bible is a growth. It is not the product of one man or a council or a decree from some human authority. For instance, the Pentateuch, the five books of Moses, was accepted by God's people to the time of Christ. God's law in that book constituted the test of later prophets and their writings. One book after another was added till we come to the close of Old Testament times. After the Babylonian captivity, all the books over which there was no question, which were generally accepted, were collated and arranged by Ezra, Nehemiah, and their colaborers. These were the Holy Scriptures in the time of our Lord. They are referred to by Josephus, in "Against Apion," and are everywhere approved by Jesus. The New Testament was added in the same way, book by book, epistle by epistle, from men filled by the Spirit of God, and bearing the eternal test, "To the law and to the testimony." Before any council acted upon the Scripture canon, as early as 170 A. D., practically all the books as we now have them were accepted as according to the Scripture rule by the early church, while as many others were rejected. Clement, Polycarp, Justin Martyr, Origen, and others mention different books. The famous "Muratorian Fragment on the Canon" (170 A. D.) mentions nearly all the books of the New Testament. It mentions the Gospels of Luke and John, the Acts, the thirteen epistles of Paul, 1 and 2 John, Jude, the Revelation. It omits several that are mentioned by others. The Peshito Syriac list of about the same age includes all except 2 Peter, 2 and 3 John, Jude, and the Revelation. The old Italian version, of about the same time, the Bible used by the North African churches, contained all our New Testament books except Hebrews, 2 Peter, and James. Later church councils confirmed our present list, and added others rejected by earlier Christians.

Facts Regarding the Bible.

Do you consider the whole Bible written by inspiration? Some of our teachers say that only part of it is inspired.

We have no reason to regard any part of the Bible as more inspired than any other parts. Concerning the Old Testament Scriptures, the Scriptures that were in existence in the days of the apostle Paul—for the New Testament was not written then—we read, "*All* Scripture is given by inspiration of God,"—literally, "God-breathed." 2 Tim. 3:16. We do not understand by this, however, that the translation is inspired, but the original Scriptures are inspired. The translation is simply turning the Scriptures into another language. In Acts 1:16, in referring to the Psalms, the apostle does not say that they were David's words, but "The Holy Spirit spake before by the mouth of David." The same thought is expressed in Hebrews 3:7. Peter tells us that "holy men of God spake as they were moved by the Holy Ghost." 2 Peter 1:21. The apostle Paul says of his own writings, "Which things also we speak, not in words which man's wisdom teacheth, but which the Spirit teacheth." 1 Cor. 2:13.

In many instances, inspiration records the words of others; and many times the words of others recorded in the Scriptures are not inspiration. For instance, we read in Genesis 3 that Satan said so and so. Satan's words were not God-breathed, but the record that tells us about them is. So in the case of some of Job's friends. They said many good things. They made wrong application of the good things. Their words were not necessarily inspired, but the record that gives their words is inspired.

If man were to judge as to what is inspired and what is not inspired, in a little while all the word of God would be set aside. Whatever did not agree with him, or with his judgment, or with his tastes, or with his desires, would be set aside as not of inspiration. Others would reject other parts, until nothing would be left of the Bible but the covers. Better it is, it seems to us, to regard the word even as our Lord Jesus Christ did. He ever spoke of it reverently. He never questioned. He quoted from Isaiah and Jeremiah, from the Psalms, from Moses; but He always regarded it as the word of God.

The Apocrypha.

> Upon what authority were the books of the Apocrypha eliminated from the Scriptures and rated as secular, while the rest are rated as inspired?

The books of the Apocrypha were not in the Jewish Scriptures that were held to be sacred,—the Scriptures that Jesus learned.

They sprang out of that time in the Jewish church concededly after prophets had ceased; that is, after Malachi.

They were not written in the Hebrew language.

Their style, their character, their teaching, are not up to the standard of the law and the testimony. This is evident to any devout Bible reader.

They are considered valuable as throwing light upon the time that produced them, and the books of Maccabees are valuable as history.

Catholic Version of the Bible.

> I would like to know where I can secure a copy of the "Vatican version" of the Bible, or how I can find out what it says on certain scriptures. I would like especially to know how it translates Matthew 28:19.

There were numerous Latin versions of the Scriptures in the early centuries, and some of them were not considered as satisfactory reproductions of the original text; so in the latter part of the fourth century and the first part of the fifth, Jerome, who was reckoned as an accomplished scholar, undertook the careful translation of the Scriptures into the Latin. His first translations of the Old Testament were from the Septuagint; but these met with criticism, and he finally undertook the work of making a more careful translation into the Latin from the original Hebrew. Jerome's Vulgate translation came to be the standard of the Catholic Church, having been finally adopted by the Council of Trent. Some of the earliest English translations were made from this Latin text. When the Reformation was at its height, the Catholic Church concluded that it was necessary for them to make a translation of the Scriptures into the English. This was begun at the college in Douay, in Flanders. The college for a time was driven from Douay to Reims; and while it was at Reims, the New Testament was published; hence the name, "The Reims New Testament." The college finally returned to Douay, and the complete Bible was published. The Douay is the authoritative Catholic version of the English Bible. It may be purchased at almost any large bookstore.

In the Douay Version, Matthew 28:19 reads, "Going therefore, teach ye all nations; baptizing them in the name of the Father, and of the Son, and of the Holy Ghost." It will be seen that that text does not materially differ from the translation in our Authorized Version; and the same is true, in the main, throughout the Bible.

Difference in Versions. 1 John 5:7, 8.

The King James Version renders 1 John 5:7, 8: "There are three that bear record in heaven, the Father, the Word, and the Holy Ghost: and these three are one. And there are three that bear witness in earth, the Spirit, and the water, and the blood: and these three agree in one." But the American Revised Version reads thus: "It is the Spirit that beareth witness, because the Spirit is the truth. For there are three who bear witness, the Spirit, and the water, and the blood: and the three agree in one." Why is the difference? Was something added in the one, or was it left out in the other?

There are a few very slight differences in the various original manuscripts that have been preserved of the different books of the Bible; and this is one of those places where a difference occurs. Some of the best Greek manuscripts have it as translated in the King James Version, while others have it as it is given in the Revised. Boothroyd's and Rotherham's Translations both omit verse 7. The Syriac retains the verse in the original, but encloses it in brackets. So also does Young's.

But the marvelous thing to the student of the Bible is that there are so few differences in these original manuscripts, and that none of these differences are really essential. Whether you follow the King James Version or the Revised, in this text or in any other, you get practically the same great truth. There is nothing in this text, in either one of these versions, but that is abundantly and clearly taught in other portions of the Sacred Word.

God's great Book was copied by hundreds of hands, into many languages, during the first centuries of the Christian era. These original manuscripts, in all these various tongues, as they have been passed on to us, are in substantial agreement. There is no disagreement that amounts to a contradiction. This shows the miraculous care that God has had for His word. No other book has passed through such an ordeal and come out with such a clear testimony. The way in which the Book has been preserved shows that it is divine.

It will be found not only profitable but intensely interesting to secure and read Dr. Gaussen's "Inspiration of the Bible." Another volume which gives the background and history of all the versions is "The Ancestry of Our English Bible," by Ira M. Price, Ph. D. The evidence that God's word has been miraculously preserved is of the clearest character.   A. O. T.

Reading the Old Testament Scriptures.

Should we not read the Old Testament?

Most certainly we should read the Old Testament Scriptures. The Master says, "Search the Scriptures; for in them ye think ye have eternal life: and they are they which testify of Me." John 5:39. When the Master made that statement, the only Scriptures in existence were the Old Testament writings. When He was on the way to Emmaus with two of His disciples, after His crucifixion and resurrection, He told them: "These are the words which I spake unto you, while I was yet with you, that all things must be fulfilled, which were written in the law of Moses, and in the prophets, and in the Psalms, concerning Me. Then opened He their understanding, that they might understand the Scriptures, and said unto them, Thus it is written, and thus it behooved Christ to suffer, and to rise from the dead the third day." Luke 24:44-46. Christ taught the Scriptures that were written by Moses, and by the prophets, and by David, and by the others who wrote the Psalms. This example and teaching of Christ were after His resurrection, and therefore unquestionably in the new dispensation. It is always safe to follow the example of the Great Pattern.

The End and the Beginning.

Will you please explain Zechariah 14:16-21?

It is impossible to take a few passages of Scripture, especially some of the obscure prophecies of the Old Testament, and make them clear in and of themselves. In all the great promises of God, it is well for us to remember what the apostle says in Ephesians 3:3-6,—that in time past these things were not understood as they were revealed later to the apostles and prophets by God's Spirit; and it is only in the light of the clearer later revelations that we may read the prophecies of God to His people in the past.

Some of those prophecies were fulfilled to Israel in the restoration of Jerusalem and the return from Babylon. Some of them were dependent upon conditions. See the conditions stated in Jeremiah 18:7-10, and elsewhere. If Israel complied with the conditions, the promises were theirs. If they failed to comply, certainly they could not ask God to fulfill His part.

Some of the prophecies, if fulfilled at all, must be fulfilled in harmony with the conditions of the new covenant, in times when all types had passed away. The book of Zechariah contains prophecies of these types. The passage under question points to that time when God's children have gained complete victory over all their foes, and the end of sin has come, and the beginning of the reign of righteousness is inaugurated. Other passages tell us how all the nations will come up against Jerusalem to fight.

Those who are left of all the nations will be God's remnant He has gathered out, and they will go from year to year to worship the King, the Lord of hosts. All the families that will not come up— carrying us back just a little to the time when the invitation was abroad—upon them the latter rain of God's Spirit will not fall. They shall perish. Though they may belong to some great nation, like Egypt, and have received great light, they shall be smitten with the plagues.

On the other hand, in God's service in that future time, there will be holiness; even everything that takes part in that service will be holy. Then in the service of God that shall follow throughout eternity there shall come in no more corruption. The Canaanites had crept in among the children of Israel. See Ezra and Nehemiah to show how corruption had come into the very service of the temple. But that would be so no more in the glorious reign that lies before. The passage itself shows that the long reign of sin will end, and only those will have part in the reign of righteousness who have met God's conditions.

Judas Maccabeus.

Who was Judas Maccabeus? And are the books of the Maccabees a part of Scripture?

The Maccabees are sometimes called Hasmoneans, and sometimes Asmoneans, from Hashmon, the great-grandfather of Mattathias. But the family received their name from the title given to Judas, the third son of Mattathias. He was called Judas Maccabeus, that is, Judas the Hammerer, because of his vigorous assaults upon the Syrians. The title gradually included all the members of the family of Mattathias and their descendants. The family came into leadership against the attempt of Antiochus Epiphanes to force Greek worship upon the Jews in the years 175 to 164 B. C. The revolt arose in the little town of Modin, where Mattathias and his five sons were living. The idolatrous altar was overturned, and Mattathias and his five sons were forced to flee to the mountains. In the year 167 B. C. the leadership was committed to Judas; and, under the loyal Jews who supported him, he won victory after victory, and three years afterward restored the temple worship. Then he began to fight for political independence, and at last fell in the Battle of Eleasa in the year 161 B. C. His brother Jonathan succeeded him. They were in a way kings, and yet later more or less dependent upon Rome. The books of the Maccabees relate the history of those times. They are not considered as inspired Scriptures. In one place prayer for the dead is spoken of; but even the translation of this is questionable. They were doubtless brave, loyal men. Especially was this true of Judas; but they are in nowise guides for us in theology, nor are the writings to be taken as inspired Scripture.

Is Revelation 20:5 Spurious?

The first sentence of Revelation 20:5, "The rest of the dead lived not again until the thousand years were finished," is by some said to be spurious, not being found in the earliest manuscripts, or before the fourth century. What ground is there for this?

We reply in brief: The earliest New Testament manuscripts are as follows: 1. The *Codex Sinaiticus,* now in the British Museum in London. It contains the whole of the New Testament. It was discovered by Tischendorf in the monastery of St. Catherine, on Mount Sinai, in 1859. It was written, in all probability, in the fourth century, not later than the fifth. It once contained the whole Bible.

2. The *Codex Alexandrinus,* now in the British Museum, written in the fifth century. It contains the whole Bible.

3. The *Codex Vaticanus,* now in the Vatican, known also as Vatican MS. No. 1209. It was probably written in the latter part of the fourth century or in the fifth. It contains the whole Bible, with exceptions of parts of the New Testament, among which is the Apocalypse.

4. The *Codex Ephraemi Rescriptus.* This is what is called a "palimpsest," the original writing of which has been erased in order to use the parchment for another. In this manuscript part of a Greek Bible was used on which to write some of the works of

Ephraem, a Syrian "father." (So have the "fathers" in other instances obliterated the word.) But by chemical reagents the old writing has been partially restored. It was written in the fifth century, and contains about two thirds of the New Testament.

5. Then we have the Peshito Syriac version; but some scholars contend that "there were no [Syriac] copies extant which were written so early as the oldest of the Greek manuscripts."

Now of the above, Revelation 20:5 is found in the first, we believe, and in the second and fourth. The third does not contain the Revelation at all. The Syriac omits the passage, and so does Vatican MS. No. 1160, of the eleventh century. Thus the three oldest Greek copies which contain the Revelation at all have the text. The Emphatic Diaglott, based on Griesbach's text, has the following footnote on the first part of Revelation 20:5: "These words were probably omitted by oversight in Vatican MS. [No. 1160] as they are found in A, B, C, though not in the Syriac." By "A" is meant *Codex Alexandrinus;* by "B," *Codex Vaticanus,* No. 2066, of the seventh or eighth century; by "C," *Codex Ephraemi Rescriptus.* Finally, the best Greek text, that of Westcott and Hort, contains the passage; and neither have the Revised Versions nor any of the critics, so far as we know, even questioned it. The revisers adopted for their revision the text "for which the evidence is decidedly preponderating;" and when that differed from the Greek text "from which the Authorized Version was made, the alteration be expressed in the margin." (See Preface to Revised New Testament, Division II, par. 4.) But there is not even an indication of doubt over Revelation 20:5. The clause in question is considered spurious only by those who have a doctrine to prove which the text condemns.

"The Book of Jasher." Joshua 10:13.

How could the record of the sun's standing still be written in the book of Jasher before it occurred? Who wrote the book of Jasher, and where can I obtain it?

Joshua was not written till several years after the events occurred related in chapter 10. In the meantime the song in the poetical book of Jasher may have been written, from which Joshua quotes. The word "Jasher" means "The Upright;" and the book seems to have been one in which Israel recorded in song the deeds of her heroes. See reference to it also in 2 Samuel 1:18. That book, as well as others referred to in the Bible, is not now known to exist. There are four works extant, claiming to be the book of Jasher, appearing respectively in 1394, 1544, 1625, and 1751. Of the last, Smith's Dictionary remarks: "A clumsy forgery in English, which first appeared in 1751, under the title of the 'Book of Jasher,' deserves notice solely for the *unmerited* success with which it was palmed off upon the public."

References in the Revised Version.

I have an American Standard Revised edition of the Bible, and there are some things in the reference column I cannot understand. The first place the difficulty appears is in Matthew 1:1. After the reference to Isaiah 9:6, is the letter "f.," in small type; then in Matthew 1:7, after reference to 1 Chronicles 3:10, is a double "f." (ff.).

Surely, when we have a good tool or machine, we ought to know how to use it. The letter "f." after a Scripture reference means that the verse next following is included; as, for example, "Isaiah 9:6 f." means Isaiah 9:6, 7. The "f." takes less space than the figure "7" and the comma. The double "f." (ff.) means verses (plural) which immediately follow the reference; that is, all the verses which follow and pertain to the subject. For instance, "1 Chronicles 3:10 ff." means "1 Chronicles 3:10-24," the genealogy of one line of Solomon down through the Captivity to Ezra's time.

Interesting Facts About the Bible.

The Bible has 66 books; 39 in the Old Testament, 27 in the New. It has 1,189 chapters; 929 in the Old Testament, 260 in the New. It has 31,173 verses; 23,214 in the Old Testament, 7,959 in the New. The Apocrypha has 14 books, 183 chapters, 6,081 verses. The middle verses of the Old Testament are 2 Chronicles 20:17, 18; of the

New Testament, Acts 17:17; of the Bible, Psalm 118:8. The original language of the Old Testament is Hebrew, with the exception of Ezra 4:8 to 6:18 and 7:12-26; Jeremiah 10:11; Daniel 2:4 to 7:28, which are Chaldean. The New Testament is Greek, not the classical Greek of the scholars, but the Greek used in everyday conversation.

"Fountains" and "Traditions."

> Please explain the following scriptures:
> "My people have committed two evils; they have forsaken Me the fountain of living waters, and hewed them out cisterns, broken cisterns, that can hold no water." Jer. 2:13. "Therefore, brethren, stand fast, and hold the traditions which ye have been taught, whether by word, or our epistle." 2 Thess. 2:15.

Read the context. It meant with Israel of old that they had not only forsaken God, the Living Fountain, but had gone after other gods, which could be of no more value than broken cisterns. In time of need, the gods could give no help; in time of drought, the cisterns would furnish no water. The text is just as true in this present age concerning those who leave God's word for the errors of men.

The second text teaches that the brethren in Thessalonica should hold fast to the teaching of the apostles, whether by word of mouth or by epistle. The word from which "tradition" comes is *paradosis*, and means "delivery, handing over, transmission," "what is transmitted in the way of teaching, precept, doctrine." See 1 Corinthians 11:2, where the word is translated "ordinances." The word "traditions," in 2 Thessalonians 2:15, refers to what Christ delivered over, or transmitted, to His apostles to teach. That we might know what was taught by spoken word, God has given us the written word. The text does not refer to erroneous tradition which claims to be apostolic. All such should be tested by the written word.

Apparent Contradiction Dissolved.

> Please harmonize 2 Samuel 24:24 and 1 Chronicles 21:25—(1) the names, and (2) the price paid for the threshing floor.

To answer the second query first: Two distinct transactions are recorded in the scriptures cited. (*a*) Fifty shekels of silver were paid for the actual threshing floor and the oxen. "So David bought the threshing floor and the oxen for fifty shekels of silver." 2 Samuel 24:24. And (*b*) six hundred shekels of gold were given for the entire place, or property, within which the threshing floor was located. "Grant me the place of this threshing floor, that I may build an altar therein unto the Lord: thou shalt grant it me for the full price. . . . So David gave to Ornan for the *place* six hundred shekels of gold by weight." 1 Chron. 21:22, 25.

Fifty shekels of silver (at 72½¢) amounts to $36.25, far too low a price for the entire land. Compare the four hundred shekels of silver Abraham paid for the field of Machpelah. See Genesis 23. The six hundred shekels of gold (at $10.88) was equivalent to $6,528, and was the sum paid for the entire hill on which Solomon afterward built the temple. See 2 Chron. 3:1.

As to the question concerning the difference in names, "Araunah" and "Ornan" are merely two forms of the same name.

Seeming contradictions in Holy Writ usually melt away under a close scrutiny of the exact wording and the context of the queried passages.

DEITY—FATHER, SON, AND HOLY SPIRIT

Various Texts on the Deity.

   1. How are we to understand the following scriptures: Psalm 90:2; Isaiah 42:8; 1 Corinthians 8:6; Deuteronomy 6:4?

   2. Can we conclude, from Revelation 3:14 and Colossians 1:15, that our Lord Jesus had a beginning, and there was a time when God the Father was alone?

   1. Psalm 90:2 would seem to apply to our Lord. The term used is not "Jehovah," but *Adonai,* which, without question, is applied to Christ; and this is the One whom Moses is addressing. He declares, "Even from everlasting to everlasting, Thou art God." And this is in harmony with Micah 5:2. Isaiah 42:8 evidently has reference to God. It is Jehovah Himself who speaks: "I am Jehovah, that is My name; and My glory will I not give to another, neither My praise unto graven images." That is the family name of the Godhead. Sometimes our Lord is called Jehovah. This is emphatically true in Jeremiah 23:6. In verse 5, He is called the Branch. "In His days Judah shall be saved, and Israel shall dwell safely; and this is His name whereby He shall be called: Jehovah our righteousness."

   1 Corinthians 8:6 presents before us the agencies by which the earth is created, the relative positions of the two Persons: "To us there is one God, the Father, of whom are all things, and we unto Him; and one Lord, Jesus Christ, through whom are all things, and we through Him." The same thought is expressed in John 1:1-3 and in Colossians 1:16,—that all the creation was wrought by God through our Lord Jesus Christ.

   Deuteronomy 6:4 is simply an expression of the unity of the Godhead: "Jehovah our God is one Jehovah." Many times, when mention is made of God, it simply implies the Godhead. Of course, there is absolute unity in that, just as truly as though there were but one person; and therefore it is spoken of as one. Our Lord's prayer in John 17 indicates the same thing: "As Thou, Father, art in Me, and I in Thee." And then He prays that the same unity may exist among His followers.

2. Yes, some do conclude, from Revelation 3:14, that there was a time when the Son did not exist, save in the all-comprehending purpose and potency of God. Yet there are others who still hold— and there is nothing to the contrary in the text—that "the beginning of the creation of God" means the One in whom the creation began, as declared in Colossians 1:17, "He is before all things, and in Him all things consist." The finite cannot grasp the infinite. Let this suffice,—that our Lord is God with the Father "from the days of eternity;" that "He is before all things, and in Him all things consist;" and He brings to all those who believe in Him the plenitude of the power of the Deity according to our needs.

Of course, sometimes expressions such as that used in Colossians 1:15, "the first-born," refer to pre-eminence rather than to priority. God calls Ephraim His first-born, although Manasseh was the first-born. He calls Israel His first-born, while Esau was the first-born of Isaac. That is, God had adopted these as such. They became pre-eminent because of character. So Jesus is called the first-born of the dead, and is pre-eminent above them all, and only by His power do all the others live.

The Pre-existence of Christ.

Was Christ a personal being before He came to this earth?

Whether our Lord existed before He was born of the Virgin Mary is a purely Biblical, not philosophical, question. If we depend upon our early teaching, upon human reason, upon some theological system, we shall go astray; if we take the literal teaching of the word, there will be no difficulty. Briefly we present the following evidences of our Lord's pre-existence as a personal being:

When God created the heavens and the earth, He addressed not creatures, but someone His equal, possessing creative power. "Let

Us make man in *Our* image, after *Our* likeness." Gen. 1:26. The very term *"Elohim,"* from which "God" is translated, is plural.

There is one Being, existing at least four hundred years before Christ, whom Jehovah designates "My Fellow," who was in future to be smitten. Zech. 13:7. The context clearly shows that the term refers to Him who became Jesus, the Great Shepherd of His sheep.

There is one Person revealed to us in the Old Testament again and again, called *"the Angel of Jehovah,"* the especial representative of God in ministering to His children. Of Him the great God declares, *"My name is in Him."* Ex. 23:21. He is called, in Isaiah 63:9, "the Angel of His presence." When this Angel came to Abraham, it is said, "Jehovah appeared unto him." Gen. 18:1. Jacob met Him by the brook Jabbok, in the night of wrestling, and said in the morning, "I have seen God face to face." Gen. 32:22-31.

This Angel-Jehovah bore a name among the angels; namely, Michael, the meaning of which is, *"Who is like God."* He is represented as a person, one who goes and comes, greater and mightier than Gabriel. Dan. 10:13. In fact, He is called "Michael the Archangel," the chief of all the angels. Jude 9. It is His voice that raises the dead. 1 Thess. 4:16. But our Lord shows that it is His own voice that will raise the dead (John 5:28, 29); the personal Michael of the Old Testament is identical with the Christ of the New.

Seven centuries before Christ, a prophet of God foretold our Lord's birth as a human being, and His birthplace. Micah 5:2. Out of Bethlehem would come "One . . . whose goings forth are from of old, from everlasting"—language that could not refer to an abstract word. It implies that the "One" referred to is as personal before that time as He was after it.

Paul, in speaking of the Son of God's love, calls Him "the image of the invisible God, the first-born of all creation," and says that "in Him were all things created," and that "He is before all things." Col. 1:13-18. Surely this language applies to a person, and fits that in Genesis, *"Let US make."* The same thing is taught in Hebrews 1:10, 11: "Thou, Lord, in the beginning didst lay the foundation of the earth, and the heavens are the works of Thy hands: they shall perish; but Thou continuest."

One more evidence from among others, the words of our Lord Himself: "And now, Father, glorify Thou Me with Thine own self with the glory which *I had with Thee before* the world was." John 17:5. "As Thou didst send Me into the world, even so sent I them." Verse 18. The apostles were persons before they were sent. Even so our Lord was a personal being.

As a member of the great Godhead, our blessed Lord stepped down to live a servant of God, an angel among the angels, a man among men, filled all vacancies with His fullness of life and character, and triumphed for every sinful soul. But all the mysteries, we may not, cannot, understand, any more than we can understand the creation of life.

Has Christ Creative Power?

Did our Lord exercise creative power in the feeding of the multitude, or was all that He did done through angelic ministration?

There are repeated evidences that our Lord exercised creative power. The angels may have done His bidding at times, but all Christ's miracles were done through the Spirit. Said the Roman centurion, "I am not worthy that Thou shouldest come under my roof: but speak the word only, and my servant shall be healed." Jesus sent His word and healed him. The poor, decaying, corrupt leper said, "Lord, if Thou wilt, Thou canst make me clean." The cleansing of that leper meant creative power, the absolute renewing of his entire being; and Jesus touched him, and said, "I will; be thou clean." There came to Jesus at another time one sick of palsy, and Jesus said, "Son, thy sins be forgiven thee." And the multitude murmured, saying that only God could forgive sins; but in order that He might demonstrate that He had the power of God to forgive sins, He said to the sick of the palsy, "Arise, and take up thy bed, and go thy way into thine house." And creative power restored the incurable of the palsy.

It was not angels that said, "Thy sins be forgiven thee," but Christ; and it was not angels that healed the sick of the palsy, but Christ. It was so when the multitude was fed. As the bread left the hands of the Master, it multiplied, and it multiplied in the hands of His disciples, through His own power. The only hope that the poor, sinful soul has is in the creative power of the Lord Jesus Christ, in the reception of His word.

This does not mean that He did not use at different times and on various occasions—and most occasions, in all probability—the help of angels. He does not do this because angels are necessary, but in order that there may be that blessed and divine co-operation which will make other hearts glad as well as His own. Even so He uses human beings. He could have said to Paul: "Thy sins are forgiven thee. Arise and be baptized." But He wanted Ananias to have a part in it, and He wanted His angel to have a part in it, and so He sent an angel to Ananias, and Ananias told Paul, and both of them were blessed in Christ in the work which they did; but the power was of Christ. "If any man be in Christ, he is a new creature,"—literally, a new creation.

The Genealogy of Jesus.

> I would like light on the genealogy of Jesus, as there is a very great difference in the record of Matthew and that of Luke.

There are two objects in giving the genealogies.

1. That of Matthew is to give the kingly side of the genealogy, and show that Jesus is the rightful king, the rightful heir of Abraham. Some of the generations are omitted. The Spirit thought it wise to divide them into three groups of fourteen generations each. It may be said, however, that it is not an uncommon thing in the Bible to omit a generation. Sometimes a grandfather is called a father, because he was the leading type, just the same as the Jews are called children of Abraham, though many generations intervened between those so called and Abraham himself. The kingship came through the male line. Joseph was the legal father of Jesus, and he therefore is given as the ancestor of our Lord. Christ received legally the kingship through him.

2. Luke, however, gives the mother's side, with a different object in view—to show that Jesus was of man, of the human family. But as it was not customary to trace the genealogy through women, the male members are mentioned instead of the female, the husband of Mary instead of Mary herself. And through this side of the family, the human side, the genealogy is traced back to Adam, the very first man, and still back of Adam to God Himself. So the Son of God was truly the Son of man. When the two lines are compared from David on, it will be seen that they meet in Zorobabel and Salathiel (Matt. 1:12; Luke 3:27), so that the blood of Solomon as well as the blood of Nathan was in both Joseph and Mary.

The Brothers of Jesus.

> Some Bible readers are puzzled over the question of the brothers of Jesus. Was Jesus the older? Or were His brothers older than He?

While the original word *adelphos* means brother, one born of the same mother, it is used in the New Testament in a far broader sense, for brothers in the faith or of the same nation. This is its general use, especially in the plural. See Luke 22:32; John 20:17; Acts 2:37; 7:23; 1 Cor. 8:13; 16:12. Members of the same family or household could properly be called brothers. This has led some to believe that the "brothers" of Jesus were His cousins.

That Jesus was the first-born of Mary is very clear from the record in Luke 1.

The "brothers" of Jesus seem to have been older than He. If younger, brought up with Him as they were, they would naturally believe on Him; but for some time they did not. John 7:5.

Assuming to advise Him as to His duty would indicate they were older. John 7:3, 4. They felt that He needed to be controlled. Luke 8:19; Mark 3:31; Matt. 12:47.

That so many of the brothers of Jesus were well known, and that in the mention of them in connection with Him, He alone is designated as the son of Mary, would also indicate that they were older than He, by another mother. See Matt. 13:55; Mark 6:3. The other scriptures, such as 1 Corinthians 9:5 and Galatians 1:19, are not out of harmony with this.

Then, too, if Mary had had other sons, would Jesus at His death have commended His mother to John? John 19:26, 27. Joseph must have died long before this, as we find no mention of his living after the early days of Jesus.

Therefore, it seems to us, the easiest solution of the problem is that the brothers of Jesus were sons of Joseph by a former marriage. A far more important question with each of us is, Are we brothers and sisters of Jesus? We may be. See Matt. 12:50.

Christ on the Cross. 1 Peter 2:24.

> Did the wrath of God, and man, and Satan all meet on our Saviour as He hung upon the cross? or was it *we* who "esteemed Him stricken, smitten of God, and afflicted"? Was He not that same beloved Son in His darkest hour as He was at His baptism?

Christ bore our sins in His own body on the tree, as the apostle declares. 1 Peter 2:24. See also Isa. 53:4, 5, 6, 11. God made Him to be sin for us, and therefore He bore the consequence of sin, which is death. In this sense only did the wrath of God rest upon Him. Of course it was Satan's hope that He might be destroyed, and so it was the hope of Satan's agents,— wicked men. The prophet, speaking for the Jews at the time of the crucifixion, says, "We did esteem Him stricken, smitten of God, and afflicted," but He was not so because of His own sins, but because He bore our sins. He was indeed the same beloved Son when He hung upon the cross and the horrors and darkness of death were around Him as He was at His baptism and His transfiguration. The crucifixion was but the culmination of all that He did for man. He humiliated Himself for man, even unto death. Death was the climax of all. But in it all He was submissive to God's will, and in it all God regarded Him with the most tender favor. It was our sins that He bore, that hid from Jesus, through His humanity, the Father's face, and caused Him to cry, "My God, My God, why hast Thou forsaken Me?" Sometimes an overwhelming sense of our own sins brings the same feelings to us; but that does not mean that God has forsaken us.

"Made Like Unto His Brethren." Heb. 2:14-17.

Was it no special advantage to Christ that He was of divine origin, "the only-begotten Son of God"? How can we who are born in sin be what He was, when He knew no sin?

Jesus was not only divine, but human. He was as truly human as any man who walks upon the earth. Let us consider:

He was one with the Father "before the world was," God's "Fellow," the One in whom "were all things created," the eternal Logos. John 17:5; Zech. 13:7; Col. 1:16; John 1:1-3.

"From the foundation of the world" Christ gave Himself, "emptied Himself," that He might break the power of sin, unify God's broken creation, and save man. Rev. 13:8; 1 Peter 1:20; Phil. 2: 5-8. When He did this, He gave up all, "counted not the being on an equality with God a thing to be grasped;" He *emptied* Himself," laying aside His Deity, "taking the form of a servant."

In this step the eternal Logos "became flesh," the same as we; for He was "born of woman, born under the law," under its condemnation, as a human, having the flesh with all the human tendencies; a partaker of the "flesh and blood" of humanity; "in all things" "made like unto His brethren," "suffered being tempted." Phil. 2:7; John 1:14; Gal. 4:4; Heb. 2:14-17. And He met all the temptations even as you and I must meet them, by faith in the will and word of God. He overcame all the tendencies found in the flesh of humanity.

Was it no special advantage to Christ that He was of divine origin, "the only-begotten Son of God"? That He was of divine origin was no special personal advantage, for He used no inherent divine power in His conflict with evil. His victory was of faith. His divine origin was against Him; for all the powers of evil were hurled against Him as against no other. But it was of special ad-

vantage to be the Begotten of God; yet that same advantage comes
to every soul of earth who will accept of Christ. For "as many as
received Him, to them gave He the right to become children of
God, even to them that believe on His name: who were born [mar-
gin, "begotten"], not of blood, nor of the will of the flesh, nor of
the will of man, but of God." John 1:12, 13. And thus, though we
were born in sin, we by faith "become partakers of the divine nature having escaped from the corruption that is in the world by
lust." 2 Peter 1:4. God thus places us on "vantage ground" in Christ
Jesus, and so He will every soul who receives Him. He "emptied
Himself" of all His glory and deity, so far as using it in His own
behalf, to become one with us, in order that we might empty ourselves from all our selfishness and become one with Him. "Him
who knew no sin He [the Father] made to be sin on our behalf;
that we might become the righteousness of God in Him." 2 Cor.
5:21. "In Him dwelleth all the fullness of the Godhead bodily, and
in Him ye are made full." Col. 2:9, 10. If the work were of ourselves, we might well be discouraged; but if *we* are *willing,* He will
make us what He was and what He is. God gives us in Christ
Jesus all the vantage ground that He possessed; shall we not accept it, and rejoice in it? Of course it means conflict and struggle;
it did to Jesus; but He conquered for us, that He might conquer
with us and in us. See Heb. 2:9-18; 4:14-16; 5:7-9; 7:25.

Christ's Age at Baptism.   Luke 3:23.

Please explain Luke 3:23 in the Revised Version. Jesus
was baptized at the age of thirty. His ministry began
27 A. D. Did His ministry begin three years before His
baptism?

Our inquirer has confounded the beginning of the Christian
era with Christ's birth. The beginning of the Christian era is about
four years this side of the birth of Jesus. It was not placed there
until the thirteenth century. Roger Bacon found that the paschal
full moon 33 A. D. fell on Friday, and this circumstance led him
and several others, as Scaliger, Ussher, Pierson, to conclude that
this was the year of the crucifixion; but Dr. Hales' Chronology

shows rather that it was not the year of the crucifixion. Christ began His ministry at about thirty years of age, in the autumn of the year 27 A. D. He closed it in the spring, 31 A. D., three and one half years later. The Christian era was invented by a Scythian monk, Dionysius Exiguus, in the sixth century, and has been quite generally adhered to although it is everywhere recognized that he was in error as to Christ's birth about four years.

The Personality of the Spirit.

    1. Some say the Holy Spirit is a person; others say He is a personality; and others, a power only. Till how long should this be a matter of discussion?

    2. Some say that Christ was both divine and human while on earth; others say, No, He was only a man, and that miracles were performed through Him by the Holy Spirit. Which is correct?

1. The personality of the Holy Spirit will probably be a matter of discussion always. Sometimes the Spirit is mentioned as being "poured out," as in Acts 2. All through the Scriptures, the Spirit is represented as being the operating power of God. "The Spirit of God was brooding upon the face of the waters." Gen. 1:2, A. R. V., margin. Job tells us that God by His Spirit garnished the heavens. The psalmist, in speaking of the death of living creatures, and their restoration, declares that God sends forth His Spirit and "they are created." By that same Spirit Jesus was begotten. By that same Spirit He went about doing good. By the gift of that Spirit men are begotten again, regenerated; and by the same Spirit there are bestowed upon them gifts for service.

We cannot define too closely God or the Godhead. We must not try to do it, because it is beyond our limitations. We may know this,—that there is a great threefold manifestation of Deity. Jehovah is our God and Father; Christ Jesus, His only-begotten Son, is our Saviour and Elder Brother, bringing to us all the potency of the Godhead; the Holy Spirit is our regenerator, and the constant companion of every soul who believes in Christ Jesus.

The reason why the Scriptures speak of the Holy Spirit as a person, it seems to us, is that it brings to us, and to every soul that believes, the personal presence of our Lord Jesus Christ. Jesus said (John 14:18), "I will not leave you desolate," or orphans. "I come unto you." He tells us in verse 16 how He will come. The Father will "give you another Comforter, that He [the Father] may be with you forever." In verse 23, He declares that the Father and He will come to the man who loves Him and keeps His word, and that They will make Their abode with him. But both the Father and the Son come by the Holy Spirit. To the Holy Spirit is given power to make the Father and the Son present to the believer.

We may perhaps obtain a clearer idea of this from the following illustration: Suppose the President of the United States wishes to speak to all the people of the country at once, as he has done from time to time in recent years. He notifies the broadcasting companies of his desire, and at the appointed hour the air is cleared for him. People sitting by their radios in all parts of the country hear his message at practically the same instant. Everybody recognizes his voice. In a certain sense he is present with every one of them. He seems to speak personally to all. In the near future, when television is perfected, and moving pictures of the speaker himself are transmitted simultaneously and appear upon a screen in every home, this impression will be still more deeply marked.

Wireless telephony furnishes perhaps an even better example still, for in this case the distant person can not only be heard, and perhaps seen, but answered. Wireless telephony has been practiced between God and His children for ages.

If mortal, finite man can do such things as outlined above, what cannot the infinite God do! When Jesus was here upon the earth, His personality could be present in only one place at a time. His disciples could not comprehend any power beyond that. Even those who loved Him so intensely, as did Martha and Mary, said, "Lord, if Thou hadst been here, my brother had not died." They could not grasp the idea that He could exercise power apart from His immediate personal presence. It was left for a Roman centurion to seize the truth. He said, "I am not worthy that Thou

shouldest come under my roof; but only say the word, and my servant shall be healed." He could understand that Christ had power
which could be exercised at a distance. And Jesus said, "I have not
found so great faith, no, not in Israel."

Because of the lack of faith, it was "expedient," necessary, that
He should go away; for He declared, "If I go not away, the Comforter will not come unto you; but if I go, I will send Him unto
you." John 16:7. His disciples could not realize the presence of
the Spirit of God as long as Christ was with them personally. In
that sense, He could be with those only who were in His immediate
presence. But when He went away, and the Spirit came, it could
make Christ present with everyone, wherever that one was—with
Paul in Athens, Peter in Jerusalem, Thomas in India, John in
Patmos.

These are simply illustrations. Wherever God's children are,
there is the Spirit. That Spirit is placed upon God's messengers,
the angels; but the angels are not the Spirit. That Spirit is placed
upon God's servants, His human messengers; but the human messengers are not the Spirit. They are possessed by the Spirit, and
used by the Spirit, and have within them the power of the Spirit;
but they are not the Spirit. The Spirit is independent of all these
human or material agencies. Why not leave it here? Why not
know that that Spirit, the Spirit of God, the Spirit of Christ, the
Spirit of Deity, goes out into all the earth, bringing the presence
of God to every heart that will receive it?

2. Our Lord, while here upon the earth, was both divine and
human. He did not lose His identity. He was the Christ of God.
There are various scriptures upon this. We read but one. Jesus
asks His disciples, "Who say ye that I am?" "And Simon Peter
answered and said, Thou art the Christ, the Son of the living God."
What did Jesus says to this? "Flesh and blood hath not revealed
it unto thee, but My Father who is in heaven." See Matt. 16:15-17.

It is an utter perversion of God's truth to say that one of the
Deity came down here to earth, and lost His identity, so that He
was only a human being while He was here; and that when He
returned to heaven, He became Deity, and lost His humanity.

Read the blessed story in brief form in Philippians 2: "Have this mind in you, which was also in Christ Jesus: who, existing in the form of God, counted not the being on an equality with God a thing to be grasped, but emptied Himself, taking the form of a servant, being made in the likeness of men; and being found in fashion as a man, He humbled Himself, becoming obedient even unto death, yea, the death of the cross. Wherefore also God highly exalted Him, and gave unto Him the name which is above every name." Verses 5-9.

And He it was that in the fullness of time was born of a woman, born under the law, that He might redeem them that were under the law. Gal. 4:4. He it was who died, and all creation responded to the agony in the great earthquake that took place. He it is who gives us this message from glory: "Fear not; I am the first and the last, and the Living One; and *I was dead,* and behold, *I am alive* forevermore, and I have the keys of death and of Hades."

Being divine and using His divine power are two different things. Our Lord, we may believe, wrought His miracles through the Spirit. He met temptation by His faith in God's word. He did all His work by the power of the Spirit in response to faith. But He was still the divine Son of God.

Could Christ Have Sinned? Heb. 2:14-17.

Was it possible for Christ to have sinned during the temptation of Satan, and during His life?

The simple words of Scripture are, that He "was in all points tempted like as we are, yet without sin." That is, though thus tempted, He did not sin. Was it possible? Truly it was; else where the temptation? For He was not only tempted in all points as we are, but "it behooved Him *in all things* to be made like unto His brethren." "Since then the children are sharers in flesh and blood, He also Himself *in like manner* partook of the same." He "was born of the seed of David according to the flesh." The temptation cost Him conflict, "prayers and supplications with strong crying and tears unto Him that was able to save." But He overcame, prevailed. He took man's nature with the awful risk. As long as the will of God reigned supreme in His life, He could not fail. But if He had sought His own pleasure, He would have failed. Read Hebrews 2 to 5.

Spiritual Bodies.

> Can a spiritual body be made visible to mortal eyes?
> See Luke 24:39; John 4:24.

There is a difference in the meaning of the various uses of the term "spirit." Sometimes it means simply the life, the life God-given; sometimes it means a spiritual being. In such a way it is used in John 4:24, "God is a spirit," or, as the margin of the Revised Version reads, "God is spirit."

Spiritual beings have the power to make themselves visible or invisible to humanity. Angels of God are around His children on every occasion. "The angel of the Lord encampeth round about them that fear Him, and delivereth them." Ps. 34:7. Sometimes these angels have been made visible. Generally they are not. Sometimes they appear as men. Our Lord, as a spiritual being, walked with the disciples on their way to Emmaus, sat with them at the table, and then vanished from their sight. He returned an invisible being with them to Jerusalem, although they did not know that He was present. But shortly after they had met with the disciples at Jerusalem, He again appeared to them, and said to them, "Handle Me, and see; for a spirit hath not flesh and bones, as ye see Me have." The evident thought implied in Luke 24:39 is that the disciples themselves thought Jesus was a ghost.

It is pre-eminently true of fishermen that they are superstitious; so they thought it was a ghost they saw when Jesus walked on the sea. His purpose in eating before them was to show that He was not a mere phantom; He was a real being with substance—flesh and bones. He showed them His hands and His feet that had the marks of the nails.

In fact, spiritual beings are more real than these mortal beings. They are composed of finer material, but it is not the less substantial. "The first man Adam became a living soul. The last Adam became a life-giving spirit." 1 Cor. 15:45. And so, according to the previous verse, there is the natural body and there is also a spiritual body. Mortal man, corruptible man, shall not inherit the kingdom of God; but the purified spiritual beings shall enter it.

Blasphemy Against the Holy Spirit.

Please explain the meaning of blasphemy against the Holy Spirit, as referred to in Mark 3:29.

God has but two agencies for saving men. These agencies are the blood of Christ for the washing away of our sins, and the eternal Spirit by which we are sanctified and made strong to serve Him. If man utterly rejects these, the Lord has no other means of reaching him. He has chosen his own doom. In other words, he has "counted the blood of the covenant, wherewith he was sanctified, an unholy thing, and hath done despite unto the Spirit of grace." Heb. 10:29.

Read the context in Mark 3. Jesus had been among the Jews, and wrought such miracles as they had never known before. All these miracles were in harmony with their own Scriptures; yet right in the face of the blessed and divine working, these Jews, who should have been a light to the world, declared that He cast out demons by Beelzebub, the prince of demons. In other words, they attributed to the devil the work of the Spirit of God.

The Lord did not arbitrarily cut them off because of that. He does not arbitrarily cut anyone off; but when man comes to that place where he will declare that the manifest working of God's Spirit is of the devil, he by that act cuts himself off from the very means which God has of reaching him. That is what sin against the Holy Spirit is. It is setting aside the work of the Spirit of God as though it were wrought by the evil one. Doubtless there have been many who have done this in ignorance, and God has accepted them, just as He did the apostle Paul (1 Tim. 1:13); but he who does that and persists in it, shuts himself off from eternal life, and commits an eternal sin.

SECTION III

THE NATURE OF MAN

Have We Eternal Life Now?

> Am I mistaken in the teaching of John 5:24 and 1
> John 5:10-13, that we have everlasting life in this life by
> believing in Christ?

That the believer has now everlasting life the following propositions and Scripture texts clearly show:

Mankind by nature are "children of wrath" (Eph. 2:3), being sick with sin (Isa. 1:5, 6; Rom. 3:23).

The disease of sin (unless divine power interposes) ends in death. "Sin, when it is finished, bringeth forth death." James 1:15.

Because men are sinners, they are ignorant of the righteousness of God (Rom. 10:3); being victims of sin, "children of wrath," or death, they are "alienated from the life of God" (Eph. 4:18); for righteousness is life (see Rom. 5:17, 18).

Therefore, they who through Christ receive the righteousness of God by faith (Rom. 3:22), receive also the life of God, from which they are no longer alienated.

Again, Christ is the manifestation of God to us (John 14:9), or, in other words, "God was in Christ" (2 Cor. 5:19); Christ was, therefore, the righteousness of God and the life of God (John 14:10).

When we accept of Christ by faith we have the "righteousness of God" (Rom. 3:22), and the life of God, or everlasting life (John 3:36). So Jesus says, "Verily, verily, I say unto you, He that heareth My word, and believeth on Him that sent Me, *hath* everlasting life, and shall not come into condemnation; but *is* passed *from* death *unto* life." John 5:24. "He that hath the *Son* hath the *life;* he that hath not the Son of God hath *not* the life. These things have I written unto you, that ye may *know that ye have eternal life,* even unto you that believe on the name of the Son of God."

1 John 5:12, 13, A. R. V. Says the regenerated Paul, "I am crucified with Christ: nevertheless I live; yet not I, but *Christ liveth in
Me:* and the *life* which I now live in the flesh I live by the faith of
the Son of God." Gal. 2:20.

Was not the life of the sinner real? Were not his sins real? Is
not the righteousness of Christ just as real? Is not the life of
Christ just as real?

God's Holy Spirit is life; and God puts that Spirit within those
who believe (Ezek. 36:27; Rom. 8:9); and "the Spirit is *life* because of righteousness" (Rom. 8:10). That Spirit gives us a new
heart and a new spirit (Ezek. 36:26), makes us a new creature
(2 Cor. 5:17); and as is that Spirit in nature, so is that which comes
from the Spirit.

To use another illustration: We are born of the "incorruptible"
seed of the word of God, the gospel which abideth forever. 1 Peter
1:23-25. Says Jesus, "The words that I speak unto you, they are
spirit, and they are life." John 6:63. Peter says that we are to
feed upon "the sincere milk of the word," that we may grow
thereby. 1 Peter 2:2. Now if we are born of this incorruptible seed,
if we feed upon spirit and life, shall we not be like the food of
which we are partakers, upon which we grow, which has been
made a part of our very being? Therefore, as in that word is the
life of God, so in partaking of that word we are partaking of the
life and Spirit of God. This is shown from the fact that, while out
of Christ we were children of disobedience and death, in Christ
we are quickened, or made alive, with Christ. Col. 2:13. Being
crucified with Christ, the child of wrath dies, and the person is
born of God, a son of God. Does not the son partake of the life of
the father? If we are children of God, do we not share His life?

But may we not lose this life, although it be real? We may. It
is given by faith; it abides by faith, by God's word abiding in us.
If His words abide in us by faith (John 15:7), that faith will work
by love (Gal. 5:6), that love will keep God's commandments (1
John 5:3; John 14:15-17); and by this last text we learn that with
all this God's Spirit, or life, abides with us forever.

But if we go down in death, what then? We commit our life

to Christ; and when Christ our life shall appear, we shall appear with Him in glory (Col. 3:4), not only with everlasting life, but with immortality. In fact, the grave cannot hold us. Death could not hold Christ (Acts 2:24), for the righteousness of God was upon Him; no more can it hold us, for the righteousness of God through Christ is upon us. In Him all fullness dwells; we have Him, He is ours, and we are "complete in Him." Praise God for His un-speakable Gift, and for that *life* from which we are no longer alienated, and which gives power over sin and death.

Mortal or Immortal?

> Can immortal create mortal? Did God, who is im-perishable create perishable beings or things? and as "in Him is no sin," and "He is the life and light of men," how can life create death? Were Adam and Eve created mortal?

We do not know what God could do; but we do not believe, nor do we see how, He could create mortals. By "immortal" we under-stand "deathless, incorruptible;" by mortal we understand "sub-ject to death, corruptibility." We do not believe that mortal, perish-able, corruptible beings were in God's plan, because all these are the fruits of sin; and sin is no part of His plan. "In Him is no sin." How, then, did God create Adam? Not immortal; for there ex-isted the possibility of sin, and it was not in God's plan to have im-mortal sinners. Neither did God create Adam mortal, for it was not *His* plan that man should die. What then? God created man neither mortal nor immortal, but a candidate for immortality. He was a perfect being, possessed of eternal life, held by faith in God. If sin had not come in, faith, by the power of God's life, would have developed an incorruptible character which God would have owned by bestowing upon it physical immortality. Such will be the gift when Christ comes. Everlasting life is given actually now, that we may have power to conquer sin; but it will not be given absolutely till character is immortal, and then man's temple of character will correspond with his character.

The Word "Soul."

> Will you please explain the term "soul of man"? The
> Bible says in regard to creation that man was made from
> the dust of the earth, and God breathed into him the
> breath of life, and he became a living soul. Some tell us
> that the soul is the spirit of man, something within him
> that never dies.

The word "soul" is used in the Bible in different meanings.
Sometimes it means the whole person. Man who was made of the
dust of the earth became a living soul. The breath of life made him
a *living* soul. He was a soul, or person, before, but *lifeless*. The
breath of life made him living. So we read in 1 Peter 3:20 that
there were eight souls saved in the ark; in Revelation 16:3, "Every
living soul died in the sea"—that is, every living creature.

"Soul" is used to express the thoughts and affections common
to man; all men; the physical life. "Bless the Lord, O my soul:
and all that is within me, bless His holy name." Ps. 103:1. "Soul"
also means life. It means simply the animal life, common to all
creatures. An instance of this is found in Matthew 16:25, 26. The
words "life" and "soul" in the King James Version come from
the same Greek word; but nowhere in all the Bible is that soul
said to be immortal, never-dying, or deathless, but always that
which we may lose. We can therefore give three comprehensive
definitions of the word "soul": a living person; the natural mind,
thought, intellect, and affections; and mere life, or vitality.

Between Death and the Resurrection. Ps. 6:5.

> Will you kindly state whether or not Adventists believe
> that the personal identity of the soul continues after death,
> or is disintegrated, annihilated, at death? If the former,
> what is its state during the interval? In other words,
> please state plainly and succinctly your exact belief upon
> the subject, with scriptural references or otherwise.

While we are sure that the answer will disappoint our querist,
we can give no other. We know no place where Adventists, Sev-

enth-day or otherwise, have ever formulated any precise, succinct, or exact belief regarding the condition of man between death and the resurrection. They have preferred to let it rest on the Bible statements without attempting to formulate the Scriptures into a creed. Hence different persons, if called upon so to do, would define in a different way. But all are agreed in accepting the literal statement that "in death there is no remembrance of Thee [God];" that when death occurs, man's "breath goeth forth, he returneth to his earth; in that very day his thoughts perish." See Ps. 6:5; 146:4; Eccl. 9:5. The condition between death and the resurrection is a dreamless sleep, from which only Christ, the Life-giver, can awaken the sleeper. As to just how God preserves identity, whether by the absolutely accurate life record of the individual which is indelibly stamped upon the resurrection body, or some other way, we may not know, nor need we concern ourselves about it. We know that man dies; that "the dead know not anything;" that Christ will bring them back from the power of death and the grave at His coming. The Bible makes Christ's second coming and the resurrection of the dead necessities in God's plan for the redemption of the human race, contrary to the teaching of much of modern theology.

"Shall Never Die." John 11:26.

> Will you kindly give me some light on the following text? "And whosoever liveth and believeth in Me shall never die. Believest thou this?"

The text in question is intimately connected with the three verses which come before. Jesus said to Martha, "Thy brother shall rise again." Martha replied, "I know that he shall rise again in the resurrection at the *last day*." Evidently the words of our Saviour in response to Martha had reference to that time as well as to the present. He declared to her that the One who raised the dead at that time had power to raise the dead at the present; and therefore He replied, "I am the resurrection, and the life: he that believeth in Me [that is, in the last day], though he were dead, yet shall he live." All those who sleep in Christ who died in faith will then come forth, and "whosoever liveth and believeth in Me [at that time, the righteous living] shall never die." This to us is the simplest meaning of the text. When Christ comes, there will be the two classes who will live forever,—those who sleep in Him, and those who will be looking for Him. And He who will give life then can give it now.

Enoch and Elijah. Matt. 17:1-3.

> The Bible says Enoch and Elijah were carried up to heaven without dying. Do you suppose they will be all the good people who will get to heaven before the second coming of Christ? Please explain the first three verses of the 17th chapter of Matthew.

Yes, both Enoch and Elijah were translated; of these the Bible gives us a record. There may have been others thus taken; we do not know. When Christ died, the graves of many were opened; and when He rose from the dead, many came out of their graves and appeared to people. Matt. 27:52, 53. When Jesus ascended, this multitude of those who were once Satan's captives ascended with Him. Eph. 4:8, margin. Matthew 17:1-3 reveals that there was yet another who had been raised; namely, Moses. The transfiguration on the mount was to reveal to the disciples what the kingdom of Christ would be at His coming. See Matt. 16:28. There will be in that kingdom Jesus Christ glorified. There will be the righteous raised from the dead, represented by Moses, who died and the Lord buried him. When Christ, or Michael, the Archangel, came to raise him from the dead, Satan resisted Him. But the words, "The Lord rebuke thee" triumphed, and Moses came forth from the dead, and appeared a living, glorified man on the mount. Those who never taste death will greet Christ when He comes. Elijah represented these. Read 2 Peter 1:16-18, where the purpose of the transfiguration is stated; namely, to set before the disciples the power and coming and surety of the Lord Jesus Christ.

Returning to God.

When the body dies, can an impure, unholy, and defiled soul return to God who gave it?

We nowhere read of the soul's returning to God. We do read
that the spirit returns to God. Eccl. 12:7. The soul, in one sense,
might be said to return to God. That depends on the definition we
give "soul." If by "soul" we mean person, certainly the person does
not return to God defiled and unclean. If we mean simply life,
why, life came from God, and it goes back to God. It could not
be spoken of as defiled, in the abstract. That life God will give
back at the resurrection; but we are nowhere told that that life has
form, or character, or personality, apart from the body. Ecclesiastes 12:7 seems to have reference to the ordinary, common life
which man loses at dissolution, though there are some who hold
that it has reference to the higher life, that which God gives to His
believing children. God does not in anywise count a man a double
being or a triple being. The normal man has body and soul and
spirit, but it takes the three to make the full man. When these
are separated, death ensues, and the dust returns to the earth as it
was, and the spirit goes back to God. It came from God as life;
it goes back to God as life. It did not come from God a living, conscious entity, nor does it go back to God in that way. A simple
understanding of the fundamentals will meet all these objections.

Feeding Upon Christ. John 6:51.

Can those die who truly partake in faith of the body
and blood of Christ?

We feed upon Christ truly by faith only. And Jesus declares,
"If any man eat of this bread [that is, of Himself, the living Bread],
he shall live forever." John 6:51. But that He does not mean by
this that the one who so eats shall not die, He continues, "He that
eateth My flesh and drinketh My blood *hath eternal life* [a present
possession]; and I will *raise him up at the last day*." Verse 54. See
also verses 33, 40, 47, 57, 58, 63. There are those who will be trans-

lated, without tasting death, when Christ comes. Of course these will be children of faith. There will be those who are not the less children of faith who will fall asleep before He comes. God does not count His people dead; they sleep in Him, with life "hid with Christ in God." Col. 3:3. There will be those who will sleep— not children of faith—on through to the second resurrection. There are those—not of faith—who will live to see Christ's coming. Let not that soul who faces death in Jesus be discouraged; "for God appointed us not unto wrath, but unto the obtaining of salvation through our Lord Jesus Christ, who died for us, that, whether we *wake* or *sleep*, we should *live together with Him*." 1 Thess. 5:9, 10. He lives better physically who rightly lives by faith; but living by faith, feeding on Christ by faith, he may still fall asleep in death. Rev. 14:13.

Death and the Body of Moses. Deut. 34:5, 6.

What information do we have regarding the death and resurrection of the body of Moses.

The record of Moses' death is given in Deuteronomy 34:5, 6,— a death at which only spiritual beings were present. The old warrior lay down and went to sleep.

Those who are in a condition of death are counted as the prisoners of Satan, inasmuch as death is the result of sin. Of Satan, or Lucifer, it is said that he "let not loose his prisoners to their home." Isa. 14:17. In Jude 9 we read that there was a dispute between Michael the Archangel and the devil about the body of Moses. Michael (the meaning of which is "Who is like God"), the Archangel (meaning the "Chief of all the angels"), was none other than the Son of God. This we learn by comparing Daniel 10:13, 21 with Jude 9; John 5:28; 1 Thessalonians 4:16. It will be seen by comparison of these texts that it is the voice of the Son of God that wakes the dead, and that this is the voice of the Archangel. The Archangel, Michael, the great Prince that stands for the children of God's people, must therefore be Christ, the Son of God. We could conceive of no reason why there should be a dispute over the body of Moses unless it was over its resurrection from the dead. It is Satan's ambition to keep forever dead all those who are the children of God. It is God's gracious promise that they shall live again. We can also readily understand that at that dispute between the devil and Michael, Michael came off conqueror, and therefore the body of Moses was raised from the dead. As evidence of this, see Mark 9:4: "And there appeared unto them Elijah with Moses: and they were talking with Jesus." Now Elijah was translated without seeing death. He and Moses were on the mount of transfiguration; the one representing that class who at Christ's coming will be raised from the dead; and the other those who, when Christ comes, will be translated without seeing death. Therefore Moses was raised from the dead,—a pledge of the resurrection for all time. Our correspondent has concluded rightly that Moses was taken to heaven. There is absolutely no proof that God gave his body to the devil, as some have affirmed. All this is pure supposition.

The Literal Resurrection. Isa. 26:19.

Do Seventh-day Adventists believe that the resurrection taught by Christ, His apostles, or anywhere in Holy Scriptures, refers to a literal resurrection of the material body at a long period of time after death? Do the following Scripture quotations refer to such material, literal, and general resurrection of mankind or the redeemed: John 11:24-26; John 20:27; Acts 24:14, 15; Rev. 1:16, 17, last part; two first sentences of the 18th verse; 1 Cor. 15:20-22; Dan. 12:2; Job 14:13, 14?

Yes; Seventh-day Adventists believe in the resurrection of the body. The body returns to dust, to death and decay; God will call it back from dust. "Thy dead men shall live, together with my dead body shall they arise." Isa. 26:19; see also Hosea 13:14. Jesus rose again, so did Lazarus and others. Have we any reason to believe that the resurrection of all others will be less literal? Some of the above texts refer to a *general* resurrection, some to *special* resurrections, but all to a literal resurrection. John 20:27 and Revelation 1:18 refer to Jesus after He was raised from the dead. The whole hope of the future life is based by Paul on the fact of Christ's literal resurrection, and the resurrection at the last day.

But not all will be raised from the dead at the same time. There is first the resurrection of the righteous, and one thousand years after, the resurrection of the wicked. Rev. 20:4-6. But the righteous do not rise from the grave with their corrupt, mortal bodies, but with glorious, immortal bodies like Christ's. See 1 Cor. 15: 51-55; Phil. 3:21. The wicked, raised one thousand years after, come up from the grave with the same mortal body which all men possess. The resurrection of the dead is one of the great elements in the Christian's hope. Take the word of God as it reads.

Brought With Christ From the Dead.

Please explain the meaning of the 14th verse of the 4th chapter of 1 Thessalonians.

The verse reads, "If we believe that Jesus died and rose again, even so them also which sleep in Jesus will God bring with Him." The subject under consideration by the apostle is the second coming of Christ and the resurrection to take place at that time. Therefore he promises that as surely as Jesus died and rose again, just so surely would those who sleep in Jesus rise by the power of Christ's resurrection. The text does not mean that God will bring those who sleep in Christ from heaven with Him, but that He brings them from the dead with Christ, or through the resurrection, the same as He brought Christ from the dead, and through the same power. An expression in Hebrews 13:20 throws light on this text: "Now the God of peace, that brought again from the dead our Lord Jesus, that Great Shepherd of the sheep;" and as He has brought the Shepherd, so will He bring the sheep. "Knowing that He which raised up the Lord Jesus shall raise up us also by Jesus, and shall present us with you." 2 Cor. 4:14. When Christ comes, He brings His people up out of their graves and takes them to heaven. Ezek. 37:13, 14; John 5:28, 29. If those who sleep in Jesus are in heaven, the resurrection is made void. It is only by a resurrection out from among the dead, the power of Christ's resurrection, that they live or have any hope. See 1 Cor. 15:12-19. The Emphatic Diaglott renders the verse in question, "For since we believe that Jesus died and arose; so also [we believe] that God, through Jesus, will lead forth with Him those who fell asleep." The leading forth, or bringing, is from the dead to the glory which awaits them. Heb. 13:20.

"Eternal" and "Everlasting."   Matt. 25:41, 46.

Would you please give me the true definition of the two words "eternal" and "everlasting," and tell me what bearing the term "everlasting" has upon the fate of the ungodly in the future?

In the New Testament, as in Matthew 25:41, 46, both words come from the same Greek word, *aiōnios,* literally, "age-lasting." The word is derived from *aiōn,* meaning "age." Bagster thus defines it: "A period of time of significant character; life; an era; an age; hence a state of things marking an age or era; the present order of nature; the condition of man, the world; *ho aiōn,* illimitable duration, eternity." "*Aiōnios,* indeterminate as to duration, eternal, everlasting." Liddell and Scott define *aiōn* as "a period of existence; one's lifetime; life; a long space of time, an age; a space of time clearly defined and marked out, an era, age, period of a dispensation, this present world." *Aiōnios* is defined to mean, "lasting for an age, perpetual, everlasting, eternal."

The corresponding Hebrew word *olam* Young defines as "age, age-lasting." For its use see Gen. 17:7, 8, 13, 19; Ex. 40:15; Num. 25:13; Deut. 33:27. The meaning of the word, it will be seen, is to be determined by that to which it is applied. If applied to God, it means without end; if to a man's life, it ends with his life or age; if to the Levitical priesthood, it ends when that priesthood expired at the close of that age or dispensation; if to the Christian era, it terminates when Christ comes. Where "world" comes from *aiōn,* it would have made a clearer sense if it had been translated *"age."* As applied to the punishment of the wicked, it evidently means just the same as when applied to the salvation of the righteous; that is, both are everlasting, or eternal. But one is eternal life; the other is eternal death. Many would make the text teach "eternal punish*ing;*" but the Bible declares it to be "everlasting destruction." 2 Thess. 1:9. Says the Revised Version, "Who shall suffer punishment, even eternal destruction." The "eternal fire" which Jude says fell upon Sodom and Gomorrah (Jude 7), and which thus made their punishment an example to the ungodly, Peter says turned those cities "into ashes, condemned them with an overthrow, having made them an example unto those that should live ungodly." 2 Peter 2:6, R. V. The salvation of the righteous is eternal *life,* which never terminates, or ends, in death; the punishment of the wicked is just the opposite state, but equal in duration, eternal *death,* which will never know life. Much more might be said, but this covers the principle.

"Spirits in Prison." 1 Peter 3:19.

> Please explain the text, "By which He went and preached unto the spirits in prison."

The quotation is 1 Peter 3:19. Let us question the text:

To whom does the "He" refer? "Christ." Verse 18.

To what does the "which" refer? The Spirit; "Christ . . . made alive in the Spirit." Verse 18.

Who were the spirits? The souls shut up in the prison house of sin, with no power to save themselves. For this Christ came. Compare carefully Galatians 3:22; Isaiah 61:1. What put them in prison? Sin; "that aforetime were disobedient." 1 Peter 3:20.

When did He preach to them? "*When* the long-suffering of God waited in the days of Noah, *while* the ark was a preparing." Verse 20.

Through whom did He preach by His Spirit? "Noah," "a preacher of righteousness" "by faith." 2 Peter 2:5; Heb. 11:7.

What was the result of the preaching? "Few, that is, eight souls, were saved." 1 Peter 3:20. That preaching also "condemned the world,"—those who did not believe. Heb. 11:7.

Not Able to Kill the Soul. Matt. 10:28.

Kindly explain to me how I can harmonize what you say regarding the condition of man in death with Matthew 10:28, "Fear not them which kill the body, but are not able to kill the soul."

The text says nothing concerning the condition of the man in death—absolutely nothing. The Bible nowhere tells us that the soul, as it is generally spoken of, has consciousness apart from the body. We might say that the word from which "soul" is taken, *psuche,* in Matthew 10:28, is the same word that is translated "life" in Matthew 16:25, and "soul" in Matthew 16:26. It simply means life, and nothing else. Man cannot take away our life finally. He can bring temporary death, but our life rests with God. Man cannot take away future life; but God can, and the very fact that He can proves that the soul is not immortal. If we would only get the Bible idea of what is meant by "soul,"—not a being of itself within the man, but just simply life, that which makes a man a living creature, as used in the text under consideration,—we would have no trouble regarding man's future. The Creator gives man life that he may use it to God's glory; and if man refuses to do that, God takes it away, and man dies, and eventually eternally dies. This is reasonable and just. "Soul" is sometimes used for the whole person in the Bible, but not in these texts.

The Gospel, to Whom Was It Preached?

Please explain 1 Peter 4:6. Does it mean that the gospel was preached to some who were dead?

Notice, the text does not say that the gospel was preached to them that were dead, but "for this cause *was* the gospel preached also to them that *are* dead." It was preached to the antediluvians (2 Peter 2:5); it was preached to Abraham (Gal. 3:8); it was preached to the unbelieving Israelites (Heb. 4:2); it was preached through God's word and works to all others (Psalm 19). But it was preached to all who are now dead or who were dead at the time the above text was written, but *when* the *dead* were *alive.*

What utter futility it would be to preach to the dead! "His breath goeth forth, he returneth to his earth; in that very day his *thoughts perish.*" See Ps. 146:4, and other scriptures. They could hear nothing. No; all of the blessed, living gospel messages God has sent have been sent to persons who were alive.

Souls Under the Altar. Gen. 4:10; Rev. 6:9.

> I would like you to explain Genesis 4:10 regarding Abel's blood crying to the Lord after Abel was dead; and Revelation 6:9, where John saw the souls of them that were slain in heaven.

There are various figures of speech recognized by all students of language. One of these is personification, by which a thing having no life is made to speak and talk as though it did have life. This figure is often used in the Bible. For instance, in the second chapter of Habakkuk, the stones in the house are represented as crying out, and the beam that is in the house as answering the stones. That is, the house was builded in iniquity. It is so evident before God that He speaks as though the very stones were crying out against it. So regarding Abel. Cain had shed his blood. The hitherto innocent earth, that had never known bloodshed, was made to drink of the evidence of his crime. Cain thought to hide that crime from God; but the Lord wished to show the guilty man that his sin was just as evident as though the very blood were crying it audibly from the ground.

Of course, no one thinks for a moment that the blood was alive or speaking, but God remembered it just as truly as though that were the case. This same figure of speech is used in Revelation 6:9 under the period of the pale horse, Death. During the time of the persecution of the Dark Ages, thousands of God's children were slain. John is represented as seeing these underneath the altar. This altar was not in heaven. Only the altar of incense is represented as being there. Rev. 8:3. The altar of sacrifice was on the earth; and the martyrs are represented as being underneath the altar of sacrifice, consequently were not souls that were in heaven.

The awful sin of putting these souls to death was so great in the sight of God that the inanimate beings who had suffered are represented as crying to God. It is the cry of justice against such wickedness. And God cares for them and hears in their behalf just as truly as though they were speaking audibly. That is all that is meant by it; for we certainly could not conceive for a moment that if those souls were in heaven, they would be crying out for vengeance against their persecutors. We could not conceive heaven to be a place of happiness if that were the case. Those souls would know that in a little while the wicked would be doomed, anyway, and it would be utter folly, yea, more than that, hardheartedness and contrary to the Spirit of Christ, for them to be crying out against their enemies. The text indicates how God feels and cares for His oppressed and persecuted children. He may seem to forget them, and centuries may pass since the crimes have been committed against them; but God remembers them just as truly as though they were audibly crying to Him from the places where they were sacrificed for His sake.

The Thief on the Cross. Luke 23:43.

A friend tells me that we have no right to change the punctuation in the text, "Verily I say unto thee today, shalt thou be with Me in Paradise." This friend uses the thief on the cross as a strong proof of the immortality of the soul.

There are several conditions in the understanding of this text. 1. What did the thief request? "Jesus, remember me when Thou comest into Thy kingdom." But when would Christ come into His kingdom? "When the Son of man shall come in His glory, and all the angels with Him, *then shall He sit on the throne* of His glory." In Luke 19:11-13 He tells us by a parable that He did not take His kingdom when He ascended up on high; but He went to do a work at the close of which He would receive the kingdom, and then come again. In Daniel 7:13, 14 we learn that the receiving of that kingdom takes place in connection with the judgment, and that at the end of earth's history He takes the kingdom under the whole heavens, which is the earth, and reigns. See also Luke 1:32, 33; 2 Tim. 4:1. Doubtless the thief had heard our Lord teach in regard to these very things, and with utter abandonment of soul he throws himself on the mercy of Christ, and pleads, "Lord, remember me when *Thou comest into Thy kingdom*," that is, when Christ should come again.

2. Our Lord's answer, "Verily I say unto thee today, shalt thou be with Me in Paradise." Where is Paradise? According to Revelation 2:7 it is where the tree of life is. According to Revelation 22:1, 2 that tree is near the throne of God, and will eventually descend again upon this earth when the New Jerusalem comes down from above. Rev. 21:1-5. Yet Jesus told Mary, the third day after His crucifixion, when in glad greetings she was about to clasp His feet, "Touch Me not; for I have not yet ascended to My Father." John 20:17. Therefore Jesus did not mean that the thief would be with Him that day in Paradise.

3. Still further, it was a very rare thing for an individual to die upon the cross the day he was crucified. When the soldiers came to break the legs of the criminals lest they should get away, they found Christ already dead, and they wondered at it. They broke the legs of the criminals, as they had doubtless often done before to others, and left them to die in lingering agony. Therefore it is not at all probable, in the very physical nature of the case, that the thief died on that day.

What, then, is meant by the text? Simply this, that the thief, knowing of the glorious kingdom of Christ to come, and that the Master would come back to earth to take that kingdom, asked that he be remembered of the King at that time; and the King, dying upon the cross as a malefactor with no power seemingly to fulfill a single promise, on a day when His own disciples had lost faith in Him, promised the dying man that his wish should be gratified: "Verily I say unto thee today [the day above all days when seemingly I cannot keep the promise that I shall make, the day when My own professed disciples have forsaken Me and fled, the day when I am dying as thou art dying, as thou hast faith to ask I have faith and assurance to promise, that when that time shall come that I enter My kingdom], shalt thou be with Me."

There would be no trouble with this text at all if it had not been wrongly punctuated. There should be no comma after "thee;" it should be after "today." The adverb "today" modifies the verb "say" rather than the verb "shall be." There is no inspiration in commas. For centuries there was no division even between words, to say nothing about the parts of sentences. Of course the men who punctuated the Bible punctuated it according to their understanding; but investigation of this subject, as our brief study clearly shows, indicates that the comma should be after "today" and not before.

Parable of the Rich Man and Lazarus.

>   Please explain the case of the rich man and Lazarus as
>   recorded in Luke 16:19-31. How about his torment?
>   How about the gulf? How about Lazarus going to Abra-
>   ham's bosom at death?

In the first place, the story is one of a series of parables spoken by our Lord to teach certain lessons; and it is a well-settled rule of interpretation (1) that no parable should be used as a basis for doctrine. It is used to enforce truth established by plain Scripture, but is in itself not designed to establish or to reveal truth. Oftentimes it is in itself pure fable or allegory, in which inanimate things are made to act and speak, though in reality they may not even be alive. (2) Parables should not be made to "go on all fours." Certain features must be brought in to make the parable consistent with itself; but these things often have no part in enforcing the lesson for which the parable was given.

The parables of the supper, the ninety and nine, the prodigal son, the unjust steward, and the rich man and Lazarus, were all given to rebuke the indifference, the pride, the selfishness, the unfaithfulness, the exclusiveness, of the Jewish people, and to set over against all these the all-comprehending love of God.

In the last of this series Jesus uses the belief of the Jews, erroneous though it was, to show, *according to their own view,* how utterly unreasonable was their pride of wealth, and contempt of the poor, and their national pride and contempt of the Gentiles.

1. The belief of the Jews at that time, according to Josephus, was that *Hades* was a subterranean region "not regularly finished," in which none of "the light of this world shines," a region of "perpetual darkness." Here souls are taken by the angels, "who distribute to them temporary punishments." Here also is a lake of unquenchable fire, in which as yet no one will supposedly be cast till the judgment day. As the souls go into *Hades* the wicked are "dragged" to the left hand by the angels, within the very sound of hell itself; while the righteous are taken to the right hand, a place of happiness. "This place we call Abraham's bosom." Between the two classes there is a great gulf which cannot be crossed by souls on either side. All this we know is neither true nor Biblical. When man dies, he dies. "In that *very day* his thoughts perish." His love, his hatred, his envy, are all perished till the resurrection day. Yet Jesus used this erroneous belief to show the Jews how utterly inconsistent they were, and what their judgment as individuals would be according to their own theory.

By and by the rich man dies. Lazarus dies. According to their own theory, he who had lived for himself, must suffer. He who had trusted God, according to the same theory, was placed in Abraham's bosom. The fixing of characters prevented forever any change in their condition. Such, *according to their own view,* would be their ultimate fate.

But Jesus taught more than this. In the light of all the prophets they rejected Him of whom all the prophets spoke. They counted themselves as children of Abraham. John 8:33, 39. According to their view, which Jesus on another occasion used, they counted the Gentiles as dogs. Mark 7:27. Lazarus (whom God aids) well represents our Lord, who came to His own personally and in His apostles, but "His own received Him not." Since that very time facts have demonstrated the truth of the parable. The Jewish people have been in trouble, in pain, in anguish, but still holding between them and the Christ of God the great gulf of their own national pride and exclusiveness and self-righteousness, elsewhere

symbolized by the veil upon the heart. They want Lazarus to relieve them, but He must come in their way. They are still in "torment" *(basanos,* trial, testing), yet unwilling to yield and cast
themselves wholly upon His mercy. His salvation will not span
their unbelief. They cannot cross upon it to Him. And God will
work no marvelous signs while they refuse to believe His word.
John 5:41-47.

Two Difficult Texts. Phil.1:21-23; 2 Cor. 5:6-8.

> Will you please explain Philippians 1:21-23 and 2 Cor-
> inthians 5:6-8? Do these texts teach that the soul goes to
> God at death?

Philippians 1:21-23 reads as follows: "To me to live is Christ,
and to die is gain. But if I live in the flesh, this is the fruit of my
labor: yet what I shall choose I wot not. For I am in a strait betwixt two, having a desire to depart, and to be with Christ; which
is far better."

2 Corinthians 5:6-8 reads thus: "Therefore we are always confident, knowing that, whilst we are at home in the body, we are
absent from the Lord: (for we walk by faith, not by sight:) we
are confident, I say, and willing rather to be absent from the body,
and to be present with the Lord."

Turning to Philippians, notice what the apostle says in verse
20, that Christ shall be magnified in his body whether it be by
life or by death, and therefore for him to live is Christ, and to die
is gain for Christ. In either case God would be glorified, in either
life or death. Therefore the apostle declares he did not know which
to choose of those two. If he were to live, suffering awaited him;
if he were to die, still God would be glorified in his death, and he
would rest from all the suffering. Therefore which I shall choose
of the two, the apostle declares, "I wot not"—he knew not. "For
I am in a strait betwixt two," that is, the dying and the living.
But he did have a desire for a third thing, "to depart, and to be with
Christ; which is far better."

When the apostle expected to be with Christ he has very clearly shown in other scriptures, as, for instance, 1 Thessalonians 4:13-18. He there tells us that when Christ comes the second time, the living shall be changed and the dead shall be raised, and so shall we ever be with the Lord. The same thought is expressed in 2 Timothy 4:8,—it is "at that day," when Christ shall come; also Philippians 3:21, when Christ "shall change our vile body, that it may be fashioned like unto His glorious body." Jesus teaches the same truth in Matthew 16:27. "The Son of man shall come in the glory of His Father with His angels; and then He shall reward every man according to his works." This was the thing which the apostle desired, a translation either at or before the second coming of our Lord. The original word rendered "depart" comes from the same root as does "return" in Luke 12:36. The word "return" in that text clearly refers to the second coming of Christ.

2 Cor. 5:6-8

Now as regards the second scripture. Study the context, 2 Corinthians 5:1-10. Note the three states or conditions which the apostle there presents.

First, our earthly condition here, indicated by the following terms: "our earthly house of this tabernacle," "in this we groan," "in this tabernacle," "mortality," "at home in the body," "absent from the Lord."

Secondly, the condition of death, indicated by "dissolved," "found naked," "unclothed."

Thirdly, the future state for which the apostle longed: "the building of God," "an house not made with hands, eternal in the heavens," "clothed upon with our house which is from heaven," "swallowed up of life."

These we are sure will be clear to the reader—these three conditions. One, in which the apostle and all other mortals are, a condition subject to trouble and trial and sickness, sadness, and death, in which all groan and long for some other condition.

Secondly, the condition of being "unclothed," or "dissolved," having no dwelling place, so to speak, dead,—an utterly undesirable condition.

Thirdly, being at home with the Lord, or forever with Him, where mortality is swallowed up of life. Compare this with 1 Corinthians 15:51-54, when "this mortal shall have put on immortality," and "this corruptible shall have put on incorruption," "at the last trump," at the second coming of Christ. Note also again the parallelism between verses 2 and 4 and Romans 8:23, where the apostle declares that we also who "have the first fruits of the Spirit, even we ourselves *groan within ourselves,* waiting [not for death but] for the adoption, to wit, the *redemption* of our *body.*" That occurs at the resurrection, when "mortality might be swallowed up of life." Therefore the apostle tells us that while here we walk by faith, not by sight. Looking forward to the glorious hope and culmination of the Christian warfare, he labored that, whether present or absent, whatever his condition when Christ came, whether living or dead, he might be accepted of Him; "for we must all appear before the judgment seat of Christ." That is the climax of the apostle's statement, and it was to that time that he looked as a time not of condemnation, but of joyful triumph in his Lord. Therefore neither of the passages, when properly understood and explained by other scriptures, teaches the immortality of the soul, or the soul's conscious existence apart from the body; but they very emphatically teach that the only hope of the Christian is the second coming of our Lord.

"His Soul Within Him Shall Mourn." Job 14:22.

Please explain Job 14:22. Does it mean that his soul within him shall mourn after he dies?

No, it does not. The connection must be taken into consideration. Job is telling us of the sorrowful state of man. He will come to nothing. He looks constantly forward to the change which will take place, when he goes down into silence. In that condition of silence, "his sons come to honor, and he knoweth it not; and they are brought low, but he perceiveth it not of them." The 13th verse reads, "O that Thou wouldest hide me in the grave, that Thou wouldest keep me secret!" Chapter 17:12 expresses a very similar thought: "If I wait, the grave is mine house: I have made my bed in the darkness."

The 22d verse refers to his condition before that. While he is contemplating his end, "his flesh upon him shall have pain, and his soul within him shall mourn." Spurrell's translation of Job 14:22 is, "Surely the flesh upon him shall consume away, and his soul shall lament over it;" previous, of course, to his death.

According to the unscriptural theory of the condition of the soul after death, the soul has no flesh upon it; it is absolutely free. Therefore, according to that theory, this text could not refer to the condition after death. It must refer to a time when one is in the flesh; and the time to which Job refers is when man is decaying, and hastening on to his death. When death comes, then it is darkness, silence, unconsciousness, sleep.

"Undying Worm"—"Unquenchable Fire."

Will you give me some light on the expression, "Their worm shall not die," as mentioned in Isaiah 66:24; Mark 9:43-48?

The term "hell" in Mark 9:43-48 comes from the Greek word *Gehenna,* and that from the Hebrew Valley of Hinnom, south of Jerusalem, called also Tophet, or Topheth. See Jer. 19:2, 6, 11, 12. This valley, says Bagster's Greek Lexicon, was "once celebrated for the horrid worship of Moloch, and afterward polluted with every species of filth, as well as the carcasses of animals and dead bodies of malefactors, to consume which, in order to avert the pestilence which such a mass of corruption would occasion, constant fires were kept burning." Isaiah 66:24, it will be noticed, speaks *not* of live men upon whom worms feed, but the carcasses, or dead bodies, of men. See Isaiah 37:36, where the Hebrew word is rendered "corpses;" and Jeremiah 31:40; Amos 8:3, and other places where it is translated "dead bodies," which is what the word everywhere means. The terms "shall not die" and "neither . . . be quenched" simply indicate that these agents of destruction will not cease until they do their appointed work; for the worm shall eat them up

(Isa. 50:9; 51:8), and the fire shall burn up the chaff (Matt. 3:12; Mal. 4:1; Rev. 18:8). For an instance of this use of "unquenchable fire" see Jeremiah 17:24-27 and 2 Chronicles 36:19, 21. The former text declares that if the Jews would not observe the Sabbath, the Lord would kindle a fire in the gates of Jerusalem which should not be quenched. In the latter it states that this fire "burnt the house of God," and "burnt all the palaces thereof with fire," "to fulfill the word of the Lord by the mouth of Jeremiah." The undying worm and the unquenchable fire are symbols of utter and complete destruction. These arguments will likewise apply to Mark 9:43-48. Gehenna, as Wilson remarks, "symbolizes death and utter destruction, but in no place signifies a place of eternal torment."

SECTION IV

PROPHECY AND SECOND ADVENT

"The Earth Abideth Forever." Eccl. 1:4.

> Will you please explain the last clause of Psalm 78:69
> and Ecclesiastes 1:4? In the former text we read, "The
> earth which He hath established forever;" and in Ecclesi-
> astes 1:4, "The earth abideth forever." But is it not true
> that the earth will burn up with its wicked inhabitants?

No. When God created the earth, He did not create it to be
destroyed. He bases His very existence upon His power to preserve His work. See Isaiah 45:18: "For thus saith Jehovah that
created the heavens, the God that formed the earth and made it,
that established it and created it not a waste, that formed it to be
inhabited: I am Jehovah; and there is none else." Again in Psalm
115:16: "The heavens are the heavens of Jehovah; but the earth
hath He given to the children of men." In Psalm 37 we have the
promise repeated over and over, that the righteous shall receive
their reward in the earth; not only the righteous, but the wicked.
"The meek shall inherit the land, and shall delight themselves in
the abundance of peace." "The seed of the wicked shall be cut off.
The righteous shall inherit the land, and dwell therein forever."
Our Lord echoes the same thought when He declares in the Beati-
tudes, "Blessed are the meek: for they shall inherit the earth."

In referring to the glorious triumph over sin, the prophet Daniel
declares, "The kingdom and the dominion, and the greatness of
the kingdoms under the whole heaven, shall be given to the people of the saints of the Most High: His kingdom is an everlasting
kingdom, and all dominions shall serve and obey Him." Read
also Revelation 21, 22, where the new heavens and earth are por-
trayed before us,—in other words, the heaven and the earth re-
newed by the power of God.

"World" in the New Testament of the King James Version,
often comes from a Greek word meaning "age." The world, or

age, will end; but the earth, the material earth, purified by the fires of the last day and the power of God, will abide forever. Sometimes "world" comes from a word meaning "the inhabited earth." Of course, there will come a time when it will be without an inhabitant; but sin shall not work its will in the domain of God. "World" comes also from a word meaning "order, beauty, arrangement." This, too, comes to an end. The earth will be purified from sin and will continue forever.

Warning the Antediluvians. Gen. 6:3.

Will you please explain Genesis 6:3?

The text reads as follows: "The Lord said, My Spirit shall not always strive with man, for that he also is flesh: yet his days shall be an hundred and twenty years." This text is generally understood to express this: "The time of that generation was limited to the period named in the text, that during that one hundred twenty years God would, by the preaching of His servant and the sending forth of His Spirit, endeavor to bring men to repentance, before the Flood came upon the earth. The Lord never brings judgment upon men unwarned. Amos 3:7. It was not His desire that the antediluvian world should perish; but their wickedness had become so great that one or the other of two things was necessary,—the truth of God would be lost to the earth, and sin would completely triumph, or the judgment of God must fall upon those who were wicked, and sweep them from the earth.

It is not the Lord's plan that righteousness shall perish from the earth or that sin shall eternally triumph; and He therefore gave that generation the privilege of turning to Him. He sent out Noah, "a preacher of righteousness" (2 Peter 2:5), who preached the righteousness of Christ by faith (Heb. 11:7), by the power of the Spirit of God (1 Peter 3:19, 20), for one hundred twenty years. At the end of this time all upon the earth had either accepted or rejected the message of the gospel. Those who rejected, identified themselves with sin, and chose to perish. Those who accepted, were carried over the Flood by the ark. So it will be in the last days before Jesus Christ shall come again. God's "Spirit shall not always strive with man," for "as it was in the days of Noah, so shall it be also in the days of the Son of man." That day of judgment will as surely come as it did in the days of Noah.

"The End of All Things Is at Hand."

Why did Paul and the other apostles in their day say that the end of the world was at hand, and that they were living in the last days, as in 1 Peter 4:7? How long has it been since the end of the world has been said to be imminent?

Christ's second coming is life to His people. Even though they may sleep in death, that sleep is but for a moment, so far as consciousness is concerned. To him who falls asleep in Jesus the next moment of consciousness is seeing Jesus come. Therefore Christians in all ages ought to be prepared for that coming, ready to meet their Lord.

The apostles wrote for all time. The word was not their word, but God-breathed through them. They wrote, therefore, for the last days as well as for their own day, and for all days in view of the last great day. But that they did not believe that the Lord was coming in their day is shown by the apostle Paul in his first and second letters to the Thessalonians. In the first epistle he again and again refers to the coming of the Lord as though it were imminent. See chap. 1:10; 2:19, 20; 3:13; 4:13-18; 5:1-6. From these repeated references in the first epistle the Thessalonian brethren had come to believe that Christ's coming was impending. This the apostle corrected in his second epistle, as follows: "Now we beseech you, brethren, touching the coming of our Lord Jesus Christ, and our gathering together unto Him; to the end that ye be not quickly shaken from your mind, nor yet be troubled, either by spirit, or by word, or by epistle as from us, *as that the day of the Lord is just at hand;* let no man beguile you in anywise: for it *will not be, except the falling away come first,* and the man of sin be

revealed, the son of perdition." Chapter 2:1-3. It is very clear, therefore, that the apostle Paul did not look for the second coming of
Christ or the end of the world in his day.

The last days would be times of special peril (see 2 Tim. 3:1-5;
Luke 21:34, and many other scriptures); Satan would do all in
his power to blind the minds of men to the importance of that
great event, to its nature and its time. Therefore we have the
solemn warnings handed down to the last generation of men.
These things are confirmed by Matthew 24 and Luke 21, which
chapters clearly show that God's children may know when Christ's
coming is near. "When ye shall see all these things, know that He
is near, even at the doors."

Prophetic Time. Ezek. 4:4-6; Num. 14:34.

Why is the Jewish year reckoned as 360 days?

1. The application of a day for a year in prophecy is authorized
by Numbers 14:34 and Ezekiel 4:4-6. 2. A Bible month is shown
to be thirty days by Genesis 7:11; 8:4, in comparison with Genesis
7:24. The first passage places the beginning of the Deluge on the
second month and 17th day; the second passage tells us the ark
rested on the seventh month, the 17th day; and the third passage
shows this period to be just 150 days, a period of five months at
thirty days to the month. Twelve of such months would constitute
a year of 360 days. The twelve-month year is indicated in 1 Kings
4:7; 1 Chronicles 27:1-15. 3. There is one prophetic period mentioned seven times in the Bible, as follows: "time and times and
the dividing of time" (Dan. 7:25); "a time, times, and a half"
(Dan. 12:7); "forty and two months" (Rev. 11:2; 13:5); "a thousand two hundred and threescore days" (Rev. 11:3; 12:6); "a
time, and times, and half a time" (Rev. 12:14). If forty-two months
are identical with 1,260 days, there are thirty days to the month;
and if the forty-two months constitute three and one-half times, or
years, there are twelve months to the year, of thirty days each. This
is conclusive as to prophetic time. In the later Jewish calendars a

short month, Veadar, was added occasionally to correct the calendar, which, of course, would make correct the *average* Jewish year.
See Smith's Bible Dictionary, article, "Month."

Signs of His Coming. Matt. 24:33.

> You speak of general increasing wickedness as a sign
> of the times. Has not the world always been wicked?
> Have there not been many earthquakes before, and de-
> structive ones? and so with other so-called signs of His
> coming?

Yes, most of the experiences that we are passing through have
been duplicated at one time or another in the world. In and of
itself the prevailing wickedness is not a sign that the coming of
the Lord is near. The Bible declares that "the whole world lieth
in wickedness;" "lieth in the wicked one," some versions give it.
It is like a child lulled to sleep in the arms of its nurse. Satan is
lulling to sleep the whole world in that way. The unregenerate
heart has always been in rebellion against God and not subject to
the will of God. Sometimes this wickedness has been unrestrained,
the same as in the closing days of the Roman Empire, as in Sodom
and Gomorrah, as in other ages of the world. Sometimes when
God's children were living as near to Him as they ought and His
Spirit was resting upon them, their very presence has been a re-
straining influence in the world.

The sad fact at the present time is that all the sins that are mentioned by the apostle Paul in Romans 1 as being in the heathen
world, are in the last days to be found in the Christian church,
among those who have a form of godliness but deny the power
thereof. See 2 Tim. 3:1-5. So the perils of the last days are not
because there is wickedness in the world, nor because wickedness
in the world is increasing; but it is because wickedness has come
into the church of Christ, and all the evil principles of the unregenerate heart are manifest among those who ought to be a restrain-
ing influence by their very presence. If the salt have lost its savor,
how can it help to save that in which it is cast? When the professed church of Christ sets aside God's standard, and has none

other save the wishes of the natural heart, times are indeed perilous. And this is what the apostle points out.

There have been earthquakes before, great and terrible ones, destructive of life. These earthquakes have nearly always been confined to few localities. We hear more of them now than we did before because instruments have been perfected; and yet the very best records show that there has been a tremendous increase in the number of destructive earthquakes. Our Lord tells us that when these earthquakes occur in divers places, they are the beginning of sorrows, or, literally, the beginning of the birthpangs which shall issue in the destruction of things earthly and the coming of the Master.

The great evidence at the present time is not that there is simply one sign or two signs of Christ's coming, but *a great aggregation of signs,* a concentration of a score or more of signs all *focusing right down in this time of the end,* in which we are living; and it is the Master's words which declare, "When ye shall see all these things, know that He is near, even at the doors."

The Millennial Reign. Rev. 20:1-6.

> Do not Revelation 20:6 (last part) and Revelation 5:10 prove that the reign during the one thousand years will be on this earth?

Not at all. Revelation 5:10 declares in that anticipatory song, "We *shall* reign on the earth;" but it does not say when. The thousand years' reign in the New Jerusalem in heaven is the beginning of the eternal reign; but it differs from what comes after in that it is a work of judgment based on what is written in the books with respect to the wicked. John 13:36; 14:1-3; 1 Thessalonians 4:16, 17, with Revelation 14:1-3; 15:2, 3; 19:1, conclusively show that at Christ's second coming the saints are taken to heaven, to the many mansions in the city of God. The sea of glass and the throne, Revelation 4:1-6 shows to be in heaven. During this time the earth lies empty, desolate of inhabitants. And yet the saints have entered upon their inheritance, for the glorious city which they have sought (Heb. 13:14) is a part of the eternal kingdom (Heb. 11:14-16; Rev. 21:1, 2). John 17:24, to which our correspondent refers, takes in not only Christ's work in heaven during the thousand years, but the whole eternal reign.

The Kingdom of God. Luke 17:20, 21.

> What is meant in Luke 17:20, "The kingdom of God cometh not with observation," and the next verse, which says, "The kingdom of God is within you." Are the kingdom of God and the coming of Christ the same? Or what is meant?

The kingdom of God is revealed in different aspects. "Jehovah hath established His throne in the heavens; and His kingdom ruleth over all." Ps. 103:19. That kingdom includes: (1) God, the King; (2) His territory, the universe; (3) His throne, or center and seat of government; (4) His law, or rule of government; (5) His subjects, those who are loyal to Him. That kingdom is now in operation, and always was, and the throne of the everlasting Father is "the throne of grace." Heb. 4:16.

Christ has not yet taken His kingdom, and will not until He comes again. He now sits as priest on the Father's throne, gathering out subjects for His kingdom. Compare the following: Luke 19:11, 12; Dan. 7:13, 14; Ps. 2:7-9; Ps. 110:1; Heb. 8:1; Rev. 3:21; 11:18; Matt. 25:31.

Now it is evident that while the kingdom of God is literal, it is also spiritual. Before one can be a citizen of that kingdom, He must accept God's rule; God's law must be in the heart; and it is the work of grace to write this law in the heart.

This work is not heralded by pomp, or power, or display; it "cometh not with observation." Man opens his heart, and God, by His Spirit, comes in, and the man becomes a citizen of a heavenly kingdom. The Jews did not know this; they would not discern the spiritual nature of Christ's kingdom. "How can a man be born again?" was the language of darkness and unbelief. The

King, God in Christ, was there; but they knew it not. None said to them, "Lo, here! or, There! for lo, the kingdom of God is in the midst of you" (R. V., margin), or, as the margin of the Authorized Version reads, "*among* you." See the following, where the same word is rendered "among": Matt. 20:26, 27; 26:5; Luke 1:28, 42; John 1:26. Vincent says: "*Within:* Better, *in the midst of.* Meyer acutely remarks that '*you* refers to the Pharisees, in whose hearts nothing certainly found a place less than did the ethical kingdom of God.' Moreover, Jesus is not speaking of the *inwardness* of the kingdom, but of its *presence.*"—"*Word Studies in the New Testament.*"

Christ's kingdom is not His coming; but it is then set up.

A View of the Coming Kingdom. Matt. 16:28.

"Verily I say unto you, There be some *standing here,* which shall not taste of death, TILL they see the Son of man coming in His kingdom." Matt. 16:28. Who are referred to by the phrase, "There be some standing here"? Surely not those to whom Christ was speaking, was it? And, "Shall not taste of death, TILL they see the Son of man"? Was this clause intended to mean that some would be stricken dead immediately after they had seen Christ coming in the clouds of glory, the second time?

The words are found in the same connection in Matthew 16:28; Mark 9:1; Luke 9:27.

They are preceded by a prediction of Christ's suffering and death, and the necessity of following Him, and are followed by the story of the transfiguration.

Taking the transfiguration with the lesson it was intended to convey, and the lesson it did convey according to one of the apostles, we are forced to the conclusion that Christ referred to His own disciples by the "some standing here."

His promise was that they should "see the Son of man coming in His kingdom" (Matthew), see "the kingdom of God come with power" (Mark), "see the kingdom of God" (Luke).

The great essential things in the kingdom of God are the King, the subjects, and their condition. These subjects will be made up of two classes when Christ comes,—the righteous dead who have been sleeping and are then raised from the dead, and the righteous living who will then be translated. 1 Cor. 15:51-54; 1 Thess. 4:13-17.

In the transfiguration scene we have all these concomitants: there was Christ, the glorious King, whose countenance was altered and whose garments were so exceeding white and glistening as no fuller on earth could whiten them; there was Moses, the representative of those who had died and shall be raised from the dead (Rom. 5:14; Jude 9); there was Elijah, who had been translated to heaven without seeing death (2 Kings 2:11). It was the miniature representation of what Christ's second coming will be to His people.

Peter refers to this very transfiguration scene as proof that the apostles had not followed "cunningly devised fables" when they had made known "the power and coming of our Lord Jesus Christ." 2 Peter 1:16-18.

A word further: "Till" does not involve the meaning suggested. The whole scene of Christ's future kingdom was given to encourage the disciples in their coming task.

The Second Advent.

1. Does the second advent take place before the plagues come upon the wicked, and after the tribulation of the saints at the hands of the "beast"? Are the saints caught up between the tribulation and the plagues? If they are not then caught up, whence come the men in heaven not able to enter the temple on account of God's glory? Rev. 15:8.

2. Do the saints sit in judgment on the earth or in the air? Rev. 20:4. If not upon earth, when do they return to set up the everlasting kingdom? Over whom do they reign during the thousand years? Rev. 20:5, 6. If in the air, why, since the earth will be freed from the wicked if the plagues come before the saints are caught up?

1. The second advent of Christ takes place *after* the plagues are poured out upon the wicked; for those whom the plagues do not

destroy are destroyed at His presence, when He appears. See Rev.
16:17 and 19:21. His coming does not occur during the sixth
plague. See Rev. 16:15. The tribulation of the saints under the
persecuting power of the beast extended from 538 to 1798 A.D. See
Dan. 7:25 and parallel scriptures. The saints are therefore caught
up *after* both the tribulation and the plagues. Revelation 15:8 in
the original does not say "no man," but "none," or "no one." See
Revised Version. Yet there are men in heaven. When Christ
ascended, He led "a multitude of captives" (Eph. 4:8, margin),
who were raised at His resurrection (Matt. 27:52, 53). These assist
Him in His heavenly work. Rev. 4:4.

2. The saints shall sit in judgment in heaven in the holy city,
with Christ. Compare John 14:1-3; Rev. 20:4; 14:1-5; 19:1; 1 Cor.
6:2, 3. The everlasting kingdom begins in the holy city above, the
capital of the new earth, which will come down upon the earth at
the close of the thousand years. Revelation 20 and 21. The saints
shall reign in judgment with Christ over the wicked, a judgment
which will be executed at the close of the thousand years. The
last question has been answered in the foregoing.

The Number From Each Tribe. Rev. 7:5-8.

Does Revelation 7:5-8 literally mean that just an even
number of descendants of each tribe of Israel will be
saved?

The true Israel of God are not those numbered among the tribes
of earth, nor have they ever been, only as those tribes were connected with Christ by faith. There are no known twelve *earthly*
tribes now. But in God's record above, where the names of true
Israel are written, the twelve tribes still exist, not made up necessarily or largely from the descendants of the Hebrews, but from
the believing of all nations. For it is by faith that Israel shall be
saved. "And *so* ["by faith," verse 20] all Israel shall be saved."
Rom. 11:26; also 9:6-8; Gal. 3:26-29; Eph. 2:20; 3:6. All who
enter the city of God will enter as one of the twelve *heavenly tribes*.
Rev. 21:12. The numbers mentioned in Revelation 7:5-8, 12,000

from each tribe, do not refer to the earthly tribes, but to those recorded in heaven; nor does it include all that are saved under each tribe, but those who are saved out of the last generation of men. The sealing work of Revelation 7:1-8 is a work which takes place just before Christ comes, and the 144,000 of that chapter are identical with the company of Revelation 14:1-5.

Months, Not Years. Daniel 8 and 9.

How do you account for the fact that it seems improbable that Daniel 9:24-27 is an explanation of the vision of Daniel 8, when the vision of the eighth chapter was given fifteen years before that of the ninth chapter when there is no hint of such a thing in Daniel's prayer (9:1-19) or in Gabriel's expounding of the vision? What year was the third year of the reign of Belshazzar? Was it 553 B.C.? Are there tablets to prove that Ussher is wrong in his reckoning?

We answer both together. There is no fifteen-year period between the two chapters. Ussher is wrong. He supposed that Nabonidus, the last king of Babylon, mentioned in the records of history that came down to him, was identical with the Belshazzar of the Bible. If that were the case, the third year of Nabonidus was 553 B.C. This did not satisfy all Bible students. It was suggested by one devout man that there must have been a second ruler in Babylon, intimated in Belshazzar's promise to Daniel. Belshazzar promises Daniel, if he will read the writing, that he will be the third ruler in the kingdom. This implies a second ruler.

Belshazzar was the second. There must have been a first. This is revealed in the tablets. One of the tablets records a prayer written by Nabonidus for Belshazzar his son, whom he had associated with himself in his kingdom. Belshazzar reigned but three years, and in the third year of his reign he was slain and Babylon was captured. There is also a tablet recording the capture of Babylon and the death of Belshazzar, or the son of King Nabonidus. Therefore the time between the visions of chapter 8 and chapter 9 is but a matter of a few months instead of fifteen years.

You will note in the eighth chapter that the vision was explained to Daniel with one exception, and that was the *time*. Gabriel, who was commissioned to make Daniel understand the dream, did so as far as Daniel was able to bear it; and the angel explained all but the matter of the time, when Daniel fainted. Daniel was still anxious to know the rest of the vision; therefore his prayer. He seemed to have connected the seventy years of captivity with the vision to some extent, and so he prayed for understanding.

The angel who had been commissioned to make Daniel understand came again. That he had reference to the vision of the eighth chapter is clearly evident from his very first words to Daniel: "At the beginning of thy supplications the commandment went forth, and I am come to tell thee; for thou art greatly beloved: therefore consider the matter, and understand the vision." Then he says, "Seventy weeks are determined [cut off] upon thy people;" that is, seventy weeks of the 2300 days. This seems to us very clear indeed. If there is no connection between the chapters, then Gabriel left the vision of Daniel 8 unexplained, and there is no pertinency to the words of Gabriel as he meets Daniel the second time.

The Two Witnesses. Rev. 11:3.

What is the meaning of Revelation 11:3, and who are the two witnesses?

God's law of witness is that there shall at least be two witnessing to the same thing. Deut. 19:15; Matt. 18:16; 2 Cor. 13:1. The two witnesses of Jesus Christ were God's word in the Scriptures, and God's word in the life and works of Christ. John 5:36, 39. Thus the Father and the Son witnessed to the same thing. John 8:17, 18. Thus the Old Testament, the Scriptures which were known before Christ came, and the New Testament, in which are recorded the life and works of Christ, are God's witnesses of the ages. In a still broader sense, the two witnesses of God are His written word and the living epistle of His true church, in whom that word is inwrought and revealed. It was dimly revealed during the 1260 days of Revelation 11:3. This was prophetic of the Dark Ages of the union of Church and State—538 to 1798 A. D.—when the enemy, through an apostate church, endeavored to destroy the witnesses of God's word. They prophesied in sackcloth, in mourning, in persecution, but they were not destroyed. Their power is in God, and the oil of the grace of His Spirit supplies the power so that every word will prove effectual, every prophecy will be fulfilled.

God's Throne. Rev. 21:3.

Will God's throne be on this earth? Rev. 21:3. Is it the throne of God the Father or God the Son?

The context would indicate that it is the throne of the Father. "Behold," says the heavenly voice; a new thing is to be seen,—"the tabernacle [dwelling place] of God is with men, and *He* will dwell with them, . . . and God *Himself* shall be with them." "And the throne *of God and* of the Lamb shall be therein." Rev. 22:3. How supremely fitting it is that the place where the Son of God suffered and died should be the most exalted in all the universe! Where sin's curse lay the heaviest, there God's grace will restore it, a fitting place for His throne. The time of Revelation 21:3 is after the millennium; 1 Corinthians 15:24 is before the thousand years.

Destruction of "Beast" and "False Prophet."

When were the "beast" and the "false prophet" of Revelation 19:20 cast into the lake of fire and brimstone?

Before the millennium. The "beast" and the "false prophet" are symbols of systems which will be destroyed by the glory of Christ's presence when He comes. At that time "a fire shall devour before Him," and the earth shall be set on fire at His presence. See 2 Thess. 2:8; Ps. 50:3; 97:3; Isa. 30:33. The last text shows that when the unveiled presence of God shall be revealed to the sin-cursed earth, the earth will be set on fire, though not universally so. But all the works of man will be broken down and consumed, and thus all earthly systems, prominent and predominating among which are the "beast" and the "false prophet," will be destroyed. They live and seemingly prosper till the great day of the Lord breaks upon the world, but are then taken by the calamities and snares of their own wickedness, and perish in the fires kindled by God's presence. Rev. 19:20. At the end of the thousand years the whole earth will be converted into a vast lake of fire, which will consume all of sin; and all who have identified themselves with sin will be cast into the lake of fire, where "the beast and the false prophet are [were cast]," at the beginning of the thousand years. Before the millennium these *systems* and their devotees perish as a consequence; but after the millennium the people meet the full fruition of their evil deeds as *individuals*.

The Pronouns in 1 Corinthians 15:25.

Please explain 1 Corinthians 15:25: "He must reign, till He hath put all enemies under His feet."

Who must reign? Who subjects the enemies? Under whose feet? In Psalm 110:1 David says: "Jehovah saith unto my Lord [Adonai], Sit Thou at My right hand, until I make Thine enemies Thy footstool." This was fulfilled when Jesus ascended on high after His resurrection and took His place at the right hand of the Father, as priest-king. Eph. 1:20, 21. So Jesus declares in His message through John, "He that overcometh, I will give to him to sit down with Me in My throne, as I also overcame, and sat down with My Father in His throne." Rev. 3:21. While on the Father's throne, Jesus reigns as priest-king. Heb. 8:1, 2; Zech. 6:12, 13. When His work as priest is ended, He will then take His own throne, and reign thereon forever. Dan. 7:13, 14; Matt. 25:31. To help the reader, we paraphrase 1 Corinthians 15:24-28, as follows: "Then cometh the end [of Christ's reign as priest in the gospel dispensation of grace, Matt. 24:14; 28:18, 20], when He [Christ] shall [as king-priest] deliver up the kingdom [of grace] to God, even the Father; when He [the Father] shall have abolished all rule and all authority and power [according to His promise in Psalm 110:1]. For He [Christ] must reign [on His Father's throne, Zech. 6:12, 13], till He [the Father] hath put all His enemies under

His [Christ's] feet. The last enemy that shall be abolished is death. For, He [the Father in purpose] put all things in subjection under His [Christ's] feet. But when He [the Father] saith, All things are put in subjection, it is evident that He [the Father] is excepted who did subject all things unto Him [Christ]. And when all things have been subjected unto Him [Christ], then shall the Son also Himself be subjected to Him that did subject all things unto Him, that God may be all in all." Studied in the light of Christ's priesthood, the subject is perfectly clear.

Were the Old Testament Prophets Mistaken?

Were the Old Testament prophets mistaken in their predictions concerning Israel, as in Isaiah 11:11-16; Jeremiah 16:14, 15; 31:31, and other prophecies?

There are certain principles which will help us greatly to understand the prophecies of the Old Testament concerning Israel, if we will learn and apply the principles. Otherwise all is confusion.

1. Many of God's promises and covenants in the Old and the New Testament are to Israel. They come through the Jews to Gentiles. They are not to the Gentiles as such. Rom. 9:4. The Gentile, the stranger, the foreigner, is blessed only as he takes hold of God's covenants. Isa. 56:1-8; Eph. 2:11-22; Rom. 11:17. "Salvation is of the Jews." John 4:22.

2. Some of these promises and prophecies of the ancient prophets were fulfilled in the restoration from Babylon.

3. Some of these predictions are what may be called double prophecies, in which the prophet's vision included events close at hand and some far off, just as in one's view of the mountains, two peaks appear as one, though when we reach them, we find them separated by miles of valley. The prophecies fulfilled before Christ were fulfilled under the typical covenant conditions then existing; those fulfilled after Christ, according to the confirmed, antitypical covenant conditions. In the times previous to Christ, the Jews as a nation occupied the center of the field; since Christ, it is the Israel by faith, God's remnant church wherever found.

4. Some of these prophecies are conditional, depending upon Israel's acceptance or rejection. These conditions are very clearly stated in Jeremiah 18:7-10. The prophecy of the sanctuary of Ezekiel (chapters 37 to 48) is one of these. That sanctuary will never be built.

5. He who attempts to read the ancient prophecies of God concerning Israel without taking into consideration the clearer revelations of the New Testament is bound to go astray. Read the emphatic words of Paul: "By revelation He made known unto me the mystery; . . . which in *other ages was not made known unto the sons of men,* as it is now revealed unto His holy apostles and prophets by the Spirit; that the *Gentiles should be fellow heirs,* and of the *same body,* and *partakers* of His promise in Christ by the gospel." Eph. 3:3-6. It therefore follows that whoever fixes up a theory that excludes God's great gospel work to the world, for all alike, in which *"there cannot be Greek and Jew,* circumcision and uncircumcision, barbarian, Scythian," is astray, and is bound to go farther astray.

In harmony with these principles, our inquirer will have no trouble in settling many difficulties. He may find many obscure texts. Let him abide by the principles; the texts will sooner or later fall into line. The new covenant of Jeremiah 31:31 was confirmed by the death of Christ upon the cross. See Heb. 8:8-10. Its blessed fruitage is forever, and all brought in by it will be of Israel.

The "Seven Times."

Kindly give an explanation of Leviticus 26:27, 28. What is the meaning of the "seven times"?

The expression "seven times" is used repeatedly in this chapter. It is sometimes said to refer to seven different years, these years, of 360 days to the year, meaning 2,520 prophetic days, or literal years; but that is not the evident thought of the expression. One reading the text will see that it states not that God is going to punish seven times and then seven times more and then seven times more. It signifies sevenfold, that is, to the very fullness. Seven is the number of completion. The term in the original simply indicates seven, or sevenfold. The Hebrew word is used in the sense of sevenfold. See Genesis 4:24—Cain avenged sevenfold. It is used in most cases simply as a number. Spurrell renders "sevenfold" in each of the four instances where the expression occurs in this chapter. The clear, evident meaning is that, on account of the sins of the people, God would visit upon them full and complete punishment.

The Earth Desolated.

> Is the earth desolate during the millennial period? What of the wicked? Where do the saints dwell during that period?

That the earth will be desolated by the destruction of the wicked is clearly shown by such texts as Isaiah 24:1-3; 34:8-15; Zephaniah 1:2, 3; and other scriptures. This is declared by the prophet to occur at the presence of the Lord (Jer. 4:23-27); and by the apostle, at Christ's coming, which is the same thing (2 Thess. 2:8; Rev. 19:21). The reader will notice that those who have not been slain by plague and battle ("the remnant," those who remain) are destroyed by the presence of Christ and the words He speaks. Also in connection with Christ's coming, the righteous dead are raised, and all the righteous are changed to immortality, and are taken by Christ to the mansions He has gone to prepare, in the New Jerusalem, the city of God in heaven. See 1 Thess. 4:16; compare with John 13:36; 14:1-3.

In harmony with this, we are told that the saints "have in heaven a better and an enduring substance." Heb. 10:34. In holy vision, John saw them there before the throne of God, on the crystal sea (Rev. 14:1-3), and heard the sound of the multitude of voices praising God (Rev. 19:1). Then, as the righteous are taken to heaven and the wicked all slain, the earth must be desolate. How long it is desolate is shown by two scriptures,—"many days" (Isa. 24:21, 22), "until the thousand years were finished" (Rev. 20:5). At the end of this period, the wicked are raised from the dead; the New

Jerusalem, the capital of the new earth, descends from heaven with the saints; Satan and his host strive to take the city (Rev. 20:7-9), and the devouring fire of God's presence destroys them. The earth is then restored for the eternal inheritance of the righteous. Rev. 21:1-7. Thus the righteous are "recompensed in the earth: much more the wicked and the sinner." Prov. 11:31.

During the Thousand Years.

> Will you please explain Isaiah 34:11-15? Does the fire
> destroy all the animals that live at the coming of Christ?
> Or are there animals on the earth at that time?

There seems to be no evidence that when our Lord shall come the second time all life on the earth will be destroyed. All human life will be destroyed. Not only does Isaiah teach that, but Jeremiah 4:25 declares, "I beheld, and, lo, there was no man." See also Rev. 19:21. Of those left on the earth after the great wars that sweep over the inhabitable part of the globe have wrought their work, it is said, "The remnant were slain with the sword of Him that sat upon the horse." That is, they will perish in the glory of Christ's presence. But there are beasts that remain.

The fire is not, then, universal. It is kindled here and there, and the whole earth becomes a desolate wilderness; but Isaiah 34, which clearly seems to use Idumea as a type of that desolate condition, would indicate that there will be wild beasts and birds of prey which will inhabit the earth during that time. It is to these that the call goes forth to come and devour the carcasses of the men upon the earth. See Rev. 19:17, 18.

Then when the glory of God shall appear the second time, the whole sinful earth, with the exception of that place where the city stands, which has been made holy by the feet of the Son of God, will become one great lake of fire. The Scriptures do not say that the lake of fire will begin at the beginning of the thousand years, or at the beginning of the day of the Lord, but it will come in the day of the Lord. And so we read in 2 Peter 3:10, "The day of the Lord will come as a thief in the night; *in the which* the heavens shall pass away with a great noise, and the elements shall melt with fervent heat, the earth also and the works that are therein shall be burned up."

Elijah the Prophet. Mal. 4:4-6.

Will Elijah the prophet come down from heaven and preach the truth in the last days?

The prophecy of Malachi is of twofold application. One of these applications was met in John the Baptist. The angel said of John, in Luke 1:17, "He shall go before His [Christ's] face in the spirit and power of Elijah, to turn the hearts of the fathers to the children, and the disobedient to walk in the wisdom of the just; to make ready for the Lord a people prepared for Him." In Matthew 11:14, Jesus expressly says of John, "And if ye are willing to receive it, this is Elijah, that is to come." Yet John was not the actual Elijah, as he expressly tells us in John 1:21, but he was Elijah in the sense of the fulfillment of that prophecy at the first advent of our Lord.

But that which was fulfilled in a single individual then, takes a great deal wider scope in the last days. One individual could go to the Jewish nation and bring before all the people of that nation God's message concerning Christ's first coming. But there is to go to the world a message concerning His second coming. Rev. 14: 6, 7. No one man can bear that message to the world; and so Elijah and John the Baptist are types of the people whom the Lord calls to bear His last message to the world.

Conditions in the world will be the same as Elijah and John the Baptist found. For instance, there was the strongest kind of union of church and state, contrary to God and His truth, in the days of Elijah. We have Jezebel, the corrupt, idolatrous, sun-worshiping queen, urging on Ahab to the persecution of the Lord's people. We have, in the days of John the Baptist, Herod, influenced by Herodias, the wicked woman whom he had married. In Elijah's day, we have the backsliding of Israel and their turning away from the true God to sun worship. So it was in the days of John the

Baptist; God's people had departed from Him, and were sunken in cold, dead formalism, making void the commandments of God by their traditions.

Those are the conditions that exist today; and God is asking His faithful people to give to the world the great threefold message of Revelation 14:6-12. That message meets all the conditions that are in the world, and that message will go and is going with "the spirit and power of Elijah," just as John the Baptist went. Consequently the antitype of Elijah is not some man who may call himself Elijah; it is not vested in one individual, but in the whole people that will carry God's message to the world.

Another thought: the important thing is not the messenger, but the message. This has been true in all ages. The important thing was not Elijah—the mere man; it was the message from Jehovah which he bore to Ahab. John the Baptist, as a man, was not the important thing; and when the Jews asked him who he was, he declared, I am not this, and I am not that; but when they demanded who he was, he said, "I am the *voice* of one crying in the wilderness." The important thing was to be the voice of God. And so in the last message that shall go to the world, the important thing is the message, and not the persons that give it; but it will be given by an entire people, in the spirit and power of Elijah.

The Seven Last Plagues.

> When the plagues begin to fall, can a person tell whether he will be saved or not? Will the first plague, the noisome and grievous sore, have any effect on God's people?

According to the ninety-first psalm, God's children will be saved from the fearful plagues that fall upon the earth; and this is also indicated in Revelation 14, 15, 16. Certainly when the plagues begin to fall, God's children will know that they are safe. They will suffer by seeing others suffering. They will have more or less suffering all through the time of trouble, but the plagues will not fall upon them. "Only with thine eyes shalt thou behold and see the reward of the wicked. Because thou hast made the Lord, which is my refuge, even the Most High, thy habitation; there shall no evil befall thee, neither shall any plague come nigh thy dwelling." Every sin will have been confessed. Every wrong thing will have gone beforehand to judgment, and the righteousness of Christ will cover all. Doubtless there will be feelings of deep unworthiness, feelings sometimes of almost despondency. The righteous will cry, as did Jacob at the brook Jabbok, "I will not let Thee go, except Thou bless me." In the language of Jeremiah 30:7, "It is even the time of Jacob's trouble; but he shall be saved out of it."

Identity of the Horns.

> Will you kindly inform me as to whether the ten horns of Revelation 17 represent the same powers symbolized by the ten horns of Daniel 7?

Not all of them are identical, though some doubtless are. The ten horns of Daniel 7 refer to the nations into which Rome was divided during the fourth and fifth centuries, three of which were plucked up to make way for the supremacy of the papacy. Never among those original ten was there unanimity of mind or coalition of effort to exalt the papacy. Three of the kingdoms were openly Arian, or antipapal. Never did these three give either moral or military support to the papacy.

But the ten horns of Revelation 17 are contemporaneous, and are united with the beast for at least one prophetic hour, during which brief period they "have one mind, and shall give their power and strength unto the beast." Rev. 17:13. This confederacy is as yet future. These ten horns are "ten kings, which have received no kingdom as yet; but receive power as kings one hour with the beast." Verse 12.

The ten horns of Daniel 7 refer primarily to the European nations associated with the rise and reign of the papacy during the Middle Ages. The ten horns of Revelation 17 are associated with the restoration of the papacy shortly before the return of Christ. Their brief triumphal reign will end in this wise: "The ten horns which thou sawest upon the beast, these shall hate the whore, and shall make her desolate and naked, and shall eat her flesh, and burn her with fire. For God hath put in their hearts to fulfill His will, and to agree, and give their kingdom unto the beast, until the words of God shall be fulfilled." Rev. 17:16, 17.

European powers will yet fulfill the specifications of this prediction. Just what international changes must precede the movement, we do not know. In all probability, some of the present nations of Europe will be numbered in the great coalition.   L. E. F.

Who Is "Taken Out of the Way"?

> Please explain 2 Thessalonians 2:6-8. Who is he that "now letteth," or is "taken out of the way"?

The text reads as follows: "And now ye know what withholdeth that he might be revealed in his time. For the mystery of iniquity doth already work: only he who now letteth will let, until he be taken out of the way. And then shall that wicked be revealed, whom the Lord shall consume with the spirit of His mouth, and shall destroy with the brightness of His coming."

When the Bible was translated, the word "let" meant to restrain, or to hinder. The Revised Version renders the word, "restraineth."

To understand the text, it will be necessary to consider verses 3 and 4. The "man of sin [shall] be revealed, the son of perdition; who opposeth and exalteth himself above all that is called God, or that is worshiped; so that he as God *sitteth in the temple of God,* showing himself that he is God." This is the development of "the falling away," the chief exponent of which is the papacy.

"The temple of God" is the church of God. See 1 Cor. 3:16; Eph. 2:19, 22.

God in Christ dwells in the church by dwelling in the hearts of the individual members by faith. Gal. 2:20; Eph. 3:17.

Just as long as faith abides in the church, just as long as Christ in His word is held paramount by the church, it must be evident to all that the man of sin could not reign or exalt himself *in the church.* If Christ is there, there is no room for another. Christ, therefore, must be the one who "withholdeth," or, as the Revised Version reads, "restraineth," the revelation of the man of sin *in the temple of God,* the church. But when Christ is rejected, when an apostate church tells Him to go, then the mystery of iniquity comes in. Or when the church opens the door of her heart to bid the mystery of iniquity to enter, Christ departs as an unwelcome guest. Therefore all that can or that ever did prevent the man of sin from exalting himself *in the temple of God* is Christ in the heart by faith.

In harmony with this, we suggest the following paraphrase of the Revised Version of 2 Thessalonians 2:6-8: "And now ye know that which restraineth [the mystery of God, Col. 1:27], to the end that he [the man of sin] may be revealed in his own season [foretold by the prophets, Dan. 7:25]. For the mystery of lawlessness doth already work [it had begun to come into the church through unconverted men, 1 Tim. 1:19, 20; 2 Tim. 2:17, 18; 1 John 2:18; Gal. 4:8-10]; only there is one [Jesus Christ] that restraineth now, until He be taken out of the way [by unbelief]. And then shall be revealed the lawless one [as during the Dark Ages and since], whom the Lord Jesus shall slay [consume] with the breath of His mouth [Rev. 19:15], and bring to nought by the manifestation [forth-shining, brightness] of His coming [personal presence]."

"This Generation."

> Does the term "this generation" in Matthew 24:34 refer to the generation to which Christ was speaking, or to some other? The term "this" would seem to make it apply to His own day.

Let us consider these particulars: First, that which Jesus gave was a prophecy of His coming and of the signs of His coming. He was answering the threefold question of the disciples, "When shall these things be? and what shall be the sign of Thy coming, and of the end of the world?" Consequently He was not speaking for that generation alone, but for all other generations down to the time of His second coming.

Second, inasmuch as it was the Spirit of Christ that inspired all the prophets, the Master must have taken into consideration all the various prophecies that pointed forward to His second coming. The Book is one book, the prophecies all have the one object —the second coming of Christ and the fulfillment of God's promises in Him. Therefore, in this great literal prophecy that is recorded in Matthew 24, Mark 13, and Luke 21, our Lord not only gave various literal signs of His coming, but also presupposed more or less knowledge, on the part of those who would live just before His coming, of other great events pointing to the same climax.

Third, Jesus knew, because His Spirit inspired the prophets, that all the prophecies given by Daniel, and those to be given later through John, and Paul, and others, would be preached prior to His second coming; that the message of Joel would go forth, "Blow ye the trumpet in Zion, and sound an alarm in My holy mountain;" that the 2300 days of Daniel 8:14 would reach their fulfillment in 1844; that the days foretold by the prophets, as expressed in Revelation 10:7, would be fulfilled,—in fact, that all the various lines of prophecy would culminate right down in these last days in which we are now living. He knew that these things would be proclaimed by His faithful servants, in obedience to His command, so that all the world would hear the message of His coming; and these signs, therefore, that He gave, would simply be corroboration of all the other prophecies given in His word. So "this generation" would apply not to the generation who listened to His words, but to the generation in which these prophecies culminated. The term "this" does not necessarily apply to the thing then present. The present tense and the things expressing present time are often used for the future.

Take, for instance, Exodus 12:2, "*This* month shall be unto you the beginning of months." That, of course, was at the very beginning of the first month, Abib. Instruction is then given regarding the Passover. Then note the twelfth verse, which applies fourteen days later: "I will pass through the land of Egypt *this* night, and will smite all the first-born." The *"this"* night" does not refer to the particular time at which the Lord talked with Moses, but fourteen nights from that time. These instances, and others that might be given, show conclusively that the term "this" is used in referring to the future, as well as to the present.

Our Lord carried His disciples down through a variety of signs, some of which would not at all indicate that His coming was near, some of which would increase in intensity as that day approached, and three of which would but little precede His coming—the darkening of the sun and of the moon, and the falling of the stars. But the darkening of the sun and of the moon, and the falling of the stars were to be seen not merely with the physical eye, but in the light of the prophecy. There have been many darkenings of the sun and of the moon; there have been various star showers. But that to which the Master referred was to come at a particular time, —"in those days, after that tribulation,"—that is, after the long tribulation caused by the persecution of the Dark Ages. Just prior to the time in which the days of that persecution—the 1260 years of Daniel 7:25 and Revelation 12 and 13—should end, came the darkening of the sun and of the moon; and a few years later came the falling of the stars.

Now those signs must be seen in the light of our Lord's prophecy, in order to be signs of the end, and they could not be seen until after the falling of the stars had taken place, November 13, 1833,— the most remarkable "star shower" within the records of astronomical phenomena.

But the message which should bear to the world the tidings of the second coming of Christ, which should prepare the world for that coming, could not be said to go forth until it went forth in its fullness, after the end of the 2300 days, in 1844. That is the beginning of the time of the last great threefold message recorded in Revelation 14:6-14, a positive feature of which is, "The hour of His judgment is come." Therefore this generation to which our Lord referred was the generation that should bear to the world the last message of mercy, and proclaim the Lord's coming, with all the accompanying signs, given not simply in Matthew 24, Mark 13, or Luke 21, but in all the various prophecies of His word.

Now, just as the generation to which Noah bore witness of the coming Deluge did not pass until the event foretold occurred, just as the generation to which our Lord first came heard the message of His coming, just so truly will the last generation to which is borne the message of His coming witness that coming. He delays it long in order to give the world opportunity to repent. The vision seems to tarry; but it is because of God's long-suffering, in pity for men who have not repented.

SECTION V

THE MORAL LAW

A Question on the Law. Matt. 5:17.

1. Matt. 5:17.—What law was Christ talking about?
2. Matt. 5:18.—When will it all be fullfilled?
3. Matt. 5:19.—What commandments was Christ talking about?

Here is the whole scripture, Matt. 5:17-20:

"17. Think not that I am come to destroy the law, or the prophets: I am not come to destroy, but to fulfill.

"18. For verily I say unto you, Till heaven and earth pass, one jot or one tittle shall in nowise pass from the law, till all be fulfilled.

"19. Whosoever therefore shall break one of these least commands, and shall teach men so, he shall be called the least in the kingdom of heaven: but whosoever shall do and teach them, the same shall be called great in the kingdom of heaven.

"20. For I say unto you, That except your righteousness shall exceed the righteousness of the scribes and Pharisees, ye shall in no case enter into the kingdom of heaven."

1. Christ is talking about the moral law of God, the standard of righteousness. Verse 20. God's royal law is summarily comprehended in the Decalogue, or Ten Commandments. See James 2: 8-12; Rom. 7:7; Ex. 24:12; 31:18; Eccl. 12:13, 14.

2. All will never be fulfilled. The law is fulfilled when man fully keeps, or fills up, its eternal breadth and depth. Only One did this, Christ Jesus. We can do it only in Christ. The prophets —that is, what they prophesied—will never be fulfilled; for they prophesy of a glorious eternity as long as the days of God, and eternity will never be filled up. Therefore *never* a jot or a tittle will pass from the law.

3. The commandments of God's law may be summarized in love to God and love to man (Deut. 6:5; Lev. 19:18; Matt. 22: 36-40). Mere outward observance, is not keeping the law. This is

self-righteousness, the righteousness that falls short (Matt. 5:20). God requires heart righteousness, the keeping of the law from the heart by the Spirit (Matt. 5:21-28; Rom. 1:16, 17; 8:4; 1 John 5:3). Dr. Albert Barnes well remarks that he who considers that any command of God is too small to be obeyed is unworthy of His kingdom.

Deeds of the Law. Rom. 3:20.

> Please explain Romans 3:20. What are the deeds of the law spoken of here?

The deeds of the law spoken of in Romans 3:20 are efforts which man puts forth to save himself. Verse 19 declares that all the world is guilty before God; and verse 9, that Jews and Gentiles are all under sin. Therefore no deeds which they can do will meet the requirements of the law; for they are as imperfect as the mortal sinful man who does them. Thus man cannot be justified by his imperfect deeds. He can only be justified by One who has wrought out for him perfect righteousness, and that One is our Lord Jesus Christ. But the Lord places His righteousness upon us for all the sins of the past, and His righteousness within us to change us from sin, in order that we may, by the same grace, walk above sin in the future. Sin has dominion over us when we are transgressing God's law and committing sin, and so only. It is God's desire that His grace shall so fill our hearts, not simply for forgiveness of the past, but for strength to live for Him in the future, "that the righteousness of the law might be fulfilled in us, who walk not after the flesh, but after the Spirit." Rom. 8:4.

Justified Without the Law. Rom. 3:28.

> Please explain Romans 3:28. Why should we keep the law if we are justified without the deeds of the law?

Justification, or counting that just which is not just, has reference to the past. Here is a man who has been a criminal—a bank robber—for forty years. He desires to be a good citizen. He cannot say, I will keep the law from this time forward, and then I will be accounted a good citizen. This would not do. The judge would say: Your future obedience will satisfy only the future; it will not change the past. It cannot undo the crimes you have committed. No deeds of the law you can do will ever restore you to citizenship; but the governor is a merciful man, he will pardon all your crimes. He goes to the governor; and in his goodness of heart, the governor pardons or justifies the criminal, and he does this without the fulfilling of the deeds of the law on the part of the criminal. Should the pardoned bank robber now say: Well, the governor has pardoned me for my crimes, which I could not undo; why should I keep the law in the future? I will go back to robbing banks again. We all know that everyone would condemn a course like that. The governor pardons that men may obey the law. Christ forgives what we may not undo,—not that we may sin again (Rom. 6:1), but that we may keep the law (Rom. 8:4). He not only forgives sin, but He changes the heart so that it will not hate God's law (Rom. 8:7), but love it, and love to obey it (1 John 5:3). He who feels that he is justified of Christ in order that he may again go into sin, has misunderstood the purpose of the law and forgiveness, and is not justified at all.

"Under the Law," and "Without the Law."

What does Paul mean in 1 Corinthians 9:19-22?

The passage reads as follows:

"For though I be free from all men, yet have I made myself servant unto all, that I might gain the more. And unto the Jews I became as a Jew, that I might gain the Jews; to them that are under the law, as under the law, that I might gain them that are under the law; to them that are without law, as without law, (being not without law to God, but under the law to Christ,) that I might gain them that are without law."

What do the terms "under the law" and "without the law" mean? Where "under the law" occurs in verse 20, the first three times, the meaning is the same,—under condemnation by the law, or under sin. The term in these instances comes from the Greek words *hupo nomon*. "Under the law" in verse 21 comes from *en- nomon, in* the law, or subject to the law. "Without the law" means "lawless," "without law," and is used of the Gentiles (Rom. 2:12), who were without God's written law. It refers to the heathen in this text.

The apostle says that in his labor he put himself in the place of others as far as it was possible, so as to win them to Christ. The Jew's prejudices were taken into consideration, as Paul, a Jew, could well do. The sinner's condition was appreciated, for Paul knew what it was to be under the power of sin. See Romans 7; 1 Tim. 1:15. Those who did not know God's law, who were igno- rant of the true God, Paul met on their own ground, as a man by nature on the same level with them. See Acts 14:15-17.

Paul, however, says that while he did everything in his power to meet all these cases, he did not sin in so doing, he did not do evil that good might come. He was *not* without law to God, for he knew God's law. Christ had become his surety, his righteousness, and he labored for all in the spirit of his Saviour that he might win all. This is what the text is designed to teach.

The Law and the Prophets. Luke 16:16.

> Please explain Luke 16:16. Some say that there were
> to be no more prophets after John; also that this statement
> does away with the moral law.

It does not mean that there were no more prophets after John, for the apostles, some of the apostles at least, if not all, were proph- ets. See Acts 2:17, 18; 19:6; 21:9, 10; 1 Cor. 14:29-32. It does not mean that the law of God was then done away. In fact, nearly all those who make this claim contend also that the law was abolished at the cross, over two years later. It was after this that our Lord said, "If thou wilt enter into life, keep the commandments." Matt. 19:17. Who would charge Christ with teaching obedience to an abolished law? He tells us in the very connection of Luke 16:16, in fact, the next verse, "It is easier for heaven and earth to pass,

than one tittle of the law to fail." We have found that it does not
mean that prophets were no more or the law abolished; what does
it mean? It means, "The law and the prophets [were preached]
until John: since that time the kingdom of God is preached, and
every man presseth into it." Before John came, the teachers of God
taught the law and the prophets,—the Scriptures,—but did not see
all that they meant; but when John came, he preached the fulfillment of many of these prophecies in the advent of the Messiah.
The Royal One of David's line was born, the present truth for that
time was proclaimed (Matt. 3:2, 3), Satan was working as never
before, and only the earnest and persevering would enter the kingdom.

"Under the Law." Rom. 6:14.

What is meant by being "under the law"?

This is quite clearly shown in the passages where the expression
occurs, as, for instance, Romans 6:14; Galatians 5:18: "Sin shall
not have dominion over you: for ye are not under the law, but
under grace;" "but if ye are led by the Spirit, ye are not under the
law." In the first scripture we are told that sin does not have dominion over those who are not under the law, and that those who
are not under law are under grace. God's object of grace is the
forgiveness of sins. This is shown in an abundance of passages.
See Rom. 5:1, 2; 3:20-31. Grace is unmerited favor. By the unmerited favor of God our sins are taken away. The one thing
which points out sin, is the law. "Nay, I had not known sin," declares the apostle, "except the law had said, Thou shalt not covet."
Rom. 7:7. "Where no law is, there is no transgression." Rom. 4:
15. "By the law is the knowledge of sin." Rom. 3:20. Therefore,
grace brings us into harmony with God's law: first, by forgiving
all the sin which the law points out, for which the law condemns
us; and secondly, by placing within us God's Holy Spirit in harmony with His law, to write that law in our hearts (Heb. 8:10),
and so enable us to keep His law, not in our strength, but in the
strength of the Spirit.

Those, then, who are "under the law" are those who are condemned by the law, who are still in their sins. Those who are not "under the law" are those whose sins are forgiven and who by the power of the Spirit of God are keeping the law. "For this is the love of God, that we keep His commandments: and His commandments are not grievous." 1 John 5:3. And that love is born within our heart by the Holy Ghost which He has given us. Rom. 5:5.

It is one of the saddest things in this world to hear a Christian say, when confronted with the duty of doing God's commandments, "I am not under the law," using an expression which shows liberty from sin as an excuse or license to disobey. The only thing in this world which leads the soul to disobey is "the carnal mind," which "is enmity against God;" "is not subject to the law of God, neither indeed can be." Rom. 8:7. Therefore the man who declares, as an excuse for disobedience to God, that he is not under the law, is confessing by that very thing that he has the carnal mind; while, on the other hand, those who walk in the Spirit and fulfill the fruits of the Spirit, the apostle assures us in Galatians 5 are not under the law, for "against such there is no law." Why? Because they are keeping the law of God.

Commandments Before Moses.

Is there evidence that certainly shows that God gave His law to the people before the time of Moses, or that any kept the law or the commandments before that time?

Surely there is, plenty of evidence, of which we briefly give a part:

God is ever the same, of unchangeable, righteous character. Mal. 3:6; James 1:17. His law, His requirements, must therefore be the same in all ages.

He asks men in all dispensations to be like Him. When He said to Israel of old, "Ye shall be holy: for I the Lord your God am holy" (Lev. 19:2), He meant the same kind of holiness, of the same standard, as He did when He said through Peter, "Be ye holy; for I am holy" (1 Peter 1:15, 16).

When God said to Abraham, "I am the Almighty God; walk before Me, and *be thou perfect*" (Gen. 17:1); when His word said, "Noah was a just man and *perfect* in his generations, and Noah *walked with God*" (Gen. 6:9); when it was said to Israel, *"Thou shalt be perfect* with the Lord thy God" (Deut. 18:13); when Jesus said, *"Be ye therefore perfect,* even as your Father which is in heaven is perfect" (Matt. 5:48); when Paul said, *"Be perfect,* be of good comfort, be of *one mind"* (2 Cor. 13:11),—all must have meant the same perfection, the same standard, the same kind of walking, the same mind; for how "can two walk together, except they be agreed?" All were, therefore, required to keep God's perfect, holy law. See Ps. 18:30; 19:7; Rom. 7:12. These scriptures clearly show that God's requirements are the same in all dispensations.

The negative side proves the same. "Sin is the transgression of the law." 1 John 3:4. "Nay, I had not known sin, but by the law: for I had not known lust, except the law had said, Thou shalt not covet." Rom. 7:7. "The wages of sin is death." Rom. 6:23. "Sin, when it is finished, bringeth forth death." James 1:15. Therefore, wherever there is death, there is sin; and wherever there is sin, there is law. "And so death passed upon all men, for that *all* have *sinned,"* all have transgressed the law. Rom. 5:12. "Until the law" in the next verse means until it was given at Sinai. Paul proves that the law existed before it was there given, by the very fact that men were counted sinners, and died; for "sin is not imputed when there is no law."

Every commandment of the Decalogue can be traced before Sinai, either by its observance or by its transgression. Note them in order: (1) Joshua 24:2; (2) Gen. 31:30, 34; (3) Jacob's family must have taken God's name in vain when they worshiped idols (Gen. 35:2, 4); (4) Ex. 16:4, 25-28; (5) Gen. 9:21-25; (6) Ex. 1: 16, 17; 2:14; (7) Gen. 39:7-9; (8) Gen. 31:32; (9) Gen. 31:30; (10) Gen. 3:6; 6:2. All the law of God was broken by the antediluvians. Gen. 6:5, 11. Most of its principles were transgressed in the Garden of Eden.

There is one more evidence. God said of Abraham, "the father of all them that believe," "Abraham obeyed My voice, and kept My charge, My commandments, My statutes, and My laws." Gen. 26:5. See also Gen. 18:19.

Surely this evidence "certainly shows" that God gave His law to the people before it was given from Sinai.

The Heathen and the Law. Rom. 2:14, 15.

If the heathen have received the law in their hearts, why is the Sabbath not found, as well as other precepts? Rom. 2:14, 15.

The scripture itself reads, "For when Gentiles that have not the law do by nature the things of the law, these, not having the law, are the law unto themselves; in that they show the work of the law written in their hearts, their conscience bearing witness therewith, and their thoughts one with another accusing or else excusing them."

The great principles of the law summed up in the Old Testament, and by our Saviour approved, are supreme love to God and equal love to our fellow men. The heathen who has that to the fullest sense of his capacity certainly will be excused by his own conscience. Yet during that very time he might have a multitude of wives. During that very time he might be doing other things that conventionalities of this age would not permit, that greater light from the word of God would condemn, just as did Abraham, just as did Jacob. The law written in their hearts is primarily not complete knowledge, but complete principle of doing right. God has expressed this in 2 Chronicles 16:9: "The eyes of the Lord run to and fro throughout the whole earth, to show Himself strong in the behalf of them whose *heart is perfect toward Him.*"

That is what God asks—the perfect affection, the perfect heart. The one dominant thing that moves the man is his affection, his love. He may know scarcely anything. He may have seen but one ray of light from the throne of God; but that ray of light dominates his life, and the man who yields himself to that ray of light is accepted of God. But the man who has a knowledge of all the Ten Commandments of God's law, and yet yields himself to one sin, however small it may seem, turns away from the light. If he continues in such a course ultimately he will be rejected. It is not knowledge that saves us—that is, mental knowledge, intellectual knowledge; it is the life of God in the soul, which comes by our yielding ourselves absolutely to all the light we see. The heathen who has that in his heart will yield to all the light that comes to him—to the sixth commandment, the seventh commandment, the eighth commandment, the fourth commandment. It is to him, then, only a matter of revelation as testing the love that is in his heart; and that love is held by the Master for obedience to God's law.

"End of the Law for Righteousness." Rom. 10:4.

Please explain Romans 10:4 so as to show definitely
the meaning of "the end of the law."

The one who has faithfully studied the book of Romans up to Romans 10:4 will have no question about the meaning of "the end of the law." Chapter 1 shows that the world is condemned, that the only hope is the gospel of Christ; chapter 2, that the Jews stand with the Gentiles—that although they have "the form of knowledge and of the truth in the law," still they have transgressed it. Chapter 3 brings both of them together; tells us that all the world is guilty before God, condemned by the law. And that chapter closes with the great thought that only by faith can we be justified, because no law can justify its transgressor. Chapter 4 shows how Abraham found relief by believing in God; chapter 5, that faith brings us peace and justification and hope.

Chapter 6 discusses baptism and what it ought to mean to the sinner, that his sins are buried, but his whole life is yielded to Christ; that now he lives the new life in Christ Jesus. But the new life must be just such a life as Christ led, and Christ kept all God's commandments.

Chapter 7 is a further development of the subject, showing that not the law, but the sinner, is bad; and the law, having no salvation in itself, drives the sinner who longs to be saved to the Lord

Jesus Christ. Therefore, while the sinner has no hope in the law, he finds hope in the grace of Christ.

Chapter 8 is an amplification of that glorious freedom in Christ. It expressly tells us that the only mind that is at enmity with God and against God's law is the carnal mind, which cannot be subject to God's law. And it brings before us the acme of Christian experience,—love to God; and love is exemplified in obedience to God's law. I John 5:3.

Chapter 9 carries the same thought further,—that the Jews sought righteousness by their works, not by faith. And Romans 10:4 is a climax to the argument that has been presented before,—that the very thing the Jews sought and could not find, is found in Christ Jesus our Lord; that Christ is "the end of the law for righteousness." "End" is not used here to signify the limit, or the last of a thing. It does not mean that the law is no more when we come to Christ. "End" is used in the sense of object, just as James says, "Ye have heard of the patience of Job, and have seen the end of the Lord" (James 5:11),—that is, the object of the Lord in afflicting Job.

It is a sad thing, is it not, that the text should be used to justify sin,—to teach that when we reach the Lord Jesus, we may disregard His law? But the text does not say that Christ is the end of the law for transgression. The object of the law is not that we may break the law, but "Christ is the end of the law *for righteousness.*" The law drives us to Christ, that in Him we may find the righteousness which the law demands. To that righteousness the law witnesses, as we are told in the twenty-first verse of the third chapter. That is, the righteousness that we have through our Lord Jesus Christ is declared by the law to be perfect. The man who is made righteous will keep the righteous law.

Decalogue—or Law of Ceremonies?

To what law does Paul refer in Galatians 3:19, 24-26?
Also in chapters 2:16-21; 3:2-5, 11-13; 4:4, 5?

It is impossible, in the space that we have, to attempt a detailed explanation of all these texts. What will help our inquirers, we are sure, will be one or two preliminary considerations: First, what is the general subject of the epistle? Doubtless all will agree that it is justification by faith in Christ, with the emphasis on *"in Christ;"* not justification by doing, not justification by any law whatsoever, but justification by faith in Christ Jesus our Lord. It is the enforcing of the same truth that is taught by Romans. Second, this point also is emphasized: that law cannot justify; and in some cases, it seems to us that the apostle is talking of law in general. No law can justify the transgressor. It matters not what it is or what its nature is. Any law, given by any authority, which has been transgressed by any person subject to that authority, condemns that person. He cannot be justified except by the grace of the one in authority. But when the apostle brings it right down to the very sinner himself, the law which condemns must be the law which points out sin; and the only law which points out sin is the law of Ten Commandments.

In chapter 2:16, he could say to the Galatian brethren that they knew that a man is not justified by the works of the law, but by the faith of Jesus Christ; and that if a man should say, "I will be justified by works that I can do," whatever those works were, he was building again the things which he had destroyed, he was making Christ a minister of sin, and that he could not do. Righteousness could not come to the sinner by the law; it must come through Christ. In Galatians 3:19, the question is asked, "Wherefore then serveth the law?" In other words, What was purposed in speaking the law? The only trouble to our inquirers, we apprehend, is the term "added;" but that expression seems to be clearly parallel with Romans 5:20: "Moreover the law *entered, that the offense might abound,*" that sin might be exceeding sinful. The consciences of men had become so perverted that they could not be trusted. The law which God wrote in man's very nature in the beginning had become so effaced by sin that man's conscience must be brought to a standard which was unperverted and unpervertible. Consequently, when God brought His people out of Egypt, He gave them the great moral standard, in order that they might know what sin was; and that moral standard was the Ten Commandments. It *entered* then in its *written form,* "that the offense might abound," that sin might be seen to be exceeding sinful. It was spoken to that people. Heb. 12:19.

The Greek word rendered "added" in Galatians 3:19 is the same as that rendered "spoken" in Hebrews 12:19. The law was *spoken* by God in order that sin might be more clearly seen. It was *added* because of transgressions; that is, that transgression might be known to be what it really is. It is the same Greek word in the Septuagint in Deuteronomy 5:22, "He *added* no more," referring directly to the Ten Commandments. That Greek word is *prostithemi.* It is defined by Baxter, "To put to, or near to, lay with, or by the side of, to add, superadd, adjoin." What it refers to in these texts, is that God added the law in its written form.

It was given in written form until a certain time, designated as "till the Seed should come to whom the promise was made." The promise is that of the inheritance, or the new earth. Rom. 4:13. That is the promise which was given to Abraham. In that new earth state God's law will be written in the hearts of all His children. Every single precept will be an enabling act, in which they will find power, and grace, and pleasure to do God's will. But until sinners are no more the law is needed, and needed in the form in which God has given it.

When Christ came the first time He came as our sacrifice, came to give Himself for us; He came as "the way." He is coming again as the life, as the king; and then He will say, "Inherit the kingdom prepared for you from the foundation of the world." That coming is set forth in Ezekiel 21:25-27. Referring to Zedekiah, whose throne was just overturned by Babylon, the prophet says: "And thou, O deadly wounded wicked one, the prince of Israel, whose day is come, in the time of the iniquity of the end, thus saith the Lord Jehovah: Remove the miter, and take off the crown; this shall be no more the same; exalt that which is low, and abase that which is high. I will overturn, overturn, overturn it: this also shall be no more, until He come whose right it is; and I will give it Him."

After the overturning of the kingdom by Babylon came the overturning by Medo-Persia, by Grecia, by Rome; and succeeding

Rome, in all its later phases, will come the Lord Jesus Christ to take the kingdom and reign forever. Until that time comes, God's law will stand in its written form as a reproof to all sinners. Thus in Galatians 4:4 we read that "God sent forth His Son, . . . made under the law," that He might redeem all those who are under the condemnation of the law. That law prescribes all duty, forbids all sin, and is in absolute harmony with His Holy Spirit. Consequently, in him in whom the fruits of the Spirit are manifest, there is no condemnation; God's law is not against him. But if a man is doing that which is contrary to the Spirit, he is still under the law, condemned by it.

The Law in Galatians.

> Will you give me a little light on two passages in Galatians,—chapter 3, verses 9 to 13, and chapter 4:24, 25?

Galatians 3:9 declares that they who are of faith are blessed with faithful Abraham. God counts them one in His family, because they have the same faith. Verse 10: "As many as are of the works of the law are under a curse." That is, those who are depending upon the law for salvation. Why? Because they are transgressors of the law, and the law condemns such to death. No law can save a man who is transgressing it. Consequently the justice of the conclusion in the eleventh verse: "No man is justified by the law: . . . the righteous shall live by faith." That is always true; it has always been true; it was true before sin entered, that the only way by which man could live was by faith in God, with a heart open on the Godward side, receiving life and blessing from Him, and pouring it out to others. And since man has sinned, it is still true. The only hope for justification is by faith in Christ, and the only hope in right living is by the same faith.

But the man who has that faith in God will live according to God's law. That law is the reflection of God, and faith will appropriate the power of God for obedience to His law. But the law does not justify; the righteousness of God in Christ justifies. If a man could obey the law, he would live by it; but only through Christ can he obey it. Christ therefore redeemed us from the curse of the law, having become a curse for us. And He did it that upon every soul in this world, Gentiles as well as Jews, might come the blessing of Abraham in Christ Jesus; and that blessing was that Abraham believed God, and God counted it to him for righteousness.

The same faith brings also the Spirit of God. Now God made a covenant with Abraham to give him all that; and the law did not take away from the covenant. The law was not designed to take away from the covenant. The covenant was given in order that the law might be established in the heart; and that covenant abides in Christ Jesus. See Heb. 8:9, 10.

The Seed of Abraham

Abraham had different posterities; but the blessing comes through one posterity,—Christ,—wholly and solely by promise. Why, then, was the law given? That sin might be seen to be exceeding sinful, so that man might flee from the wrath, and find refuge in Christ Jesus. Paul gives a parable of Abraham's two sons —the one by Hagar, the bondwoman; the other by Sarah, a free-woman. The one was born after the flesh, through the work of man wholly; the other was born after the Spirit, through promise and power of God, and man co-operating with that promise. God promised Abraham that through his seed all should be blessed. Abraham fixed matters up in his own way; and in order to carry out his own way, he had a son by Hagar, his bondmaid. God said, "This shall not be the seed."

And that plan and scheme of Abraham's through Hagar was a type, or figure, of the covenant from Mount Sinai, that gendered, or bore, children to bondage. What the apostle means by the covenant at Sinai was Israel's promise to do God's will, relying upon power which they possessed of themselves: "All that the Lord hath said will we do, and be obedient." They felt that they could work it out themselves. See Exodus 19. They left the Lord out of the question, save in the blessings. They wanted God's blessings, but they wanted to buy those blessings, or obtain them through their own works.

But the child born to Sarah is a type of the new covenant, in which God promises, if we will but receive the promise, if we will but co-operate with Him by yielding wholly and absolutely to His plan, to save us. He brought the promised seed to Abraham by miraculous power through Sarah. And so God brings to all His children deliverance from sin when they yield wholly to His plan. We can see what the results of the two plans are. If the first were successful, man would glory in himself. If Abraham had been successful in his scheme, he would have taken the glory to himself. But as there is no success in that, and success lies wholly through God and His power, all the glory is given to God.

Hagar stands for the religion possessed by those who would work out their own salvation, not through God's working in them, but through their own power. Sarah, or Isaac, stands for the mighty power and promise of God that is able to work above all appearance, and bring out of what seems to be utterly impossible, that which is eternally true and will eternally abide. Therefore we have the comfort, "Now we, brethren, as Isaac was, are children of promise."

"Thou Shalt Not Kill." Ex. 20:13.

God's word says, "Thou shalt not kill." As war involves the taking of human life, is it any more justifiable to do wholesale killing under Federal or state orders than to kill an individual? In case one should refuse to fight, he presumably would be tried and shot. Now, should we walk up bravely and be shot rather than go and shoot others?

In ancient times, God directed His people to fight; but He Himself ruled. His people were His agents. Yet there are instances in His word which seem clearly to show that God would have interposed and preserved His people from war if they had but trusted in Him. An instance is the taking of Jericho, as recorded in the first chapters of Joshua. All that God called His children to do was to march around that city and blow trumpets. The army of heaven threw down the walls and conquered the people. When Jehoshaphat was besieged by the enemy,—Moab and Ammon and others,—he proclaimed a fast, and sought God; and word came from the prophet that they should not be afraid by reason of the great multitude that had come against them, "for the battle is not yours, but God's,"—that they had no need to fight, but should simply stand still, and see the salvation of God. And thus they went forth, with singers in the forefront of the battle, praising God; and the Ammonites and the Moabites and the Edomites destroyed one another, and God's children were saved. See 2 Chronicles 20. That was in the olden times.

Our example is Christ Jesus our Lord. He did not resist. He reproved His ardent disciple when he drew the sword. Matt. 26:51, 52. He healed the wound that Peter made. Luke 22:51, 52. He has told Christians that the weapons of our warfare are not carnal, yet they are mighty through God in pulling down strongholds that no earthly army can overthrow—the fortresses of sin within the heart. 2 Cor. 10:4, 5.

Christian nations surely ought not to be at war, and the fact that they are at war shows that Christianity is wanting. On the other hand, those who are carnal will fight; and all the nations of the earth are carnal. They will live by carnal laws. And God has ordained civil government, because He could have no other among carnal men. In these great struggles, God often overrules. He casts down one, and sets up another. He gives the kingdoms of the earth to whom He will. He makes the wrath of man to praise Him; and that which cannot be used in that way, He restrains to His own glory.

As to what the duty of an individual would be, that individual must decide for himself. If he goes to the army under the command of his ruler, he may not be obliged to kill anyone. He can act as nurse in caring for the sick and the wounded. He may be able to do a wonderful missionary work with the men around him, yet he himself cause no loss of life. The one motive which should animate the Christian should be the motive which actuated our Lord Jesus Christ,—"The Son of man is not come to destroy men's lives, but to save them."

Grace and Obedience.

There lies before us a letter from one who declares that he is saved by grace; and then he asks where there is one scripture in God's word, from Genesis to Revelation, to show that God's law of commandments was ever given to Gentiles. He tells us further that they were counted "dogs and strangers by the Jews, who had no dealings with the Gentiles;" and he asks, "Could it be possible that the Jews and the Gentiles were under the same law, and yet could have no dealings with one another?"

In the first place, there is not one single word in Scripture which shows that the Jews and the Gentiles had no dealings with one another; they had dealings with one another all the way through, even when the Gentiles were in gross idolatry and the Jews were obedient to God. Of one class it is said that the Jews had no dealings with them, and that is the Samaritans (John 4:9); but the Samaritans professed to keep the same law that the Jews did. The only difficulty between the two peoples was that one held only to the books of Moses, and the other to the entire Old Testament; one held that the holy mountain was Gerizim, and the other held that it was Zion. The Samaritans wanted to help build God's temple in the time of Ezra and Zerubbabel, but the Jews utterly refused to permit them to do so; therefore the enmity between the two factions. But these who were at enmity professed to keep the same law. See Ezra 4:1-3.

Secondly, if this inquirer will read Isaiah 56, he will there learn that the Lord gives great promises to the Gentiles who will unite with His covenant and keep His Sabbath. Note that the chapter applies to the Christian dispensation, when God's "salvation is near to come," and His "righteousness to be revealed." Then He tells us, "Blessed is the man that doeth this, and the son of man that layeth hold on it; that keepeth the Sabbath from polluting it, and keepeth his hand from doing any evil." Verses 6, 7: "Also the sons of the stranger ["foreigners," A. R. V., the Gentiles], that join themselves to the Lord, to serve Him, and to love the name of the Lord, to be His servants, *every one that keepeth the Sab-*

bath from polluting it, and taketh hold of My covenant; even them will I bring to My holy mountain, and make them joyful in My house of prayer." Certainly this is very clear and definite.

Thirdly, there is not one single promise to the Gentiles, in all God's word, of hope or salvation, save only as they become a part of spiritual Israel. Gal. 3:29. Therefore Paul, writing to the Ephesian Christians, who were once Gentile heathen, says: "Wherefore remember, that ye being in *time past Gentiles* in the flesh, who are called uncircumcision by that which is called the circumcision in the flesh made by hands; that at that time ye were *without Christ,* being *aliens* from the *commonwealth of Israel,* and *strangers* from the *covenants of promise,* having *no hope,* and *without God* in the world." That is the condition of all Gentiles, as such; but these Gentiles came to Christ, and they became a part of Israel in coming to Him. Therefore Paul says: "But now in Christ Jesus ye who sometimes were far off are made nigh by the blood of Christ. . . . Now therefore ye are *no more strangers and foreigners,* but *fellow citizens* with the saints, and of the household of God; and are built upon the foundation of the *apostles and prophets,* Jesus Christ Himself being the chief cornerstone." Surely this is clear. There is abundance of testimony along the same line. Jesus declares, "Salvation is of the Jews" (John 4:22); and the apostle Paul declares that the true Jew is he that is one inwardly (Rom. 2:28, 29).

The Bible does not say we are saved by Sabbathkeeping, or by obedience to father or mother, or by abstaining from killing or stealing, or by the keeping of any of God's commandments. No Christian who understands the word ever teaches any such thing as that. Salvation is in Christ, and in Christ alone. By Him only are we saved; but we would press home this question upon the heart: Are we saved to sin and sinning, or are we saved to righteousness? Did the Lord Jesus Christ leave heaven and die, did He bestow upon us His grace, did He bring home His Spirit to our heart, and give us hope, in order that we might go on in sin and disloyalty? Was that the object of Christ's death? or did He die in order to save us from sin and sinning, to make us loyal children, children who would delight in God's commandments, even as He delighted in them? This is the question that faces every Christian who is puzzled or troubled by the foolish objections which are brought up concerning the object of grace. The object of God's grace is to make men and women so that they will be obedient men and obedient women, true men and true women, loyal men and loyal women; and if the grace which we have received does not do that, we have received the grace of God in vain. Compare 2 Cor. 6:1 and Titus 2:11, 12; Rom. 3:21.

Let us press home another question to the heart of our querist: Would he like to live near to neighbors who do not believe that their Christianity requires them to keep God's law? Would he feel that his automobile is safe in the garage, or his chickens in the chicken house, or his potatoes in the field? It seems as though some of these questions are really practical. The Hon. Wm. J. Bryan remarked one time, in one of his lectures, that he would feel it very unsafe to leave his pocketbook around among Christians who did not believe in the authority and binding obligations of God's commandments. That was a wise and just remark. A person does not know God's grace and its purpose who cannot see that God's grace is given in order to bring us back to Him and into harmony with His holy law. Then His commandments are not a yoke of bondage, but a delight; and it is easier to observe His commandments, and walk in them, than it is to go the way of the world.

SABBATH AND SUNDAY

The Importance of the Sabbath.

> If, as Seventh-day Adventists claim, the Sabbath is of such importance, why did God wait until almost the end before calling the world's attention to it? Will not sincere Sundaykeepers be saved? If so, why do Seventh-day Adventists come over here to China and stir up all this discord?

Every truth of God is important. Albert Barnes truly says, in his comments on Matthew 5:17-20, that anyone who considers any command of God so unimportant as not to be obeyed is unworthy of His kingdom. In this world one of the problems being worked out is that of sin,—a great incident in God's eternal work. One of the factors in those problems is that any man who desires his own way shall be allowed to have it, in order that not only the people of this world, but the beings in other worlds, may see what it means to depart from God and His truth. Consequently God suffered the great apostasy of Christian times; but, in great mercy, He foretold it, told the character of that apostasy, and what that apostasy would do, how it would think to change the times and the law of God. Dan. 7:25. He forewarned men, so that they need not fall into apostasy. Yet He permitted it to come, that men might see what iniquity would do if allowed to work itself out. But just as truly as He predicted that, He also predicted the Reformation, predicted the time when those who were among His people should take their feet from the Sabbath, from doing their pleasure on God's holy day, when they would restore the breach, build up again the wall that had been broken down by this apostate power. Isa. 58:12, 13. That is the message which is going to the world at this time.

But His people during that time of imperfect light, a time when darkness reigned because of apostasy, a time when so many lost sight of the great truth of the Bible, God will judge accordingly. So was it when Jesus came the first time. Great and important phases of truth had been buried under the traditions of the Jews. Jesus said of them, "If I had not come and spoken unto them, they had not had sin: but now they have no cloak for their sin." If God did not give to the world in the last days His message concerning His Sabbath truth, He would not count as sinners those who were transgressing it, who yet with sincere souls thought they were doing God's will. But He must demonstrate to the heavenly beings and to all mankind that notwithstanding all that apostasy has done, God will restore His truth, and will gather out of the last and darkest and weakest generation a class of people who are keeping all the commandments of God and all the faith of Jesus. Rev. 14:12. To him who loves the Lord Jesus Christ, that message is a message of joy and gladness.

The everlasting gospel of which this reform is a part is the everlasting good tidings (Rev. 14:6-14); and Seventh-day Adventists, if they would be true to God, must preach this glorious, glad light which God has given them of the blessed Sabbath, the memorial that it is of a great, kind heavenly Father, and the pledge that it is of a glorious Redeemer who is able to save to the uttermost. So while sincere Sundaykeepers who have been unwarned and who do not know God's truth, who are living according to the light they have with perfect hearts, will be saved, yet God would have His children fully enlightened, and especially in these days predicted by the prophets. Hence we go to China and to all other nations because God's message for this day is to go to "every nation and tribe and tongue and people." Rev. 14:6.

The Day of the Sabbath.

Has the Sabbath been lost? Do we really know which is the true seventh day?

What evidence will we accept? The greater part of Sabbath history is covered by the Bible; will we accept that as authority? No man who believes in a Sabbath at all could consistently do otherwise; for it is from the Bible that the Sabbath idea and institution have come to us.

1. In the Beginning

"In the beginning" man knew the Sabbath. By three distinct steps the Creator founded the Sabbath. After working six days He rested upon the seventh day, making it God's *rest* day. And then He blessed and sanctified, or set apart, the rest day, for all time to come. Gen. 2:2, 3. That day was the seventh of a cycle of days. It was the maker of the week, because all days were numbered with respect to that one day. When God gave that day, man knew the day. There was surely no mistake "in the beginning."

2. At the Exodus

Admitting, for the sake of making the truth clearer, that man in his idolatry may have forgotten the Sabbath during the centuries between the Garden of Eden and the Exodus, yet God had not forgotten it; and the first thing He did when He called His people out of Egypt, was to restore to them the Sabbath which, as a nation of slaves in sun-worshiping Egypt, they had not kept.

More than this: By the fall of the manna God marked the seventh day each week by a threefold weekly miracle for forty years. God gave a double portion of manna on the sixth day; He divinely withheld it on the seventh day, the Sabbath. The manna which fell on the first five days would not keep over to the next day, but that which fell on the sixth day was divinely preserved over the Sabbath. Israel must have known God's Sabbath; for forty years it was stamped into the very life of the nation. The record of this is especially found in Exodus 16. The next month God confirmed that holy day by placing its written law in the very heart of the Decalogue. Ex. 20:8-11. It is the same Sabbath day, based on the same reasons, that we find in the beginning.

3. At the First Advent

When our Lord came, the Jews were observing the seventh day with much outward, Pharisaic ceremony. It was loaded down with rabbinical tradition till it had become a burden. From the Exodus to that time no one claims that the Sabbath was lost. The Jews were still keeping the same day, but in the wrong way. Jesus Christ, in whom dwelt "all the treasures of wisdom and knowledge," observed the same day. Moreover, He lifted it to a higher plane, or, rather, restored it to its primitive design, a blessing to mankind, instead of a yoke of bondage.

Jesus Christ observed the Sabbath. He taught the perpetuity and immutability of that law of which the Sabbath was a part, even to its very jots and tittles. Matt. 5:17-20. He taught by precept and example perfect obedience to that law. Luke 4:16; John 15:10; Matt. 19:17. He died upon the cross to vindicate its justice and perfection, and to save men from sin, its transgression. 1 John 3:4; Rom. 7:7. By His perfect obedience imputed, we, who are sinners, by faith are counted righteous. Rom. 5:19.

Surely, on the face of it, God would not leave men ignorant concerning one of the essential and important precepts of that law. Nor did He. For when His own heart was stilled in death, those who had followed Him and had been taught by Him, "rested the Sabbath day according to the commandment." Luke 23:56. The next day was "the first day of the week." Luke 24:1; Mark 16:1, 2.

Therefore, at the first advent of Christ, at the beginning of what is called the Christian church (although that church began with Adam), the Sabbath was known, and the day of the Sabbath was still the seventh, the day just before "the first day of the week."

4. Since the First Advent

What evidence is there that the day has not been lost since Bible times? Is the evidence sufficient to assure us? In reply we would say that it is simply overwhelming. Here are six considerations and proofs, every one of which is sufficient of itself:

1. The Unreasonableness of the World's Losing a Day.—It is not infrequent that a single person loses count of the days of the week. It is so rare a thing that a whole family loses count that such an occurrence is talked of for years. But whoever heard of a whole neighborhood or village or city or country losing a day and not knowing it? And to think of a world's doing such a thing is too

absurd to consider, especially when not a small portion of the world honored the first day of the week as devoted to the worship of the sun, "the wild solar holiday of all pagan times."

2. God's Care.—It is unreasonable to believe that God requires the observance of an institution, as He certainly does by the perpetual Sabbath command, and then permits the day of the Sabbath to be lost to the world. Neither has He permitted it.

3. The Jews.—At the time of the first advent the Jews were great sticklers for the Sabbath. When they were scattered to all the nations of earth at the time of the destruction of Jerusalem, they carried the Sabbath with them. They have clung to the Sabbath, more or less strictly, ever since. Go where one will,—China or America, Russia or Australia, Morocco or Timbuctu, Tartary or Alaska, England or Hindustan,—the Jew has been there first, and has, by his singular custom, stamped the seventh day as "the Jewish Sabbath," though God gave it to all men. If the Jews in one part of the world had lost the day, differences would have arisen as representatives of other countries met together. But on the authority of the late Rabbi Wise, no such differences were ever recorded.

4. Custom and History.—Nearly all the great nations have been at some time sun worshipers, regarding the day of the sun and the week. In a chart prepared by the late Rev. Wm. Jones of London, assisted by able linguists all over the world, the week and its days in 162 languages and dialects are given; all of these languages recognize the same order in the days of the week; and 102 of them call the seventh day the Sabbath, or by some equivalent term. Then, in all the histories, encyclopedias, dictionaries, chronological and ecclesiastical tables of any note, Sunday is known as the first day of the week, the day just after the seventh. According to all authentic history, ecclesiastical or secular, the day of the week is identified; there has been no change since the Son of God stamped it as divine by His life, His teaching, His death.

5. The Churches.—The early church observed the Sabbath. Of this there is no doubt. Prof. Edward Brerewood, in his "Learned Treatise of the Sabbath," Oxford, 1631, states what is said in sub-

stance by other first-day writers: "The Sabbath of the seventh day
. . . was religiously observed in the East church three hundred
years and more after our Saviour's passion." And down to the year
1000 no other day save the seventh was known by the term "Sabbath." Gradually the Sunday displaced the Sabbath, brought in by
half-converted sun worshipers. There have been Christians, however, who have observed the Sabbath all through the Christian era.
But whether Sundaykeepers or Sabbathkeepers, there has been no
dispute as to *the day* till engendered in these times to evade the
force of God's commandment.

6. Astronomy.—The science of astronomy also bears evidence to
the fact that there has been no lost time. Astronomical records and
dates, as far back as 600 B. C., agree with the computations made by
astronomers today, bearing witness to the fact that there has been
no lost time, no lost count of the order of the week.

Now, reader, here are all these evidences. Surely the order of the
days of the week has persisted from the beginning to the present.
God's Sabbath stands.

Every objection men have ever brought against it or can ever
bring against it has been met and can be met, save one, and that is
the cross. It involves a cross to keep it. Its observance demands
faith in God. But Christ will help us bear the cross, and the exercise of faith will lead the soul into a larger, clearer, more fruitful
field of heart and life than he has ever known before. And in it all
he will have Christ Jesus as companion, friend, and brother.

Reasons for Keeping Saturday.

1. What are your strongest reasons for keeping Saturday, or what we call Saturday, for the Sabbath?
2. Where is all your Scripture for doing so?
3. Does your Sabbath begin at twelve o'clock noon on
what we call Saturday?
4. Do you make a distinction between the names "Sunday" and "Sabbath"?

1. We do not keep Saturday—that is, truly converted, Sabbathkeeping Christians do not. Saturday is a civil day, beginning at

twelve midnight, and ending at twelve midnight. But the Sabbath begins at sunset on what is called Friday evening, and ends at sunset on what is called Saturday evening; consequently the days are not synchronous, or identical.

Our reasons for keeping the Sabbath are: First, the commandment of God: "Remember the *Sabbath day,* to keep *it* holy. Six days shalt thou labor, and do all thy work: but *the seventh day* is *the Sabbath* of the Lord thy God: in it thou shalt not do any work, thou, nor thy son, nor thy daughter, thy manservant, nor thy maidservant, nor thy cattle, nor thy stranger that is within thy gates: for in six days the Lord made heaven and earth, the sea, and all that in them is, and *rested* the *seventh day:* wherefore the Lord blessed the *Sabbath day,* and hallowed it." Secondly, the example of our Lord Jesus Christ, who kept His Father's commandments, who did no sin, who left us an example, that we should follow in His steps. John 15:10; 1 Peter 2:21, 22. He therefore observed the Sabbath. Luke 4:16, and elsewhere. Surely there can be no stronger reasons than the eternal law of God, sanctioned and confirmed by prophet, apostle, and Jesus Christ, and the example of our Lord Himself. See 1 John 2:3-5.

2. "Where is all your Scripture for doing so?" It is throughout the Bible. All that is said in the Bible regarding a weekly Sabbath applies wholly and exclusively to the seventh day. Take, for instance, the institution of the Sabbath in Genesis 2:2, 3, and connect with it Mark 2:27, 28: "The Sabbath was made for man," and for man in the beginning, before there was a division of races, or nations, or tribes. See Exodus 20:8-11; also the whole of Exodus 16, showing how God marked it out during the falling of the manna; Isaiah 56; Isaiah 58:13; 66:22, 23; Luke 23:56. Then regarding the whole law of God, of which the Sabbath is a part, see Matthew 5:17-20; Psalm 111:7, 8. The last generation of men, who will welcome the Lord Jesus Christ, keep the commandments of God and the faith of Jesus. Rev. 14:12. These are only a small portion of the scriptures there are to confirm the great Sabbath truth.

3. "Does your Sabbath begin at twelve o'clock?" No; as before stated, it begins at sunset. "From even unto even, shall ye celebrate

your sabbaths." Lev. 23:32. See also Nehemiah 13:15-22, which clearly shows that the Sabbath began at sunset, when the heavy shadows began to creep in; and this also is intimated in Matthew 8:16; Mark 1:32; Luke 4:40. The context shows that this day was the Sabbath. The Jews would not bring their sick to be healed on the Sabbath day, on account of their superstition; but as soon as the sun set, they came with all their sick. This shows that the Sabbath closed at sunset. This is also in harmony with the making of the days in Genesis 1,—"The evening and the morning were the first day," "the second day," "the third day," and so on, giving man, wherever he may be on the earth, a sure knowledge of the beginning and the closing of the day, and also the blessed privilege of welcoming the Sabbath when it comes, and bidding farewell to it as it goes,—something which the Sundaykeeper does not experience.

4. "Do you make a distinction between the names 'Sunday' and 'Sabbath'?" Certainly we do. "Sunday" is the purely heathen name of the first day, so called in honor of the sun, to which it was dedicated. "Sabbath" is the divine name of the seventh day, and comes from God's rest upon that day.

For a broader study, we commend "The Lord's Day the Test of the Ages," a pamphlet costing 25 cents, which covers the Sabbath in all dispensations.

What Is the Lord's Day?

The Lord's day of the Holy Scripture must be the day which the Lord claims as His. In this, the word of God is very explicit. In Isaiah 58:13, the Lord calls the Sabbath "My holy day." Exodus 20:10 expressly says, "The seventh day is the Sabbath of the Lord thy God." Matthew 28:1 and Mark 16:1, 2 clearly show that this seventh day is the *seventh day of the week,* the day just before "the first day of the week." And in Mark 2:28, Jesus Christ declares, "The Son of man is Lord also of the Sabbath." What day, then, according to these scriptures, is the Lord's day? There can be but one true answer,—the seventh day of the week, the Sabbath of the Lord.

It is admitted—it could not be otherwise—that the Bible does not say that "the Lord's day" of Revelation 1:10 is the first day of the week. Why, then, call the first day of the week the Lord's day? Because, we are told, the early fathers called it that. But shall we take a "father" of an apostate church two hundred years this side of Christ, followed by other such "fathers," as of more authority than Christ and His word? Less than forty days after Jehovah spoke with His own voice from Sinai, some of the "fathers" in Israel, Aaron among them, made an image to the Egyptian sun god Apis, and said, "These be thy gods, O Israel, which brought thee up out of the land of Egypt." And the next day they held a feast to it, which they called "a feast to Jehovah." See Ex. 32:1-5. If the "fathers" of less than twoscore days' apostasy were wrong in the face of God's testimony, may it not be that the "fathers" two hundred years this side of Christ may also have been wrong? The only safe rule to follow is the Lord's word; and the Lord's word declares that the Lord's day is the seventh-day Sabbath.

Did the Apostles Change the Sabbath?

In a religious periodical, in answer to the question, "Who changed the Sabbath?" I find the statement given: "First by the authority of the apostles, delegated them by the Lord. Matt. 16:19. They kept the first day of the week. Acts 20:7; 1 Cor. 16:1, 2. Says Neander, 'The apostles rejected the Sabbath to avoid the risk of mingling Judaism and Christianity.' And also, secondly, because on that day Christ rose from the dead and appeared no less than five times to His followers. Thirdly, the outpouring of the Holy Ghost on the day of Pentecost occurred on Sunday." Will you please explain this?

Regarding these statements, there is nothing in Matthew 16:19 to show that the apostles were delegated to do anything else than to teach the word of God. That text itself ought to be explained by the great commission given in Matthew 28, in which Jesus told His disciples to teach all things He had commanded them; but He never commanded any change of the Sabbath; on the contrary,

He declared that not "one jot or one tittle" of the law could be changed. Matt. 5:17-20; Luke 16:17. So Jeremiah was set over the nations "to pull down, and to destroy, and to throw down, to build, and to plant" (chapter 1:10); but he simply did this by proclaiming God's word concerning those nations (chapter 18:7-10).

Secondly, we have no record that the apostles ever kept the first day of the week as a holyday. Acts 20:7 simply records a night meeting held at the beginning of the first day of the week, the rest of the day being spent in regular secular labor; and 1 Corinthians 16:1, 2 does not indicate any gathering whatever, but that each man should lay by himself *at home,* on the first day of the week, as God had prospered him, the money he would send to the needy in Judea, so that it could be gathered when the apostle came.

That the apostles did not reject the Sabbath to avoid the risk of mingling Judaism and Christianity is shown again and again by the labors and teaching of the apostle Paul. In the second chapter of Romans, he declares that the Jews had "the form of knowledge and of the truth in the law." In Acts 20, he declares that he had "kept back nothing that was profitable," but had taught all things that were necessary, had not shunned to declare "the whole counsel of God;" but nowhere is there any record that he had taught the Ephesian people any change in the Sabbath. He could say, as he met the Jews in Rome, as recorded in Acts 28, that he had done nothing against the custom of the fathers; and they could say they had heard no charge against him. That is, he had nowhere transgressed the moral law, as the Jews themselves regarded it.

James tells us that we are to keep the royal law according to the Scripture, and whoso offends in one point is guilty of all. See James 2:8-12. And Peter declares (1 Peter 2:20-22) that Christ is made our example, who did no sin. That is, Christ kept the law. He is our example to follow. And John tells us that he who says he knows God, and keeps not His commandments, is a liar, and the truth is not in him; and continues by saying, "He that saith he abideth in Him ought himself also so to walk, even as He walked." See 1 John 2:4-6.

Neander lived a good many centuries this side of Christ. He had no more knowledge of the matter than hundreds of others. The very best knowledge, and the only knowledge, of what the apostles did is found in the Scriptures themselves. Jesus did rise from the dead on the first day of the week, and did appear to His disciples several times; but in no case did He tell them that that day was a holyday. He simply appeared to them on that day in order to show them that He was alive and had risen from the dead. As to the outpouring of the Holy Spirit on Pentecost, the day of the week is not even mentioned, and some good authorities contend that it was the Sabbath day. Others think that it was Sunday. But the Lord passed over one first day in the ten days between His ascension and the outpouring of the Spirit, and that fact of itself shows that not the first day was to be honored, but the antitype of Pentecost. There is absolutely nothing in God's word to indicate that the first day was set apart as a holyday, and very many first-day people acknowledge this. There is but one Bible Sabbath, that instituted and commanded of God and observed by our Lord Jesus Christ.

The Sabbath for Israel.

If the Sabbath is a law for the Gentiles and the church, why do the Scriptures say, with precision, it is a law and a sign for Israel in the past and in the future? Ex. 31:13-17; Ezek. 20:12, 13. If for the church, cite Biblical passages that ordained it.

Let us say to our readers as emphatically as we can that God has no promise for the Gentiles in His word at all, only as they become Israel. The Gentile as a Gentile is utterly without hope, and so God's word repeatedly declares. For to Israel pertain "the adoption, and the glory, and the covenants, and the giving of the law, and the service of God, and the promises; whose are the fathers, and of whom is Christ as concerning the flesh, who is over all." Rom. 9:4, 5.

Our Lord Jesus Christ was of the stock of Israel. So were all the prophets, and all the apostles; and Jesus Himself declares,

"Salvation is of the Jews." John 4:22. The very term "Israel" is of spiritual significance. It was given to Jacob because he prevailed with God, and it means "prevailer with God." "Thy name shall be called no more Jacob [supplanter], but Israel: for thou hast striven with God and with men, and hast prevailed." Gen. 32:28. Only those who have thus prevailed with God can ever keep God's Sabbath; for the Sabbath is holy, and only holy men can keep a thing holy. God does not declare that the Sabbath shall be sanctified by our keeping it. He has already sanctified it. We are to keep it holy as He has made it holy; and the only way we can keep it holy is by having a holy heart.

Our Lord Jesus Christ said, when a young man asked Him what he ought to do, "Keep the commandments." Matt. 19:17. The apostle Paul declares: "Do we then make void the law through faith? God forbid: yea, we establish the law." And in the book of Hebrews we are told that under the new covenant, God's law—the law which existed in Jeremiah's day, six hundred years before Christ—is written in the hearts of His children. Heb. 8:8-12; Jer. 31:31-34.

But the Lord does not leave outside the Gentile, called by Him "the stranger." And here is one of the promises which the Gentile may appropriate: "Also the foreigners that join themselves to Jehovah, to minister unto Him, and to love the name of Jehovah, to be His servants, every one that keepeth the Sabbath from profaning it, and holdeth fast My covenant; even them will I bring to My holy mountain, and make them joyful in My house of prayer." Isa. 56:6, 7. Without that covenant relationship with Israel, the apostle Paul declares, men have no hope, and are "without God in the world," "alienated from the commonwealth of Israel, and strangers from the covenants of the promise." Eph. 2:12.

It is only Israel that will be saved. In that glorious city which God shall give to His children, there are twelve gates, and those gates are named after the tribes of Israel; and all who pass through those gates, in God's plan, will pass in as members of one of the tribes. For "Israel shall be saved by Jehovah with an everlasting salvation." Isa. 45:17. It is utter folly to ask a man to keep the

Sabbath of the Lord who does not know the Lord. Nobody can compel one to keep the Sabbath who does not know God. What folly it is for men to attempt it!

On What Day Was Christ Crucified?

We would not take the space to answer this question were not so many agitated over it, and that needlessly. It is *assumed* from Matthew 12:40 that Jesus was in the grave three days and three nights; that He was crucified Wednesday, and therefore was raised from the dead in the closing hours of the Sabbath day; and therefore the claim that the first day should be observed, because He rose from the dead on that day, falls to the ground.

Out of the study arise these questions:

1. On what day was Christ crucified?
2. With what definiteness are we to understand the term "three days and three nights"? Do they mean absolutely seventy-two hours?
3. When do these days begin?
4. On what day did Christ arise?
5. What bearing has the time upon the Sabbath question?

1. On What Day Was Christ Crucified?

On this point Matthew says nothing. Mark expressly says, "And when even was now come, because it was the *preparation, that is, the day before the Sabbath*." Mark 15:42. In this instance the word "even" refers to the closing hours of the day, when the sun began to decline. Luke is in harmony with this: "It was the day of the preparation, and the Sabbath *drew on,*" and that very Sabbath day the women rested "according to the commandment." Luke 23:54, 56.

John gives us this testimony: "The Jews therefore, because it was the preparation, that the bodies should not remain on the cross upon the Sabbath (for the day of that Sabbath was a high day), asked of Pilate that their legs might be broken, and that they might be taken away." John 19:31. That Sabbath day had double dignity; it was a chief day of the Passover as well as the Sabbath.

Obviously, all these testimonies would fix the crucifixion on the sixth day, from 9 A. M. to 3 P. M. Then, as the Sabbath drew on, the body of Jesus was taken down from the cross, hastily wrapped in the linen cloth with myrrh and aloes, and deposited in a rock-hewn tomb immediately adjacent to the place where the crucifixion occurred. John 19:41.

2. The Term "Three Days," Etc.

Does this expression mean just seventy-two hours? or does it mean part of two days and the whole of one—that is, a part of the first day being counted, the whole of the second, of course, and a part of the third? That the latter is the case is evident from the use of the term in the various texts where this very period is referred to. The following list of quotations and citations includes every instance of its occurrence:

1. "For as Jonah was three days and three nights in the whale's belly; so shall the Son of man be *three days and three nights* in the heart of the earth." Matt. 12:40.

2. "Jesus answered and said unto them, Destroy this temple, and *in three days* I will raise it up. Then said the Jews, Forty and six years was this temple in building, and wilt Thou rear it up *in three days?* But He spake of the temple of His body." John 2: 19-21.

3. "And He began to teach them, that the Son of man must suffer many things, and be rejected of the elders, and of the chief priests, and scribes, and be killed, and *after three days* rise again." Mark 8:31.

4. "In three days." Matt. 26:60, 61.

5. "And there arose certain, and bare false witness against Him, saying, We heard Him say, I will destroy this temple that is made with hands, and *within* three days I will build another made without hands." Mark 14:57, 58.

6. *"In* three days." Matt. 27:40.

7. *"In* three days." Mark 15:29.

8. "Sir, we remember that that deceiver said, while He was yet alive, *After* three days I will rise again. Command therefore that the sepulcher be made sure *until* the third day." Matt. 27:63, 64.

There is another term, "the third day," referring to the same period, which occurs as follows:

9. "From that time forth began Jesus to show unto His disciples, how that He must go unto Jerusalem, and suffer many things of the elders and chief priests and scribes, and be killed, and be raised again the *third* day." Matt. 16:21.

10. "The *third* day." Matt. 20:18, 19.

11. "The *third* day." Mark 9:31.

12. "The *third* day." Luke 18:32, 33.

13. "But we trusted that it had been He which should have redeemed Israel: and beside all this, today is the *third day since these things were done*." Luke 24:21.

14. "The *third* day." Luke 24:46; Matt. 17:22, 23; Mark 10:34; Luke 9:22; 24:7; Acts 10:40; 1 Cor. 15:3, 4.

We have numbered the above scriptures and citations so as to make them more easy of reference. In No. 1 Jesus refers to the experience of Jonah, and applies it to an experience which would come to Himself. The only expression which would confine it to the grave is "heart of the earth," and this we will consider later. No. 2 uses the expression *"in* three days," and that is also used by the enemies of Christ in Nos. 4, 6, and 7, and its stronger equivalent, "within," in No. 5. The chief priests and Pharisees, referring to the same thing (No. 8), use *"after* three days," and then ask that the sepulcher be made sure *"until* the third day."

Jesus uses in No. 3, the expression "after three days;" but in Nos. 10, 11, 12, 14, He uses "the *third* day," showing the latitude of the various terms used. This is still more strongly manifest by No. 13, where the disciples declare at the very close of the first day of the week, "Today is the third day since these things were done." So also No. 9, and the prophecy in Hosea 6:1, 2.

From a fair comparison of all these passages we must conclude

that *"in* three days," *"after* three days," *"within* three days," *"three*
days," and until "the *third* day," simply mean three days in common parlance, including only a part of the last day, and by a parity
of reasoning, not necessarily the whole of the first day.

3. When Do the Days Begin?

While technically the beginning would seem to apply to the
death of Christ, in the fullest sense they would cover His betrayal
into the hands of His enemies, when His death was determined.
For as truly as at the crucifixion, the *death agony* for the world
began at His betrayal, and was more manifest in the Garden of
Gethsemane than on the cross. It was by physical wounds that His
blood was shed on Calvary; it was by awful death agony for the
sins of the world that it was forced from Him in Gethsemane,
where "He poured out His soul unto death." It was at the very
time when Judas was bargaining with the chief priests that Jesus
said: "The *hour is come,* that the Son of man should be glorified.
Verily, verily, I say unto you, Except a grain of wheat fall into the
earth and die, it abideth by itself alone." John 12:23, 24. And
again: "Now is My soul troubled; and what shall I say? Father,
save Me from *this hour:* but for this cause *came I unto this hour.*
Father, glorify Thy name. . . . *Now* is the judgment [crisis] of
this world: *now* shall the prince of this world be cast out." Verses
27-31. A few hours before this the broken bread and the blood of
the grape manifested the death foreordained of God and purposed
of man. A little later His agonized heart forced from His lips, "My
soul is exceeding sorrowful even unto death." Mark 14:34. The
death agony was already on. A little later still come the band to
take Him. To them He says, "When I was daily with you in the
temple, ye stretched not forth your hands against Me: but *this is
your hour,* and the *power of darkness."* Luke 22:53.

Right here, at this crisis, began the three days and nights when
Christ was delivered to death in the hands of His enemies, into
the power of the heart of the earth, into the hands of "the world
rulers of this darkness." Eph. 6:12. When He reached that hour,
His time had come. No hand, human or divine, earthly or heav-

enly, could interpose for His rescue. He had yielded all. All that followed was development in the process of putting to death. "The heart of the earth" would refer to the powers of earth, the center of which was Roman rule, led by "the prince of this world," Satan. But the *third day* from the time of His yielding to the powers of earth He was living above all the powers of darkness.

4. On What Day Did Christ Rise?

We have (1) the record of the visits to the sepulcher; and (2) positive statement. Here are the passages which speak of the visits:

1. "In the end of the Sabbath, as it began to dawn toward the first day of the week, came Mary Magdalene and the other Mary to see the sepulcher." Matt. 28:1.

2. "And when the Sabbath was past, Mary Magdalene, and Mary the mother of James, and Salome, had bought sweet spices, that they might come and anoint Him. And very early in the morning the first day of the week, they came unto the sepulcher at the rising of the sun." Mark 16:1, 2.

3. "Now when Jesus was risen early the first day of the week, He appeared first to Mary Magdalene, out of whom He had cast seven devils." Mark 16:9.

4. "Now upon the first day of the week, very early in the morning, they came unto the sepulcher, bringing the spices which they had prepared, and certain others with them." Luke 24:1.

5. "The first day of the week cometh Mary Magdalene early, when it was yet dark, unto the sepulcher, and seeth the stone taken away from the sepulcher." John 20:1.

Only one of these passages speaks of the rising of our Lord. Nos. 1, 2, 4, 5, all refer to the visit of the women in the early morning of the first day. The context of each passage shows clearly that all save the last refer to the same visit. The particulars in Matthew 28 make it evident that the meeting there recorded was on the early morning of that first day, identical with the other meetings. The Greek phrase *opsē de Sabbatōn,* rendered "in the end of the Sabbath," ought, as Bloomfield and others remark, to be explained as "after the Sabbath." The context demands it. There is, however, another explanation. The original Greek was written without division into chapters or verses or sentences. Does not *opsē de Sabbatōn* ("late on the Sabbath") belong to the previous clause, at the end of chapter 27? It would then read: "And they [priests, etc.], having gone [from Pilate], made the sepulcher secure, with the guard sealing the stone late on the Sabbath. As it began to dawn toward the first day of the week, came Mary to see the sepulcher." This is in perfect harmony with both Mark and Luke. Greenfield in his Greek Testament gives this as an alternative reading.

But Mark 16:9 clearly fixes the resurrection of Christ to the first day of the week. The Interlinear Translation by Hinds and Noble renders the text, "Now having risen early the first day of the week, He appeared first to Mary the Magdalene." Rotherham's emphatic translation reads, "Arising early on the first of the week, He was manifested first to Mary the Magdalene;" the Peshito Syriac by Murdock, "And in the morning of the first day of the week, He arose." See other translations. Surely this ought to be conclusive. "The three days" would begin Thursday night and close Sunday morning, including all of Friday, all of Sabbath, and part of Sunday.

5. Is There Any Significance to the Resurrection Day?

None whatever. No day has been divinely designated to commemorate the resurrection. When God has set apart other days, He has been explicit concerning them. The Passover, the Day of Atonement, and other yearly days of the Jews were enjoined so clearly that there could be no mistake about them. So it was with the seventh-day Sabbath. If the Lord had designed that His resurrection should furnish us another worship day, He certainly would have made it plain. That His word is utterly silent is sufficient for the child of God.

On the other hand, He has given us the Sabbath. He has commanded it in unmistakable language. It has been confirmed by the teaching and example of our Lord Jesus Christ. What more does the Christian need? "Ye are My friends, if ye do whatsoever *I command you.*"

The Rest That Remains. Hebrews 4.

> Please explain the fourth chapter of Hebrews. Apparently there was a movement afoot at that time to change the Sabbath day.

The Sabbath day is not the question of Hebrews 4. Read chapter 3. The Lord desires to bring His people home to Him to that promised eternal rest. He emphasizes again and again, in both the third and the fourth chapter, the thought that the Hebrews of old did not enter into that rest. The eighth verse of chapter 4 reads, "For if Jesus [really, "Joshua" (see the American Revised Version); "Jesus" in Greek is the same as "Joshua" in Hebrew (see also the margin of the King James Version)] had given them rest, then would he not afterward have spoken of another day,"—that is, not another week day, nor another day of twenty-four hours, but another time when God would give His people rest.

The only reason why the Sabbath is brought in at all is to show that God's plan concerning the rest of His people is from the beginning of this world; for He says, "He that is entered into his rest, he also hath ceased from his own works, as God did from His." Verse 10. And verse 4 says: "For He spake in a certain place of the seventh day on this wise, And God did rest the seventh day from all His works." That is, that finished earth, as it came from the hand of God, was designed to be the rest home of man for all eternity; but unbelief came in, and man sinned, and consequently there was no rest; for there is no peace and rest to the wicked.

But He promised them rest when they came from Egypt. If they had believed, they would have entered into it; but Joshua did not give them rest then. The entering into that rest, therefore, is yet future; it remains. Then again under Solomon and David, God would have given His people rest; but unbelief thwarted it.

Now the Lord puts it upon each soul individually through faith. "Today"—every day—God calls to enter that rest; and when man will give up his own strivings and strugglings and

9

his own work and his own sins, and yield himself wholly to the righteousness of God, he will enter into the beginning of that rest. He will find rest in Christ Jesus from all his sins and strife of soul; and that rest will be completed when man enters the earth made new at the second coming of Christ.

The only reason why the Sabbath day is mentioned there at all is that it is a pledge of God's eternal rest when His plan is completed in redemption. "There remaineth therefore a rest ["a Sabbath rest," A. R. V.] to the people of God," such a Sabbath as the Lord had when the earth was made, which includes rest from sin. See Isa. 66:22, 23.

The Sabbath and the Gentiles.

Are Gentiles under obligation to keep the Sabbath?
Was it not given to Israel alone?

As this is a frequently raised question, a few points may be worthy of consideration.

The Sabbath is a memorial of creation. This is demonstrated by such texts as Genesis 2:2, 3; Exodus 20:8-11. That creation affects all who dwell upon the earth, and all are amenable to the One who created them. The Sabbath was therefore for mankind, the whole race; for "the Sabbath was made for man" (Mark 2:27), and the "God that made the world and all things therein" also "made of one blood all nations of men for to dwell on all the face of the earth, and hath determined the *times before appointed,* and the bounds of their habitation" (Acts 17:24, 26). Among the times before appointed is that of the Sabbath, which originated at creation, and was sanctified as God's memorial; and this memorial is "throughout all generations." Ps. 135:13.

That the Sabbath is for all men is shown by the records of peoples who, before apostatizing, acknowledged its binding obligation, and kept it, as shown by ancient records, and by the names they have retained for the days of the week.

That God gave the Sabbath to Israel was true. But He did not give it to them as a people to themselves; He gave it to them as

He gave all other truth, that they might give it to others. To Israel pertained "the adoption, and the glory, and the covenants, and the giving of the law, and the service of God, and the promises." Rom. 9:4. The Gentile world worshiped idols, forbidden by the first two commands of the Decalogue. Shall we therefore reject the law, saying it was for Israel? So with other precepts of that same holy law. God ever calls the seventh-day Sabbath His day, "the Sabbath of the Lord thy God," but never "the Jewish Sabbath." The latter is man's name. Which shall we choose? On the other hand, God repeatedly calls Himself the God of Abraham, Isaac, and Jacob, the God of Israel. Shall we therefore reject Him?

But the new covenant is to Israel; all the promises are to Israel; the inheritance is to Israel; the holy and eternal city of the everlasting kingdom is the city of Israel, for after Israel are her gates named (Rev. 21:12); and Jesus declares that "salvation is of the Jews" (John 4:22). The Bible was given through Jews; and the Saviour was a Jew, and "unto Him shall the gathering of the people be." Gen. 49:10. Shall we therefore reject all these precious riches and blessings?

The fact of the case is that these Jews were the depositaries of God's truth because God saw that they could best preserve it till Christ came. They rejected it, and God cast them off; but their rejection did not affect God's truth. He simply placed the flaming torch and the sacred treasure in other hands, devoted to His service, to bear the light and the blessing to the world. But those who bear them are the Israel of God. There are no covenant blessings or promises to the Gentiles except as they become Israelites —prevailers with God—by faith. But all may become such, Jew or Greek, male or female, black or white. God is no respecter of persons.

But faith, the faith of Jesus Christ, the faith of Israel, the faith which works by love, the love that keeps the commands of God,— the same faith and love are required of all; and all who have it are Israelites indeed, true Jews, of "the commonwealth of Israel," and of "the household of God." See Eph. 2:11-19. And God is one; His law is one; His Son is one; His salvation, His Sabbath,

His mighty redeeming love and eternal inheritance, each and all are one and the same to all who will accept them. He who will not accept them, may remain a Gentile, "having no hope, and without God in the world;" for there is no other hope, no other God. But he who will, may embrace Christ, become a covenant heir of God, and a lover of God's Sabbath, an inheritor of His promises. See Isa. 56:2-8.

"From One Sabbath to Another." Isa. 66:23.

This text says, "From one Sabbath to another, shall all flesh come to worship before Me, saith the Lord." But others tell us, from Revelation 21:23 and 22:5, that there is no night there; and therefore Isaiah has no reference to the Sabbath, but one eternal rest. Please explain.

First of all, Isaiah 66:23 could not have reference to one great eternal rest, because to speak of "from one eternal rest to another" would be absurd, for an eternal rest does not leave time for any successive eternal rests. Then, too, that the Sabbath is indicated, is also shown by the connection, "from one new moon," which would also stand for one month—from one month to another, and from one Sabbath to another; or from month to month and week to week; and the great day of the week then as now will be the Sabbath.

What is meant in Revelation 21:23 and 22:5 is not that there will not be a succession of day and night, or that day will not follow day. The implied contrast is with cities of this world. Cities of this world have walls and gates, or they did in those days; and those gates were shut by night, to keep out robbers and marauders and hostile armies who would come in under cover of the darkness of night. That will not be the case in the New Jerusalem. God's glory will be so great in that city that there will be no night there, no darkness under which robbers can hide or the lawless devise or plan destruction. It will be all light. Nothing more than this is implied.

It is also spoken regarding the city itself, and not regarding the new earth. When God's children come up from all parts of the earth, where there is a difference between day and night, as indicated by Isaiah 30:26, the Sabbath will be observed there just as truly as it can be here, only with perfect holiness to the Lord. The light of the moon will fall upon that earth, but it will be like the light of the sun now; and the light of the sun in the new earth will be sevenfold what it is now. Yet when God's people come into His very presence, His glory will be so great that "the moon shall be confounded, and the sun ashamed; for Jehovah of hosts will reign in Mount Zion, and in Jerusalem; and before His elders shall be glory." Isa. 24:23. It is possible, with flood lighting, to make the night as bright as day. But it does not take away the night, nor change the succession of days; nor will God's ineffable glory, far surpassing anything artificial, or even in the natural world, take away from the earth its succession of days or months, or its Sabbath.

Old and New Style Calendar.

What effect did the change from Old Style to New Style have upon the day of the Sabbath?

The change of the calendar from Old Style to New Style was made by Pope Gregory in 1582. The computation of Julius Caesar was a bit too lengthy, and consequently by the sixteenth century the calendar was ahead of the solar year. Ten days were dropped from the calendar made by Julius Caesar, the one then in vogue in European countries, to bring the calendar year into harmony with the solar year. By this change, October 5, 1582, was called October 15, 1582. This corrected the mistake in the calendar of Caesar. England did not make the change until 1752, when September 3 of that year was called September 14. But these changes did *not* affect the *days* of *the week*. This is shown by the fact that there was no difference between the reckoning of the days of the week in Great Britain and the rest of Europe between 1582 and 1752, although the former reckoned according to the Old Style, and the latter by New Style. None of the changes in years or days of the month of the past have affected the days of the week.

A Question of Days.

    1. "One man esteemeth one day above another: another esteemeth every day alike. Let every man be fully persuaded in his own mind." Rom. 14:5.

    2. "Ye observe days, and months, and times, and years. I am afraid of you, lest I have bestowed upon you labor in vain." Gal. 4:10, 11.

    3. "Let no man therefore judge you in meat, or in drink, or in respect of an holyday, or of the new moon, or of the sabbath days." Col. 2:16.

    May we not very reasonably conclude, from the reading of the following texts, and from their connections, that the observance of the Sabbath is of very little importance, if not wholly unnecessary to salvation?

    1. Romans 14 is not a discussion of a question of days, but a question of judging, or condemning, a brother. "To his own master he standeth or falleth;" and, despite the judgment of mortals, God is able to hold him up. Even though the text did refer to the Sabbath, it would prove nothing concerning its obligation; it would simply prove that the observer or the nonobserver was answerable to God alone. But at the bar of God, all who have known God's law will be judged by the law. Rom. 2:12; James 2:8-12. But the text and the context seem to make reference to matters which of themselves made no difference, ceremonial days of the law, for example.

    If it should be said that the term "every day" of the text must include the Sabbath, it is sufficient to show that it does not in Exodus 16:4. Compare with verse 27. The "every day" meant every day of the common days given to man, of "the six working days." Ezek. 46:1. The Sabbath command is a part of God's law, of which no jot or tittle shall pass away. See Isa. 51:6, 7; Matt. 5: 17-19. The eternal Spirit of God did not contradict through Paul what it said through Isaiah and Jesus.

    2. The days and times of Galatians 4:10, 11 are heathen days and times. Read the text and the context:

    "Howbeit then, when ye knew not God, ye did service unto them which by nature *are no gods*. But now, after that ye have known

God, or rather are known of God, how turn ye again to the weak and beggarly elements, whereunto ye desire again to be in bondage? Ye observe days, and months, and times, and years. I am afraid of you, lest I have bestowed upon you labor in vain." Verses 8-11.

Before they knew God, before the gospel came to them, whom did they worship or serve? *Answer:* "Ye did service unto them which by nature are no gods." They were therefore heathen. Compare with 1 Cor. 12:2; 1 Thess. 1:9. See also Acts 14:6-18. Lycaonia was a part of Galatia. In their backsliding, what did the Galatians do? *Answer:* "How turn ye *again* to the weak and beggarly elements, whereunto ye desire *again* to be in bondage?" What were among the heathen observances? *Answer:* "Neither shall ye use enchantment, nor observe times." Lev. 19:26. "He reared up altars for Baal [the sun god]. . . . He made his son pass through the fire, and observed times." 2 Kings 21:3-6. See Ezek. 8:15, 16.

The oldest and most widespread heathen worship was sun worship, and the oldest heathen day is Sunday, dedicated to the worship of the sun. Besides this, there were monthly and yearly and other heathen feasts and festivals and holydays. The Saturnalia, from which came Christmas; the feast of Eostre, from which came Easter; and the Sunday, are good illustrations of the perpetuity of heathen customs. When, therefore, the Galatians went back to their heathen gods, they doubtless returned to their old feasts and festivals. No wonder that the apostle questioned their conversion.

3. The context of Colossians 2:16 clearly shows that the meats and drinks and fast days and sabbath days to which the apostle had reference were those which were "a shadow of things to come; but the body is of Christ." Verse 17. These yearly days, some seven in number, are mentioned in Leviticus 23, "beside the Sabbaths of the Lord." Verse 38. All the ceremonial sabbaths pointed forward to Christ; but the eternal Sabbath of the Lord was a constant memorial and sign of Christ's power to create, uphold, and sanctify. Ex. 20:8-11; Ezek. 20:20, 12. God's moral law is unchangeable and eternal, and His weekly Sabbath is a part of that law.

Do not forget the very first expression in the scripture under question, which is the core of the whole matter: "Let no man therefore judge you." Why? Because, as the previous verses show, we have acknowledged Jesus Christ the Lord, been buried with Him in baptism, and arisen to a new life in Him. The mere ceremonies of the past are nothing in Him. The sins that were recorded against us have been all blotted out; and those past ordinances, which call to remembrance our sins year by year, from time to time, are gone.

Sunday Laws and Prohibition.

Please give the reasons why a law prohibiting the manufacture and sale of intoxicants is right, and one forbidding Sunday labor is wrong. Are not both class legislation?

The design of the prohibition of the manufacture and sale of intoxicants has nought to do with class. It does not prevent anyone from drinking, if he has liquor. It does prohibit the manufacture and sale for public purposes. One of the chief reasons for doing this, from a political standpoint, is the enormous drain that the liquor business is upon the community. If those who manufacture and sell liquor met all the expense and tragedy of the liquor traffic, that would be one thing. But they do not. They impose upon the community a fearful burden, which the community itself must bear, in the drunkards and paupers they make, in the widows and orphans or worse than widows and orphans, in the crime and corruption that is fostered, in a hundred different ways, breaking down all barriers of law, of society, and loading continually heavy burdens upon the community. The saloons make necessary the great number of police in our cities and towns; they furnish a great deal of the material for the courts. The mere suggestion of these will bring to the minds of our readers very much more than we have mentioned as the result of the liquor traffic. It has to do wholly and solely with the economic problem of our cities and towns. In a long series of years, a country could better afford to pay pension to the men engaged in the liquor traffic, until they died, than to allow the traffic to go on; and this from a purely economic standpoint.

A Sunday law is altogether different. It is class legislation; it is more, it touches the rights of mankind. It touches the very highest class of those rights, the right to worship God according to the dictates of one's own conscience, and the right to earn a living for one's family, working in what way and how long one will. It does not strike directly at evils, economic or otherwise. The fact certainly has been demonstrated that the Sunday is as well kept in communities where there is no Sunday law as in communities where there is one. Neighbors get along just as peaceably; there is just as much quiet; there is far more agreement, less trouble and prejudice in every way, than where Sunday laws exist. The most serious effects of Sunday laws fall, many times, upon those who are the most conscientious and faithful.

In nearly all cases of prohibition of the liquor traffic, time is given for the saloon man to adjust his business. Adjusting his business, he has no trouble from the law. He could not say that conscientiously he must follow that business. No saloonkeeper in the world would ever make such a claim at that. Any other business equally profitable, or less, would be preferable; for few saloonkeepers would actually prefer a business like that, were they not trained to that one thing. But this is not the case at all with the Sunday law. It has to do with conscience and one's relationship to God.

Jesus and the Sabbath Commandment.

Why did Jesus not mention the Sabbath commandment when He enumerated the others?

In the first place, our Lord nowhere enumerates the Ten Commandments. He gave some of them, as in the nineteenth chapter of Matthew. He quotes those to show to the young man that he was not really keeping the commandments after all. The young man had declared, "All these have I kept from my youth up;" but Jesus showed, by the principle upon which the commandments quoted were based, and the application of that principle, that the young man really had not kept the commandments at all. He had outwardly observed them. His life was blameless, probably, so far as a negative example was concerned; yet he was wealthy, and the poor were all around him, and he had not given to their needs. But in that enumeration of commandments, we do not have any one of the first four precepts of the Decalogue, and we nowhere in the teachings of Christ have any reference to the second commandment of the Decalogue. Extrajudicial oaths are forbidden, but the third commandment is not quoted.

Why should we demand that our Lord should restate the Ten Commandments? He expressly tells us, "Think not that I am come to destroy the law, or the prophets: I am not come to destroy, but to fulfill." Matt. 5:17. There would be no change in God's government. God's moral law is perfect, and Christ came to restore men to allegiance to God. That was His sole purpose. He declares, "I and My Father are one." Again, "I came . . . not to do Mine own will, but the will of Him that sent Me." God's will is expressed in His law (Ps. 40:7, 8); and Jesus declares that those who say, "Lord, Lord," and do not the will of God, will have no part in God's kingdom. To them the Lord will say: "Depart from Me, ye that work iniquity." "I never knew you." "Iniquity" is lawlessness, doing things contrary to God's law. All the teaching of our Lord, in precept and example, in His sacrifice upon the cross, taught the immutability, the inviolability, the absolute necessity, and eternal perpetuity, of the law of God in every jot and tittle; for He declares, "It is easier for heaven and earth to pass, than one tittle of the law to fail."

The change from the old dispensation to the new dispensation, as they are sometimes called, was not the change in God's purpose or the change in God's plan. It was simply a greater development of that plan. The old object-lesson offerings, which pointed forward to Christ, ceased because the shadow reached the substance; but the government of God underwent no change. Faith was demanded before Christ came, faith in the Sacrifice and Redeemer to come; faith was demanded when He came, faith in the Sacrifice who was there with them. Obedience was demanded before He came, the obedience of faith to all God's commandments; obedience was demanded after He came, the obedience of faith, the following in His footsteps.

There was no more change in the constitution or fundamental laws of God's government when Christ came than there is when one administration is succeeded by another in the United States Government. The administration is different, but this has no effect whatever upon the Constitution. Every word and act of Christ's life confirms the Sabbath commandment with the others.

The Breaking of Bread.

> Some persons infer that the breaking of bread mentioned in Luke 24:35; Acts 2:42, 46; 20:7; 27:35, and other scriptures, refers to the holding of the Lord's Supper. Does this phrase not generally refer to a common custom at a meal?

You are quite right in your conclusions regarding these texts. The principal object in trying to make it appear that such texts refer to the celebration of the Lord's Supper is that some excuse may be had for sacredly observing Sunday. For instance, Acts 20:7 says, "Upon the first day of the week, when the disciples came together to break bread, Paul preached unto them, ready to depart on the morrow; and continued his speech until midnight." The claim is made that this breaking of bread was the Lord's Supper, and that they had come together on the first day of the week to celebrate that ordinance, and furthermore, that they would not have been celebrating that ordinance on the first day of the week if they had not regarded that day as a sacred day.

This may sound very plausible, but the text is wanting in several important particulars. In the first place, observe that the text does not say that they had come together on the first day of the week because they regarded it is a sacred day. If the breaking of bread would make a day sacred, then, according to Acts 2:46, referred to in your question, they would have observed every day as sacred, because that text says, "They, continuing daily with one accord in the temple, and breaking bread from house to house, did eat their meat with gladness and singleness of heart." They continued "daily" in breaking bread. But even if this were the Lord's Supper which they celebrated, that would not necessarily indicate that it was upon a sacred day. The Lord's Supper was not instituted on either Saturday or Sunday. It could be observed on any day; and it might have been celebrated at the time indicated in Acts 20, because of Paul's departure the next day—the Christians at Troas may have wanted to celebrate it with him before he left them. But even though this meeting was held in part at least on the first day of the week, there is strong evidence that the breaking of bread did not occur until Monday morning.

The Sunday institution rests upon such a weak foundation that it has to resort to all kinds of devices to give it any semblance of support. The Sabbath of Jehovah has a very explicit command enjoining its observance. The Sunday institution rests only upon inference. And when people begin to build doctrines upon inferences, there is no end to the absurdities that may be promulgated.

The Right to Keep Sunday.

Have I not a right to keep Sunday, according to Romans 14:5, 6? Am I not justified in keeping Sunday if I keep it to the Lord, being fully persuaded in my own mind?

We quote all of the text that pertains to days, from the American Revised Version: "One man esteemeth one day above another: another esteemeth every day alike. Let each man be fully assured in his own mind. He that regardeth the day, regardeth it unto the Lord."

Let it be noted: (1) That this chapter—and the whole epistle, for that matter—is addressed to Christians to whom the apostle had emphatically taught the perpetuity and immutability of the law of which the Sabbath precept is a part. The Jews held the true *"form* of knowledge and of the truth" in that law, and in this they knew God's will (see chapter 2:17-23); by that law, men will be judged (2:12); by that law is the knowledge of sin, and all mankind stand condemned by it (3:19, 20; 4:15; 7:7); that law witnesses to the righteousness of God in Jesus Christ (3:21, 22); faith establishes that law in the heart (3:31); grace saves from its transgression (6:1, 2, 15, 16); the demands of the law are met by those in Christ (8:4); and only the carnal heart is at enmity with its righteous requirements (8:7). Therefore the ones who heeded this epistle were Sabbathkeepers.

Chapter 14 cannot therefore refer to the Sabbath day, but to the immaterial days, such as the Passover and the Day of Atonement. The expression "every day" refers to the six working days of the week, as in Exodus 16:4, and does not include the Sabbath.

Romans 14 has for its specific purpose instructions to Christians that they should not judge one another; that all judgment rests with God, to whom each and all must give account. Verses 10-12.

So far as our responsibility to man is concerned, one has the right to keep any day or no day. One is not, cannot be, justified before God in the observance of a day contrary to God's law. God cannot justify transgression of His law. He will justify the ignorant and perfect heart despite the transgression, but not because of it.

It would seem that no day would be acceptable "to the Lord" that He Himself had not given. And no one could keep any day acceptable to God who was not fully persuaded in his own mind. There is no coercion in God's service; there must be the willing heart. The thought of the apostle seems to be that in immaterial things, there should be liberty. A transgression of God's law would take one out of God's church entirely. Let us not use equivocal expressions to evade the plainest, clearest duty, emphasized by the example of our blessed Lord.

Temperance and the Sabbath.

Is not the temperance question as important to discuss as the Sabbath question?

The temperance question is always important; so also is the Sabbath question; but a man may be truly a temperance man and not be a Sabbathkeeper or a Christian. No man can truly be a

Sabbathkeeper without being a temperance man. The latter reform always goes with the former. Why? Because the Sabbath is a memorial of God's creative power and loving Fatherhood. Had man always observed the Sabbath, he never would have been an idolater; nor would he ever have yielded himself to the abominable lusts that have carried away so many millions of the race. The Sabbath commandment is, "Remember the Sabbath day, to keep it holy." That implies the remembrance of it outside of the Sabbath day itself. Every day of the week was numbered with respect to the Sabbath. It was "One Day to the Sabbath," "Second Day to the Sabbath," "Third Day to the Sabbath," and so on, until the Sabbath itself came. Remembering that commandment in the letter and spirit of it, man could never forget God, or his obligation to God. Having yielded himself to God, he could never give himself up to the sins of gluttony or drunkenness. Every power of his being would be laid upon the altar of God. He could no more prostitute his mental and spiritual powers to the lust of appetite than he could yield himself to bow to the altars of Baal. Consequently wherever true Sabbath reform has obtained through the ages, there is connected with it true temperance.

Furthermore, it is God's time now for a Sabbath reform. Thus has every age ended. The patriarchal age ended with Sabbath reform, and connected with that was the true temperance question. As God led Israel out of Egypt, that temperance reform took hold of not simply wine and strong drink, but upon diet as well. There was true Sabbath reform in the closing of the Jewish age, when our Lord Jesus Christ showed what the Sabbath meant and should mean; and there was also true dietetic and temperance reform, during which time was given that wonderfully comprehensive rule, "Whether therefore ye eat, or drink, or whatsoever ye do, do all to the glory of God."

We are nearing the close of the Christian age. Our Lord is about to come. One of the mighty reforms which will sweep this earth, antagonizing all mere legal reforms which seek to embody in dead statute law the living principles of the gospel, is reform upon the Sabbath, the closing of the breach that has been made in

God's law; and inseparably connected with that is true temperance reform, a reform message which takes in the whole man, spirit and soul and body.

The Sabbath question is not the mere question of the day of twenty-four hours. There is connected with it the very question of divine authority and full allegiance to God in worship, and all that is highest and best in the life of the Christian.

The Great Round World.

> 1. In circumnavigating the globe one way, a day is lost, and the other way a day is gained; what is the cause of this? 2. What is the custom on board ship with the day lost or gained, when circumnavigating the globe? 3. Has the day lost or gained any effect on the days of the week, or on the date only, like the changing from the Old Style to the New Style of reckoning time?

1. Apparently the sun revolves around the earth from east to west once in twenty-four hours. It passes over fifteen degrees of the 360 into which the earth is divided, in one hour of time. If one travels around the world with the sun, he apparently gains time in proportion to the space passed over. For instance, if he travels over fifteen degrees of space, in round numbers a thousand miles, during twenty-four hours, he apparently gains one hour of time. In other words, he has lengthened his day one hour by keeping one hour longer with the sun. If he should keep that up for twenty-four days, he would have extended each day an hour. Though losing nothing in actual time, he would be a day ahead of where he was when he started, as the days are named in the week. If he were traveling eastward at the same rate, he would lose an hour, or be with the sun an hour less each day; and in twenty-four days would lose twenty-four hours, or a whole day. In the first case he would drop one day, in the second he would add or repeat a day.

2. A traveler on board ship and otherwise in journeying westward, if he came to the usual place of the change on Tuesday, would call the next day Thursday. In traveling eastward, if he came to the place of change on Tuesday, he would call the next

day Tuesday. Or he could add or drop a part of each of two days. Custom has fixed this place of change in the Pacific Ocean. From the east coast of Asia westward to the west coast of America the traveler east or west finds himself in harmony with all the people in the count of the days of the week. But crossing the Pacific Ocean westward, ships drop a day; in crossing eastward, they add a day.

3. Both the day of the week and the date are affected thereby. If the traveler should obstinately stick to his own time, it would put him out with all the rest of the world. But if he keeps himself in harmony with providential and everyday facts, he has no trouble whatever about losing or gaining days, or observing any day he wishes.

Doing Simple Duty. Eccl. 12:13.

> Is there any evidence that the Lord does not sanctify
> and bless the first day of the week, now kept by Christians,
> to their edification, rest, and utmost satisfaction?

The Lord does not expressly tell us that He does *not* sanctify and bless the first day; neither does He tell us that He does so bless and sanctify it. He does not ask men to do what He has not commanded, nor to surmise that He has done what He has given us no record that He has done. He says: "If ye love Me, keep My commandments." "Ye are My friends, if ye do whatsoever I command you." "Fear God, and keep His commandments: for this is the whole duty of man." To disregard these plain injunctions of God's word—the plain commands which He has given us concerning His holy day—and to set up in our own minds an institution which God never has given, is to do as did Saul. He thought that rendering sacrifice, doing something which pleased him, was more pleasing to God than it was to obey explicitly just what God had told him; but the words of the prophet to him were, "Behold, to obey is better than sacrifice, and to hearken than the fat of rams." 1 Sam. 15:22. To substitute something of our own for something which God has given, is to put no difference between the clean and the unclean, the holy and the profane. And it is just that thing which God charges to false teachers of Israel.

"Her priests have violated My law, and have profaned Mine holy things: they have put no difference between the holy and profane, neither have they showed difference between the unclean and the clean, and have hid their eyes from My Sabbaths, and I am profaned among them." Ezek. 22:26. See also Leviticus 10.

God's blessing rests upon His people every day; that is, upon those who walk in the light which shines upon their pathway, and who yield themselves to do His will so far as they understand it. One can obtain the blessing of the Lord in seeking Him on Thursday as well as seeking Him on Sunday. Education also has very much to do with these things. The devout Jew living in Babylon or Rome who had not heard of Christ's death upon the cross, no doubt found real pleasure, blessing, and edification in offering up his sacrifice by faith, and yet the one great Sacrifice had superseded it. The Lord only holds us responsible for what He gives us. Jesus said of the Jews who crucified Him: "If I had not come and spoken unto them, they had not had sin: but now they have no cloak for their sin. He that hateth Me hateth My Father also. If I had not done among them the works which none other man did, they had not had sin: but now have they both seen and hated both Me and My Father." John 15:22-24.

We are not condemned because we may be walking in error for which we are not responsible. We are condemned when we cling to error after God has revealed it to us as error. "And this is the condemnation, that light is come into the world, and men loved darkness rather than light, because their deeds were evil." The man who observes Sunday with all his heart, believing it to be truth, will gladly accept the light of God when it comes, and thereby demonstrate that he was before that walking in all the light he saw. "He that doeth truth cometh to the light, that his deeds may be made manifest, that they are wrought in God." But he who is actuated by selfish motives, turns from the light, condemns its searching rays, and still clings to his sins. See John 3:17-21.

The matter of feeling in the condemnation or approval of a doctrine is largely a matter of education and practice fostered by the wrong theology of the day. All God requires is faith, simple faith in His holy word. He who has such faith as will lead him to turn from everything that is condemned by the holy word, and who gives himself wholly to God, will find a joy that the follower of no human tradition can ever have. It is the experience of thousands who have embraced the Sabbath of the Lord, with all that it means, even among those who have long enjoyed God's blessing in first-day churches, that they have a sweetness of peace and a satisfaction of life which they never knew before. "Great peace have they which love Thy law: and they shall have no stumbling block." Ps. 119:165, margin. Our correspondent truly says in a postscript, "I am assured that no faithful Christian will have any choice of his own as to which day he keeps, but will accept none but God's choice, when he knows it." But how can we know it except by God's word?

Change of the Sabbath.

Where do you find that Constantine changed the Sabbath?

We do not find that he changed it, nor have we said that he changed it. We do not believe that he did change it. What we have said is this: that the first Sunday law on record is one made by Constantine in 321 A.D. That Sunday law reads as follows:

"Let all the judges and town people, and the occupation of all trades, rest on the venerable day of the sun; but let those who are situated in the country, freely and at full liberty attend to the business of agriculture; because it often happens that no other day is so fit for sowing corn and planting vines; lest the critical moment being let slip, men should lose the commodities granted by Heaven. Given the seventh day of March; Crispus and Constantine being consuls, each of them for the second time."

The original of the edict is in Harvard University Library. It is quoted in Kitto's Cyclopædia, note to article, "Sabbath," page 720, Adam and Charles Black, Edinburgh; in "Sunday," by Archdeacon Hessey, fifth edition, 1889, Cassel & Company; in "The Sabbath," by Wilbur Crafts, note 276, page 555, sixth edition;

Schaff-Herzog Encyclopedia, article, "Sunday Legislation," volume 4, page 2260; McClintock & Strong's Biblical, Theological, and Ecclesiastical Cyclopædia (Harper Brothers) refers to it (volume 10, page 18), as does also "Neander's Church History," page 336, volume 2, eleventh American edition; Encyclopædia Britannica, seventh edition, volume 6, page 301, article, "Constantine." These are all modern works, but each is good authority for a fact of this kind. Of two works before us, on the Sabbath, one by Dr. Peter Heylyn (1636), quotes the same law, pages 66, 67, part 2; and one by Dr. Francis White (1635), pages 218, 219, refers to it. The simple fact is that there is no question as regards the law. All learned men on all sides of the Sabbath question admit the law, its authenticity, and its author.

The change of the Sabbath was a gradual work. Little by little, men lost their regard for the holy day of the Lord, while Sunday was kept as a great feast day. In fact, in all the early ages of the church, Sunday was not considered a sacred day; a small portion of it was used for religious services, and the rest for labor or recreation. As late as the fourth and fifth centuries, the two days were kept together as sister days, but more than a thousand years passed before Sunday was called the Sabbath. The Sabbath was crowded out largely in the fourth and fifth centuries. At last, as in the Council of Laodicea, 336 A. D. and 364 A. D., those who kept the seventh-day Sabbath were anathematized.

Easter Sunday. Acts 12:4.

When was Easter instituted, and by whom? The claim, of course, is that now it is held in commemoration of the Saviour's resurrection.

It is almost impossible to tell just when any of these voluntary feasts and practices crept into the church. It was at a comparatively early age that the celebration of Easter began. There is no doubt that at an early date many Christians celebrated, in a way, Christ's resurrection from the dead; but they never designed to set apart a day for that purpose. That is stated over and over again by the early "fathers." The yearly celebration of that day they connected with the Passover, and it was called the paschal feast. It is an utter mistranslation which places "Easter" in the text of Acts 12:4. Instead of "Easter" it ought to be "the Passover," as it is in the Revised Version. Therefore, the early Christians kept it at the time regulated by the Passover; but at an early day, the Roman Church endeavored to place the celebration of the resurrection on Sunday instead of on the day of the Passover.

Victor, Bishop of Rome, about the close of the second century, attempted to lord it over his brethren of the East, Dowling tells us, by forcing them to follow the rule which was observed by the Western churches in the keeping of the paschal feast. He wrote them an imperious letter commanding them to observe the same days he did. But the Eastern churches answered the lordly summons by the Bishop of Ephesus, Polycrates, that they would by no means depart in this matter from the custom handed down to them by their ancestors; upon which Victor, exasperated, pronounced them unworthy of the name of his brethren, and excluded them all from fellowship with the Church of Rome. This Dowling denominates the earliest instance of Roman assumption, but it was not even at that time called Easter.

The term "Easter" comes from the Anglo-Saxon *Eostre,* the name of the Saxon goddess, worshiped in spring, as exemplifying the fruitfulness and productiveness of nature, with offerings of flowers, eggs, and other symbolical characteristics. It was sun and nature worship. As with other heathen festivals, the rapidly apostatizing church thought it would be a good thing to connect the Passover celebration with the heathen feast of Easter; so it came into the church. There is no warrant of Scripture for it whatsoever. There is no sacredness in any way attached to the day; and those who observe it in memory of the resurrection of Christ can well bring home to their hearts the question which the Lord Himself asks, "Who hath required this at your hand?"

But is it not well to celebrate the resurrection of Christ? some may ask. Surely it is; but the truest, grandest, most fitting memorial of Christ's resurrection is the godly life of His followers. The resurrection of Christ demonstrated His power over sin; and if His followers wish to keep His resurrection before the world, it will be by living the Christ life, demonstrating the power of His people over sin. That is one constant, living representation of the resurrection.

"The Mark of the Beast." Rev. 14:9-11.

What is the mark of the beast? Is it Sundaykeeping?
Do Seventh-day Adventists teach that it is?

Seventh-day Adventists do *not* teach that Sundaykeeping is the mark of the beast. There are many thousands of God's children who have observed Sunday, and are observing it. They have believed and do believe that it is a holyday, and that they are glorifying God in its observance.

In this they are in error. "The seventh day is the Sabbath of the Lord thy God." So the voice of God declared from heaven. So His finger wrote in the very heart of His holy law. The followers of God in all ages from Adam to our blessed Lord and His apostles observed it; and we are over and over assured in the Book of God that His holy law is unchangeable, even to the jots and tittles. Ps. 111:7, 8; Isa. 51:6, 7; Matt. 5:17-20. Thus God has given us law and example for the observance of the seventh-day Sabbath, and its deeper study will show that it is founded on the eternal principles of the character of God.

Sunday is an interloper. It has neither divine command nor example. By no word of Inspiration is a sacred character for it predicated or assumed. It is one of the "six working days" and no more. Religiously, it is "the wild solar holiday of all pagan times," dedicated to the worship of the sun, among the seasons and times forbidden of God. It came into the Christian church through that apostasy which should "magnify itself," and "think to change the times and the law." Dan. 8:11; 7:25; 11:36-39; 2 Thess. 2:3-7. The Roman Catholic Church declares Sundaykeeping in the church to be the mark of her power to command fasts and holydays. "That the [Roman Catholic] church hath power," she declares, is proved "by the *very act of changing the Sabbath into Sunday*."—"*An Abridgment of the Christian Doctrine*," *Henry Tuberville*.

Protestants have no other authority for Sundaykeeping than that of pagan and papal tradition. Yet many have not understood, many do not understand, that they are in error; and God blesses them, not *because* of the error, but *notwithstanding* the error, for "the eyes of Jehovah run to and fro throughout the whole earth, to show Himself strong in the behalf of *them whose heart is perfect toward Him*." True service is a matter of love; knowledge is a matter of revelation and instruction. There are many who know little but love much, and God is leading them on to greater light and knowledge. It is also sadly true that there are many who know much but love little or not at all. For them God waits. Unless the heart and affections are yielded to Him to be changed by His Spirit, knowledge will avail nothing, and the light which is in them will become darkness.

Now in God's providence and plan His great threefold message of Revelation 14:6-14 is going to the world to call men from darkness to light; it is going to Babylon to call men from confusion of cruel dogma and tradition back to the word of God. Some in every nation, tribe, and people will hear, and heed, and do; will return to "the everlasting gospel," and be found among those who "keep the commandments of God, and the faith of Jesus." Rev. 14:12. Others will abide in Babylon, will in Babylon commit spiritual fornication by uniting with civil power to enforce the dogmas and traditions of error, among which will be Sundaykeeping. Around this all the union of Church-and-State forces is gathering. This union and consequent conditions between Church and State compose the beast and the image, till organized apostasy and Church-and-State tyranny are world-wide. The mark and test of allegiance to this power will be the legal Sunday, the great mark of apostasy, the change in God's law; and he who in the light of God's word turns from that light, from that law, from that gospel and its power, to the darkness of tradition and apostasy, to the power of the civil arm, receives in his very worship and yielded allegiance the character of the power he serves, and he crowns *that* with the badge of beast authority, the mark of his servitude, *by the observance of Sunday as enforced by the beast and his image,* in contradistinction to the true service of God in the Sabbath of the fourth commandment.

This is in principle the mark of the beast. Just the particular form it may assume in the future development, we do not know. Just as what stage of character development men possess that mark and cut themselves off from God, it is not for mortals to say. Judgment rests with God, not man. It is for us to proclaim the solemn warning against false worship, the dread consequences of sin; to set forth the eternal principles of the true; to plead with men to come to Christ in the faith that changes character; to entreat that Spirit which writes God's holy law upon the heart, and makes the doing of His every command a delight. But, praise God, the judgment of those who reject His truth rests not with us, but with Him.

THE CEREMONIAL LAW

"The Law" in Acts 15:24.

What is meant by the expression "the law"?

It is worthy of note, if our inquirer will look it up, to see that the expression, "Ye must be circumcised, and keep the law," is omitted from the Revised Version and the better Greek texts. The law under discussion in the fifteenth chapter of Acts includes the Mosaic code (see verses 1 and 5), which God did not impose on the Gentiles. Every moral element in that law remained. But every moral element of the law is included in the Ten Commandment law. When Christ came, the ritual law expired by limitation. The prolific vine which had twined around the trunk of the moral law dropped off, but the tree stood,—the Ten Commandments remained,—impaired in no part of its life. There will be no trouble to our inquirer whatever, or to any other who earnestly desires to know the truth, if he will keep in mind that God's government is one, eternal, unchangeable; necessarily so from His own perfect, holy, just, loving character. His law is as His government, and that law is summarized in the great Ten Words spoken from Mount Sinai.

In order to win the transgressors back to that law, and teach them His character, and hold them to Himself, God devised the ceremonial law, by which His children could from the very beginning express their faith in Him. In the patriarchal age it was very simple. In the Mosaic age it was complex, but every act that was performed had its lesson respecting sin and salvation; and sin is, ever has been, and ever will be, the transgression of the moral law of Ten Commandments. Sometimes this ceremonial law has been so intertwined in its moral aspects with the moral law that to the casual observer they have seemed almost the same. It is like a strong-growing green vine on an oak. When the vine is cut, it falls and dies, but the oak stands just the same. The life of each is different. So it is with the two laws. We have two ordinances in this dispensation, God's simple regulations regarding baptism and the Lord's Supper. The four things imposed on the Gentiles in Acts 15 were things of moral bearing, things which those Gentile converts did not consider were part of the moral law because their minds had been blinded by generations of practice. They were imposed by the apostles because they did have a moral basis.

Sabbath for the Jews Only. Ex. 35:2, 3; 34:21.

> If the prohibition to build fires on Sabbath in Exodus 35:2, 3 is a civil or ceremonial regulation for the Jews while in Palestine *only*, why may not the prohibition in Exodus 34:21 also be limited to them? Also Leviticus 23:32 and perhaps Leviticus 11:7, 8?

The command concerning the Sabbath, and a local law respecting it, are two things of an entirely different character. The Sabbath law originated in Eden, before man sinned. Gen. 2:2, 3. The Sabbath was therefore made for man, for the race. Mark 2:27. To show its eternal, enduring nature it is placed in the very heart of the Decalogue, bulwarked before and behind by nine other moral precepts concerning which there is no question, in order that man might know that there should be no question over the fourth commandment. Of that law it is easier for heaven and earth to pass than one tittle to fail. This is shown in an abundance of scriptures. Ex. 35:2, 3 was in its nature a local regulation referring to the wilderness period. The climate demanded no fire. The manna was prepared the day before the Sabbath. To build a fire was a direct and daring act of presumption against God. See Num. 15:30-36.

Leviticus 23:32 specially applies to the Day of Atonement, a typical feast pertaining to the Levitical age; but it also states a general law as regards the beginning and ending of all days. This also is shown in many scriptures. The day began and ended at the setting of the sun. Mark 1:32.

The *law* of unclean animals is not binding, but the great facts on which it is based should guide the well-instructed Christian.

It was no arbitrary law which divided between beasts regardless of their nature. In the very nature of things the swine is unclean, and God told His people so. This distinction existed before the Flood. Genesis 7:8; 8:20. Knowing this, how should the Christian apply 1 Corinthians 10:31?

"Let No Man Judge You." Col. 2:14-17.

> Will you please explain Colossians 2:14-17? The word here is *sabbatōn*, genitive plural. It is also *sabbatōn* in the Septuagint in Exodus 20:8-10. "Ordinances" is "dogma" (Greek, "law," "decree," etc.) The bond (see R. V.) was written in the dogma, or law. Verse 17 being nominative plural and neuter in Greek agrees with "holyday," "new moon," and "sabbath." The order "holyday," and "new moon," and "sabbath" is exactly as the order is in the Old Testament in some places. When that order appears in the Old Testament, does "sabbath" mean the Decalogue Sabbath or not? Would these considerations involve the claim that Paul did not refer to the Decalogue Sabbath in Colossians 2:14-17?

To answer the last question first, it would not in anywise affect the claim that Paul did not refer to the Decalogue Sabbath. The Decalogue Sabbath is not "a shadow of things to come." It is a memorial of that which is past. It is the constant present evidence of God's power to create and to re-create.

The Greek word *sabbatōn* is used for the singular in its plural form, partly for emphasis. Perhaps this can easily be seen by tracing it in a New Testament Greek concordance. The kind of sabbaths, new moons, etc., is shown by the phrase before referred to: "Which are a shadow of things to come." This was literally true of the feast days—the monthly festivals and the yearly sabbaths.

There is another consideration that is worthy of note in this passage that the student ought not to miss, and that is the point of the apostle's teaching. He is speaking to Christians, those whom God has redeemed and re-created in Christ Jesus. They have been placed upon the true foundation of God's word, and it is the apostle's desire that they shall be rooted and builded up in Christ and established in faith. All this is in harmony with God's holy word. Our Lord Himself was that word personified, a commandment keeper, and those rooted and established in Him by faith are also commandment keepers; therefore being justified by Him, received by Him, cleansed by Him, let not man judge. Let not man condemn. In other words, whatever men may say, do not let us feel condemned by them, even though we are not walking in the ordinances of men. God's path of commandments upon which grace has placed us may lead us away from all the traditions of the church in the past, and contrary to all human laws in the present. Let not these things trouble us. Go forward, looking to Christ and to Him alone. We are not to be led away by false philosophy, nor to be puffed up by the fleshly mind, but the Christian is to hold fast the Head; and he who truly and intelligently holds fast the Head, Christ our Lord, will be a commandment keeper, not to earn salvation, but because of the life within him.

Selling It Unto the Stranger. Deut. 14:21.

> I do not understand the following text: "Ye shall not eat of anything that dieth of itself: thou shalt *give it unto the stranger that is in thy gates, that he may eat it;* or thou mayest *sell it unto an alien:* for thou art an holy people unto the Lord thy God." Deut. 14:21.

The Lord means just what He says. He told His people not to eat anything which died of itself, but gave them permission to give it to the stranger within their gates, or to sell it to the foreigner. See Revised Version. "But was not this inconsistent?" Not at all. The stranger believed that such food was good, and ate such food continually. It was given or sold to him without any deceit, as flesh of an animal which had died of itself. The Israelites were forbidden to eat blood, but that which died of itself of course contained the blood; but the other nations around them did not consider it wrong in any way to eat the blood. In all cases they evidently bought and sold such flesh for just what it was; while many times, if reports are to be believed, meat is sold nowadays for fresh, healthy meat when it is the flesh of animals that died of disease.

And few are the flesh eaters, indeed, but that eat fish and shellfish which die of themselves by slow, lingering deaths, and they find no fault with the dealer for selling such. In fact, the great majority of all fish, lobsters, clams, crabs, oysters, shrimps, etc., die of themselves, and are eaten with gusto by those who criticize the Lord's directions in Deuteronomy 12:21.

To What Law? Heb. 7:12.

To what change of what law does Hebrews 7:12 refer?

Read the context, or less, even the verse itself, and there can be no more question. It is the law relating to the priesthood. "The priesthood being changed," of course the law regulating it must be changed. The Levitical priesthood was vested in the house of Aaron, of the tribe of Levi. The time of service, the kind of man, the sacrifices he offered, were all specified in law. But when Christ began His priesthood after the order of Melchizedek, He came of a different tribe to serve after a different order. The text in question has no more bearing upon the Decalogue than it has upon the Constitution of the United States. The use of it to endeavor to prove the change of the Sabbath shows to what desperate straits error is put to defend itself.

What Days? Gal. 4:7-11.

Please explain Galatians 4:7-11. To what days does the apostle refer?

The passage is not difficult to understand if we will study the context. It will be seen from the eighth verse that the Galatians were at one time heathen; they were in bondage to them that "by nature are no gods." In Leviticus 19:26 we learn that the Lord forbade indulging in the customs of the heathen. "Neither shall ye use enchantment, nor observe times." See also Deut. 18:10.

The heathen had their days dedicated to their gods. Sunday was the day dedicated to the sun, Monday to the moon, and so with all the days of the week. The months also were named in some cases after the gods, as January for Janus, the two-faced god. Those idolatrous feasts were many times scenes of the greatest license; they were essentially bestial and low. They were carried on throughout all heathen lands. Therefore, when the Galatians turned from the Lord Jesus Christ to self-justification, they naturally fell right back to the observance of the heathen days and times. For the apostle declares, "But now that ye have come to know God, or rather to be known by God, how *turn ye back again* to the weak and beggarly *rudiments,* whereunto ye desire to be in bondage over again?" What were those weak and beggarly rudiments? It was "bondage to them that by nature are no gods," and it constituted evidence that they observed days and months and seasons and years; that is, the heathen days and times and months and seasons, hoping for salvation in them.

Are we to understand from this that God would have us observe no time? No; because He has Himself given us one time that should be observed, His great worship day, the Sabbath, the seventh day.

"Nailed to the Cross." Col. 2:14.

> Will you please explain Colossians 2:14? Does it teach that the Lord's Supper is not to be observed, and that baptism is done away—that all these were nailed to the cross?

The apostle is speaking of only those things which are against us, which are nailed to the cross. In the eighth verse he tells us, "Take heed lest there shall be anyone that maketh spoil of you through his philosophy and vain deceit, after the tradition of men, after the rudiments of the world, and not after Christ." Those things that are of the world, those things that are of men, are not the things by which we are saved. They are the things that are to be put away. They are the things which have brought us into bondage. In Christ dwells all fullness; in Him is true circumcision, the cutting off of sin. In Him we are baptized (verse 12), and we show our faith in Him by baptism, and by that baptism show to the world that we have "put off the old man" with all his workings. By His power we are raised, or made to walk in "newness of life," and we can rejoice in the fact that He has blotted out all those things which would bring us into bondage, and nailed them to His cross forever; and He has wrought all this in order that we may obey Him in perfect freedom of spirit, keeping the things which He Himself has given, instead of being bound about by the rules and ordinances of men. That would include not only the traditions of men, but it would include all those Jewish types and shadows and traditions which were done away when Christ came.

Abolishing the Commandments. Eph. 2:15.

Please explain Ephesians 2:15, "abolishing the enmity."

The thing which Jesus abolishes is "the enmity," and the place where He abolishes it is in His "flesh." He took upon Himself the flesh of those whom He saves (Heb. 2:14; Gal. 4:4, 5; Rom. 1:3); and therefore the flesh that He took was the flesh that possessed all the tendencies toward sin, just the same as the flesh which the children bear. If our Lord had followed those tendencies, He would have been led into sin, as every human being has been; but by the power of the Spirit of God dwelling in Him by faith, He overthrew that enmity, abolished it.

Man lets his mind run in harmony with his flesh, and it becomes the carnal mind, and "the carnal mind is enmity against God: for it is not subject to the law of God, neither indeed can be." Rom. 8:7. The mind therefore is in bondage to sin. Jesus began His work where man failed, in the mind; and there He abolished the enmity in the flesh, even "the law of commandments contained in ordinances."

Out of that very idea of the carnal mind have come all of the ordinances that men have devised to enable them to live better. All the various stated fasts and the crucifixions of the flesh have arisen out of human effort to earn salvation; but all these passed away in the work of our Lord Jesus Christ. Jesus abolished them, and made "in Himself of twain one new man, so making peace;" and He invites both Jew and Gentile to let that "new man" come into the heart, that they may be one in Christ Jesus.

THE COVENANTS

The Words of the Covenant. Ex. 34:28.

Please harmonize Exodus 34:28 with Hebrews 8:7 and
Ephesians 2:12-15.

There is nothing to *harmonize*. When two statements of inspiration seem to be in conflict, the difficulty is not in the statements, but in our limited understanding. *We* need to be brought into harmony with the word. Exodus 34:28 reads: "And he was there with the Lord forty days and forty nights; he did neither eat bread, nor drink water. And He wrote upon the tables the words of the covenant, the Ten Commandments." Each of the first two times that the pronoun "he" occurs in the above it refers to Moses, who was in the holy mount by the invitation of the Lord. Verses 1, 2. The last "He" refers to the Lord, who wrote the Ten Commandments, as He told Moses He would. See verse 1, where the Lord says, "I will write upon these tables the words that were in the first tables." See also Deuteronomy 10:1-4, where Moses declares that "He [the Lord] wrote on the tables, according to the first writing, the Ten Commandments." Boothroyd translates Exodus 34:28, last clause, as follows: "And Jehovah wrote upon the tables, the words of the covenant, the Ten Commandments." The Ten Commandments are not the mutual covenant, the covenant which *God made with Israel,* as recorded in Exodus 19:5-8 and 24:3-8. Yet they are called the *Words* of the covenant, and the *Ten Words* of the covenant, because the covenant was made in respect to these words. That is, Israel in that promised to keep the Decalogue. The covenant into which Israel entered depended on the Decalogue, not the Decalogue on the covenant. The covenant, the agreement which Israel made, could be broken a thousand times, but that would not affect God's law. A foreigner may promise to keep the law of this country on condition that he be received as a citizen. That law would be the law of his covenant, or promise.

He might then break his promise, or violate his covenant; but that would neither abolish nor confirm nor affect in any way the law of the land. That would stand whether he kept it or not. The covenant mentioned in Hebrews 8:7 was the covenant into which Israel entered. It was faulty, because Israel, being sinful and weak, could not keep the law. In the new covenant, old as the days of Abel, God puts the same law in the heart, and then man keeps it.

Ephesians 2:12-15 refers to the covenants and man's relation thereto. Verse 12 shows the condition of the Gentiles who do not know God. Verses 13, 14 show how they are brought nigh to God through Christ, who is our peace, to reconcile us to God. He does this by abolishing "in His flesh *the enmity.*" The "enmity" is not on God's part, but ours. "Because the *carnal mind is enmity against God:* for it is *not subject to the law of God,* neither indeed can be." Rom. 8:7. This carnal mind, Christ abolished in His flesh for us all. In other words, Christ took away the sin and all those typical services and symbols which pointed out sin, and made remembrance of it, but could not take it away. Jesus Christ in no way abolished or changed the moral law, the Ten Commandments. See Isa. 42:21; Matt. 5:17-20. It was inseparable from His heart and life. Ps. 40:7, 8.

The New Covenant. Heb. 8:7-13.

Please explain Hebrews 8:7-13.

The passage is largely a quotation from the 31st chapter of Jeremiah. Jeremiah predicts the making of the new covenant. Hebrews records what has taken place in Christ Jesus. The first covenant was the covenant made at Mount Sinai recorded in Exodus 19 and in Exodus 24. That was a faulty covenant, because it was no stronger than the weakest promise which it had—the promise of the people. Note, "For if that first covenant had been faultless, then should no place have been sought for a second. For finding fault with *them....*" It was the people who were at fault. The new covenant, which was the everlasting covenant given to

Abel, to Noah, to Abraham, and to Israel, was based upon the promises of God. Man's part was simply the yielding to those promises and the receiving of them. And when men do that, God promises not to compel them to obey, but so to place His law in their hearts and in their minds that they would have no other desire than to obey. They would love God and keep His commandments. All this is comprised in the gospel of the Lord Jesus Christ. It is, in other words, stating God's great plan of salvation through faith. The old covenant, apart from its national view, was man's effort to save himself through promise; the new covenant carries us clear over into the new state when sin shall be forever banished, and the children of the covenant shall bask in the smiles of God forever. And note, too, that the law written in the heart is the same law of God which Jeremiah knew, six hundred years before Christ. The law is eternal.

The Two Covenants in Galatians.

Please explain Galatians 4:24-31.

Galatians 4:24-31 touches upon the old and the new covenant. Hagar is the type of one, Sarah is the type of the other; the child of Hagar, the type of those who are brought in through human scheming; the child of Sarah, a type of those who are brought in solely through the promise of the Lord Jesus Christ. Hagar bore children to bondage, for she was a bondmaid; so all those who are endeavoring to save themselves by any scheme of man are in bondage. They never can break their bondage themselves, and all they save or convert to such a system as that are children of bondage. On the other hand, Sarah was a free woman, and her children were free. She represents God's order; and all those who are saved according to God's order, with faith in the promises of the Lord Jesus, are children of freedom. The two things are represented by the earthly Jerusalem and the heavenly Jerusalem. The earthly Jerusalem is representative of that kingdom which Israel tried to establish in their own righteousness under constant rebellion against God; but the New Jerusalem, to which the children have not yet come, is the

Jerusalem that is made wholly after God's order, and is free, and is therefore called the mother of the children of freedom. Hence, Paul concludes that we who have believed in Christ are as Isaac was—the children of promise. Isaac was persecuted by Ishmael, the child of the bondservant; so God's true children will meet persecution from those who are following the schemes of men. But in the glorious outcome God will save His children, and cast out those who are not of Him.

The Covenant and the Law. Gal. 3:16, 17.

> Kindly explain Romans 5:13, 14 and Galatians 3:16, 17. It has been claimed that as Abraham was saved by faith, the law, coming 430 years after, could not change the covenant of faith.

All of which is absolutely true, for all who are saved are saved by faith; "for without faith it is impossible to please Him." What is meant by the law coming 430 years after, is that it was given in written form 430 years after. Of this we are expressly told that it does not make the covenant of none effect. The covenant is God's everlasting promise in Christ Jesus. The object of the giving of Christ and that covenant is to save from sin, and sin is the transgression of the law.

There were brethren in Galatia, as also elsewhere, who seemed to think that men were saved by the law. The apostle's argument in both Romans and Galatians is to prove that man is saved, not by his righteousness, but by faith in Christ's righteousness. If this point is kept in mind, there will be no difficulty whatever with any of these scriptures, for we are saved by faith. Faith lays hold upon the righteousness of God in Christ Jesus. That was true of Abraham. It is true of every child of Abraham since that. Consequently anything that comes in through God's providence, or anything that man may do, cannot make of none effect the eternal promises of God; and this scripture shows that the law was not given to annul the promises, was not revealed in written form to Israel to change in any way God's plan of salvation. The apostle in both Galatians and Romans tells us why the law came in in written form. It was added, or spoken, because of transgression. Gal. 3:19. "Moreover the law entered, that the offense might abound" (Rom. 5:20); in order "that sin by the commandment might become exceeding sinful" (Rom. 7:13). "But where sin abounded, grace did much more abound." God's eternal moral standard is His holy law. Man's everlasting hope in all ages is Jesus Christ.

The Covenant by Sacrifice. Ps. 50:5.

> To what time does this apply? When will the gathering take place?

The gathering will take place when our Lord Jesus Christ shall gather home His people. The covenant by sacrifice is that covenant which centers in the sacrifice of our Lord and Saviour Jesus Christ. That does not mean that His people will not sacrifice. They will give all, even as they accept all; but no sacrifice can make effective a covenant save the sacrifice of our Lord Jesus Christ. His is the sacrifice, ours the acceptance; and the acceptance is the renunciation of our all upon the altar. Luke 14:33.

The New Covenant and the Sabbath.

> In Jeremiah 31:31-34 we have a promise of a new covenant, and in Hebrews 8:6-11 it seems to be fulfilled. Some say that this is where the Sabbath of the Bible was changed. Is this true?

We do not know how it could be changed through the new covenant, when the Sabbath is an integral part of God's law, and the work which the new covenant will do for the believer is to write that law within the heart. That is what the new covenant has done through all the ages. The only time reference there can be to it would be its confirmation at the death of Christ. He was that new covenant incarnate. In Him were "the sure mercies of David." Isa. 55:3, 4. He was a witness to the peoples, a leader and commander to the peoples. In His teaching He declared that it was easier for heaven and earth to pass away than one tittle of the law to fail. Matt. 5:17, 18. When the young man came to Him asking what he should do to obtain eternal life, Jesus replied, "If thou wouldest enter into life, keep the commandments." Matt. 19:17. He Himself kept the law perfectly, and thus having taught and exemplified all the principles of the covenant, He confirmed it with His death upon the cross. Paul tells us that though it be a man's covenant, if it be confirmed, no man disannuls or adds thereto. Gal. 3:15. He who seeks to crowd into that new covenant a worship day or an institution of which God has not spoken, is endeavoring to change the very hope of Christianity, and set aside the new covenant, sealed with the blood of Jesus. Oh, how much better it is to let the new covenant do the same work in our hearts that it did in the heart of Jesus of Nazareth! Then shall we say like Him, "I delight to do Thy will, O my God; yea, Thy law is within my heart."

UNPARDONABLE SIN

Unpardonable Sin.

> Please give an example of unpardonable sin. Be as explicit as possible.

Let us emphasize: An unpardonable sin is an unrepentable sin. Any soul that hates sin, that is sorry for his sinning, sorry that he has grieved God and the Holy Spirit, and longs to put away the sin, however deeply he has sinned, has not committed an unpardonable sin; for all these desires, feelings, emotions, longings, are begotten of the Spirit, to win him back to God.

Why ask for instances? No two cases can ever be just the same. But when King Saul turned from God, the only one who could save, to a familiar spirit, he committed the unpardonable sin, because there was rejection of the means of salvation. 1 Chron. 10:13, 14. When the chief priests said, "We have no king but Caesar," they rejected the only one who could save them. John 19:15; Matt. 23:37, 38. When the scribes called that power in Christ which cast out demons the Beelzebub, they set aside the only power that could save, and they could find no forgiveness, because they could never discern its source. Mark 3:29, 30.

It is the blood of Jesus Christ and the sanctifying power of the Spirit which saves. If we turn from these, what hope have we? Heb. 10:29. This is not to the discouraged soul, but to the sin-loving, Christ-hating soul. Here are three texts for every discouraged heart who has failed again and again: "As I live, saith the Lord God, I have no pleasure in the death of the wicked; but that the wicked turn from his way and live." Ezek. 33:11. "Now the just shall live by faith: but if any man draw back, My soul shall have no pleasure in him." Heb. 10:38. "The Lord taketh pleasure in them that fear Him, *in those that hope in His mercy.*" Ps. 147:11. Read also Isaiah 55:7; Micah 7:18, 19.

All forgivable sins are repentable sins; but sin which is continued under light and blessings which are used in a selfish way contrary to the appeals of the Spirit of God, only harden the heart all the more, and render it more and more unresponsive to every true appeal. This is true in the case of the wicked. How much more does it become true of one who has truly known God and yet turns away from Him and indulges in the things that are wrong! There is always hope for every soul, always repentance for every soul, who stands where the Spirit of God can convict him of his sin. There is never repentance when one identifies himself with the sin and continues on in it despite the appeals of the Spirit.

Those Who Fall Away. Heb. 6:4-6.

Please explain Hebrews 6:4-6.

The text referred to reads: "For it is impossible for those who were once enlightened, and have tasted of the heavenly gift, and were made partakers of the Holy Ghost, and have tasted the good word of God, and the powers of the world to come, if they shall fall away, to renew them again unto repentance; seeing they crucify to themselves the Son of God afresh, and put Him to an open shame."

Another text from the same book speaks similarly upon the same subject, and the texts should be studied together. It reads: "For if we sin willfully after that we have received the knowledge of the truth, there remaineth no more sacrifice for sins, but a certain fearful looking for of judgment and fiery indignation, which shall devour the adversaries. He that despised Moses' law died without mercy under two or three witnesses: of how much sorer punishment, suppose ye, shall he be thought worthy, who hath trodden underfoot the Son of God, and hath counted the blood of the covenant, wherewith he was sanctified, an unholy thing, and hath done despite unto the Spirit of grace?" Heb. 10:26-29.

Some persons are troubled over these texts, thinking possibly they may have reference to the ordinary backslider, who in his heart has never rejected the Lord, and who is continually thinking that someday he will enter His service again. And oftentimes when he begins to think seriously of taking up that service without delay, then the enemy of all souls will confront him with these texts, the same as he confronted Christ Himself with texts of Scripture, and sought to give them a wrong application.

The text is speaking of individuals who have actually been enlightened. They have really tasted the heavenly gift, and know from experience what it is. They were made partakers of the Holy Spirit. They tasted the word of God, and also the powers of the world to come. Their experience reached out to the depth of definite knowledge, so that they knew the positive grounds of the divine gift. And now these individuals break away from all this, and, according to the text quoted from the tenth chapter of Hebrews, they count the blood of the covenant, wherewith they had been sanctified, an unholy, a common, thing. They have despised the Spirit of grace.

The text speaks of an actual falling away that leads a man to renounce things that he really knows are truth, and to treat with disrespect and despite the Holy Spirit, whose influences in all their blessed realities he has felt upon his own heart and life. And having fallen away after this manner, it can be readily seen that he has broken off from all the influences that would draw him to heaven, and has purposely and with determination placed himself beyond hope, and beyond the reach of God. The text shows that he has done this willfully—he has exercised his will to do the thing.

But the poor backslider, in the place of exercising any will power, has simply allowed his will to be overcome and dethroned by the persistent attacks of Satan; and to all such the Lord sends many gracious appeals in His word, as, "Go and proclaim these words toward the north, and say, Return, thou backsliding Israel, saith the Lord; and I will not cause Mine anger to fall upon you: for I am merciful, saith the Lord, and I will not keep anger forever. Only acknowledge thine iniquity, that thou hast transgressed against the Lord thy God, and hast scattered thy ways to the strangers under every green tree, and ye have not obeyed My voice, saith the Lord. Turn, O backsliding children, saith the Lord; for I am married unto you: and I will take you one of a city, and two of a family, and I will bring you to Zion." "Return, ye backsliding children, and I will heal your backslidings. Behold, we come unto Thee; for Thou art the Lord our God." Jer. 3:12-14, 22. Of all the blessed attributes of God, there is one He has singled out as pre-eminent—"He *delighteth* in mercy." Micah 7:18.

Sinning Against the Holy Spirit. Matt. 12:31, 32.

Can you tell me what sinning against the Holy Spirit is, as mentioned in Matthew 12:31, 32; also in Luke 12:10?

Compare these two scriptures with Mark 3:28-30. It will be clearly seen, by this comparison with the words found in Mark, that the sin against the Holy Spirit on the part of the Jews was attributing to Satan the power by which Christ wrought miracles. Jesus was working miracles that only Divinity could work. It was a strong, clear manifestation of the Spirit of God in Him. His teaching was in harmony with those miracles. He taught also the things of God. To declare, as the Jews did, that He cast out demons by Beelzebub, the prince of demons, was utterly to turn away from the only power that could save them, the power of the life and Spirit of God. This is the teaching of Jesus, and this will serve to show what sinning against the Holy Spirit is.

The only reason why a sin is unforgivable is that it is unrepentable. God has but one power to save His people, one means of cleansing. He cleanses by the blood of the Lord Jesus. He gives life and power by His Holy Spirit. See Heb. 10:29.

Sin becomes unforgivable because it is unrepentable. If a soul is sinking on the sea, and a life buoy is thrown him, and he will not grasp it when he can, what help is there for him? He chooses to die. Take, for instance, the experiences of Jesus which called out these words. He had been casting out demons, relieving poor, distressed souls that had been under the bondage of Satan. He had given manifest evidence that the power which He exercised was the mighty, loving power of God. But the Jews said, "By Beelzebub the prince of the demons casteth He out demons." They attributed the work of the Spirit of God to the spirit of evil. See Mark 3:22-30. Note especially the last verse, "Because they said, He hath an unclean spirit."

Now it is possible for one who knows nothing of the working of the Spirit of God to speak against it, or blaspheme it, and still be saved. This seems to have been the case with the apostle Paul; for he declares, "I obtained mercy, because I did it ignorantly in unbelief." 1 Tim. 1:13. But to him who does it in the face of such light as the Jews themselves had, or to one who continually rejects the Spirit of God until the heart becomes hardened, there comes a condition at last that yields no response to the pleadings of the Spirit. The danger does not lie in God's unwillingness to forgive; the danger lies in our putting ourselves in such an attitude toward God that He cannot reach us.

Cannot Be Saved. Prov. 16:4; Rom. 9:15-24.

Do not Proverbs 16:4 and Romans 9:15-24 teach that some persons cannot be saved?

No. God saves character; and He calls to savable character every soul. The first scripture simply teaches that all things are fitting in God's plan. The wicked will belong to the day of wrath; but God compels none to be wicked. See His oath in Ezekiel 33:11.

God would have glorified His name through Pharaoh's submission if the Egyptian monarch had yielded, even as He did through Nebuchadnezzar and Cyrus. He raised him up, brought him to the Egyptian throne, for that purpose. Pharaoh would not submit, therefore God's Spirit left him to hardness of heart. Yet God got glory to Himself despite the king's stubbornness.

Study one expression in Romans 9:15. On whom is it God's will to have mercy? "Showing mercy unto thousands of them that love Me, and keep My commandments." Ex. 20:6. We expect that; but upon what other class is it God's will to show compassion and mercy? "Let the *wicked* forsake his way, and the *unrighteous man* his thoughts: and let him return unto the Lord, and *He will have mercy upon him;* and to our God, for *He will abundantly pardon."* Isa. 55:7. "As I live, saith the Lord God, I have no pleasure in the death of the wicked; but that the *wicked turn from his way and live:* turn ye, turn ye from your evil ways; for why will ye die?" Ezek. 33:11. Read John 3:16 and Revelation 22:17.

Ananias and Sapphira. Acts 5:1, 2.

> Acts 5:1, 2 says: "A certain man named Ananias, with Sapphira his wife, sold a possession, and kept back part of the price, his wife also being privy to it, and brought a certain part, and laid it at the apostles' feet." What was their reason for keeping back part of the price? And the fourth verse says, "Thou hast not lied unto men, but unto God." In what way did they lie to God?

Shortly after the organization of the church at Jerusalem, there were some among the believers who, on account of their faith, were cast out of their homes, and cut off from their means of support, while others had money and property of considerable value. The record says of these, in the latter part of chapter 4, that they had all things in common. Those who had possessions, sold them and put the proceeds into the common fund; and from this, distribution was made to those who were in need. The instance is cited of one, Joses, who sold his property and brought the money to the apostles. Two others, Ananias and Sapphira, under the influence of the Spirit, pledged the proceeds from the sale of certain property. Later they allowed a spirit of covetousness to come into their hearts, and concluded that they had been too hasty in making such a large pledge. They noted, however, that those who had thus sacrificed their possessions were held in high esteem by their brethren; and wishing to win for themselves this same high opinion, yet not wishing to give so large an amount, they deliberately decided to sell their property, and withhold a large share of the proceeds for themselves, while pretending to give the full amount.

In telling Peter that they had given the full amount that they had received, they deliberately lied to the Holy Spirit. It was true, as Peter said, that the property was their own, and they were not obliged to give it up—they had made the pledge of their own free will; and in attempting to deceive the apostles, they had lied to the Almighty.

This example was given as a warning against hypocrisy, to those of all ages, and that they should beware of robbing God. It is God who entrusts men with property, and He does this that they may use it in blessing others, and He will one day call them to give an account of their stewardship. He claims a certain portion, a tenth, as His own; and aside from this, He asks that men give freewill offerings to aid in the propagation of His work in the earth.

When a man has made a pledge to God, he should consider it his highest duty to fulfill it. The warning of God's word is, "Beware of covetousness, which is idolatry." A. O. T.

MARRIAGE AND DIVORCE

How Much Is Involved in Christian Marriage?

Will you kindly define what constitutes a Christian marriage? Is a marriage ceremony of any real value, and is there any importance to be attached to it by true believers, aside from the formality which custom demands of those who enter the state of wedlock? Would not a man and a woman who had solemnly, before the Lord, promised to accept and take each other as husband and wife, be as truly married as though a civil ceremony had been performed by a justice, or a civil-religious ceremony by a minister of the gospel?

It is impossible to set forth anything definite as to a form of ceremony. It seems to have been regulated by local customs, with certain essentials. In the first marriage, the Creator gave to the man his wife, under what form we know not, although we do know that there was sufficient form to convey clearly to all parties involved that a marriage had taken place, and the solemn truth was conveyed that the twain should be one flesh, and that the union was indissoluble and the relationship permanent. One of the essential things in marriage seems to have been the passing of the bride from her father's house to the house of her husband or his father. This was preceded by betrothal, and accompanied with more or less ceremony, and solemn covenant. See references to these customs in the following: Ezek. 16:8-14; Mal. 2:14; Prov. 2:17; Gen. 24:57-60; Ruth 4:9-13; Isa. 61:10; Cant. 3:11; Jer. 2:32; Matt. 9:15; 25:1-10. These and many other scriptures indicate that ceremonies accompanied the marriage, feasts were held, friends were present, pledges were given, covenants were ratified. The right of both wife and children and the good of society demand some formalities in the marriage ceremony, and this seems to have been recognized all through Bible times.

The use that is made of marriage as a symbol of the union between Christ and the individual (Rom. 7:4; Gal. 3:27), as well as between Christ and His kingdom (Isa. 54:4-6; 61:10; 62:3-5; Rev. 21:1, 2, 9, 10; 19:7-9), indicates that more should be made of the marriage itself than a mere formal contract between two parties, though the world may make too much of the ceremony and too little of the sacred union for life. The sacredness of marriage in God's sight is also indicated by its prohibitions.

While the solemn agreement between the man and the woman might, as between them and God, constitute a true marriage, they owe it to posterity and to the public to make it public and of public record. And the Bible demands conformity to civil law when duty to God does not contravene. Rom. 13:1-7.

Taking One's Brother's Wife. Lev. 18:16; 20:21.

> Does not the moral law in Leviticus (Lev. 18:16; 20:21) apply today to all Christians just as it applied then to all the Jews?

New Testament writers, such as Mark, Matthew, and Luke, make reference to Deuteronomy 25:5, but not to this passage in Leviticus. The prohibitions in Leviticus seem to be against gross and unlawful indulgence of lust or illegal marriage while the husband was yet living. If it were unlawful to marry the wife of a deceased brother, why was such an injunction given as in Deuteronomy 25:5? While the illustration which Paul uses in Romans 7:2, 3 is designed to teach a spiritual lesson, it must also have been a recognized fact in the marriage laws of the Jews. That being the case, a brother's widow is free from her deceased husband, so that she is free to "be married to another man." Compare the terms used in Leviticus 18:16 with verse 7 of the same chapter. The other text, Leviticus 20:21, evidently refers to adultery, the brother, the woman's husband, being yet alive. See 1 Cor. 7:39. We do not believe that marriage to the wife of a deceased brother is contrary to Scripture. The indulgence of unlawful lusts, forbidden in the texts to which our querist refers, is always wrong. Some have had an idea that John the Baptist reproved Herod for marrying his *deceased* brother's wife; but Herod took the wife of his brother, *while his brother was yet living*—quite a different thing. Deuteronomy 25:5, before referred to, made it a *duty* to take a deceased brother's wife, providing he died childless. If his brother did not die childless, it would naturally be the *privilege* of the widow and her former husband's brother to marry if they felt so disposed.

A Question of Divorce.

Husband and wife are legally separated by divorce, though not for scriptural cause. The husband seeks reconciliation with the wife, but is unsuccessful. She marries another. Afterward he marries, and his wife bears him children. Later he is troubled as to whether his last marriage is right, and asks what course to pursue. What shall the husband do?

There is, to our mind, only one thing for him to do, and that is to live a faithful, godly life with his present wife, the mother of his children. The legal divorce, and the action of the first wife in marrying left him free to marry as a Christian; let him so abide.

Marriage of Cousins. Lev. 18:6-18.

Will you kindly tell me if there is any Bible reason why first cousins should not marry, and where it may be found?

The degrees of consanguinity forbidden by the Scripture are named in Leviticus 18:6-18; 20:12, 14, 17, 19-21. First cousins are not forbidden to marry. One great objection to in-marrying, that is, the marrying of blood relations, is that the fruit of such union is likely to perpetuate, emphasize, and augment the unpleasant traits of the family. The fruit of such union is more likely to be affected unfavorably mentally and physically, all things being equal, than the fruit of a union between those not blood relatives. If both parents were of different temperament, strong and well physically, and well-balanced mentally, one generation would not be likely to suffer. Today medical science claims to be able, by certain tests, to determine in what cases it is safe for cousins to marry.

Putting Away and Marrying.

Will you please explain Matthew 5:32; 19:9?

Both scriptures are in perfect harmony, and teach practically the same thing. "Whosoever shall put away his wife, saving for the cause of fornication, causeth her to commit adultery: and whosoever shall marry her that is divorced committeth adultery." And the ninth verse of the nineteenth chapter reads, "Whosoever shall put away his wife, except it be for fornication, and shall marry another, committeth adultery." It seems that the exception is very clearly and definitely marked,—that if there is fornication, the guilty party could be put away, and divorce secured; and the innocent one would be free to marry again. But it does not give the guilty party the right to marry again; and whoever marries the guilty party, partakes with that guilty party in the sin. This, it seems to us, is the teaching of the text.

We know there are those who believe that persons divorced, for whatever cause, should never marry again; but in both of these cases, the Lord has given us a very clear exception, and other texts should be understood in harmony with it.

In some instances in which persons have thus separated, the guilty party has married in harmony with the laws of the world, not knowing, or realizing, or appreciating, and perhaps not caring, what is said in the Scriptures regarding such a step. This course, so far as the law of the land is concerned, has been perfectly legal. Children have been born to such marriages, and afterward the participants may have embraced the gospel message of truth. What should they do? We would say that they had better remain as they are. When they came to Christ, He accepted them as they were, and did not design to break home ties, or marriage ties, or take away from the father or the mother the responsibility of caring for their offspring.

Separation but Not Remarriage. 1 Cor. 7:15.

Will you please explain 1 Corinthians 7:15? To whom
does the instruction apply—to the man and woman who
separate after one accepts Christ or after both profess to
be Christians? In the first case, is the believer free to
marry again?

The verse reads: "But if the unbelieving depart, let him depart.
A brother or a sister is not under bondage in such cases: but God
hath called us to peace."

We learn this from verse 11: A wife, if she cannot live in peace
with her husband, and separates, should remain unmarried or else
be reconciled to the husband. The next verse tells us that if a
brother (a believer) has a wife who does not believe, and she is
pleased to dwell with him, he is not to put her away or leave her. In
verse 13, similar instruction is given regarding the wife. Then verse
15 says, "If the unbelieving depart,"—does not want to stay with the
believer,—let him go. "A brother or a sister is not under bondage
in such cases." If the unbelieving departs, the believer has no right
to marry again without a legal separation, and scripturally he would
have no ground for a legal separation in a mere matter of belief or
unbelief. There is but one cause for separation that will permit a
scriptural remarriage while both parties are living; and our Lord
states that clearly in Matthew 5:32.

Is Polygamy Sin?

God told man to be fruitful and multiply. Gen. 1:22,
etc. Was it evil, or sin, for a man to have more than one
wife? See instructions given in Deuteronomy 21:15-17.
And there were many illustrious characters who had
more than one wife. David did, and he is said to be
"a man after God's own heart."

In the first place, it would seem that if God had designed that
man should have more than one wife, He would have made more
than one wife for Adam. The record does not say that He made
them male and females, but "male and female," a female for a

male. He gave to Adam one wife, and the divine expression is, "They twain [the two, not four or five, or three even] shall be one flesh." We have no more reason to gather from the Scripture that polygamy is right than that polyandry is right. Why has not the woman just as much right to two or more husbands as the man has to two or more wives?

Secondly, God wishes man to learn some things in the providential outworkings of events, as well as by direct precept. Man had in the beginning God's plan clear and direct. He ought to have followed that plan. When males were killed off in war and strife, man began to multiply wives to himself, contrary to God's plan. And man's devices have had some sad outworkings. Good men have failed to carry out God's plan. Their hearts have been right, and God has accepted them notwithstanding their sins; but this does not excuse their sins, or their bad example, or the bad results. Abraham had many trials and much sadness on account of his two wives. He would have avoided much of his trial if he had believed God and refused to act on Sarah's suggestion. Isaac's life seems to have been a quiet and happy one; he had but the one wife. Jacob had two wives, and his life was miserable in consequence, on account of the jealousies of the wives and of the sons. David had more than one wife. He was a man after God's own heart in his sorrow for sin, in his devotion, in his faithfulness, in his willingness to receive God's reproof; but he certainly did not follow God's way in multiplying wives to himself, and went directly against the commandment of God, that the king should "not multiply wives" to himself. Deut. 17:17. But just as soon as a man has more than one wife at the same time, he multiplies wives to himself. We have only to think of the sad history of David's family, of his rebellious and wayward sons, to see the folly of his having many wives. So also with Solomon. In the teaching of Jesus, He brings us back to the original plan of Eden. "He which made them *at the beginning* made them *male* and *female,* and said, For this cause shall a man leave father and mother, and shall cleave to his *wife* [one]: and they twain shall be one flesh." Surely it is contrary to God and His truth and His plan to have more than one wife.

Unequal Marriages. Genesis 6.

> Who are "the sons of God" spoken of in Genesis, chapter 6, as marrying "the daughters of men"?

Evidently the "sons of God" are the men who profess the religion of God. Division came after sin entered. This is indicated by various expressions. For instance, in Genesis 4:26 we read: "Then began men to call upon the name of Jehovah," or, as the margin reads, "to call themselves by the name of Jehovah." The children of Seth were those who had faith in God. The children of Cain became the sons of men, and looked simply to this earth life. They did not have the faith in God that was manifest in Abel, and afterward in Seth. The one class were men of the world; the other, children of God. But the children of God, with their human desires, looked upon the daughters of men, and saw that they were fair, and "took them wives of all that they chose;" and just as Solomon's heart was weaned away from God by his wives, so the sons of God became corrupted in this way. Mighty men sprang from them, but these men were corrupt and wicked at heart.

The New Testament gives clear warning against the marriage of Christians with unbelievers: "Be not unequally yoked with unbelievers: for what fellowship have righteousness and iniquity? or what communion hath light with darkness?" See 2 Cor. 6:14-18. Such marriages have always been lacking in completeness.

The Case of Esther.

> Persians could not marry Jews. What about the case of Esther?

Our querist has turned the matter around. Persians were not forbidden to marry Jews, but Jews were forbidden to marry Persians. But in this case, it was not the choice of Esther, but the choice of the king; and the Jews were captives and slaves in the land of Persia. Esther seems to have been gathered among the beautiful maidens of the kingdom from whom the king was to take his choice; and she was chosen. It was an exceptional case, and God overruled it for the good of His children. There were those exceptional cases all the way through. For instance, Rahab, of the inhabitants of Canaan, of the city of Jericho, who housed the spies, became an ancestress of our Lord, and so also did Ruth the Moabitess. But these were exceptional cases, and did not pervert the holy seed.

ASTRONOMY

The Sun Standing Still. Joshua 10:12.

> Joshua asked the Lord that the sun should stand still; but the astronomers claim that the sun stands still all the time, and the earth moves. How should we understand this apparent discrepancy?

It is easily understood if we will allow the same usage of language in the Bible as elsewhere. We speak of the sun's rising and setting. But when we say the sun has risen, we mean that the portion of the earth upon which we are has revolved toward the sun; and when we say the sun has set, we mean that that portion has revolved away from the sun. So it was in Joshua's day. The sun did not go down. Joshua desired that it should not go down in appearance. This could have been met in two ways. The reflection of the sun could have been cast back upon the earth just as long as God desired it to, if He chose to work that way; or He could have retarded the motion of the earth, so that the day would be much longer. It was in God's power to do either.

The Sun and the Earth. Eccl. 1:5.

> I wish you would explain Ecclesiastes 1:5. I have always understood that the earth revolves around the sun.

The language of Ecclesiastes 1:5, "The sun also ariseth, and the sun goeth down," is simply the language of *appearance*. All the scientific men of the day use the same expression in speaking of "sunrise" and "sunset," The scientists of our day tell us that neither the sun nor the earth stands still, but that both are moving on through space, the sun with all its attendant planets, while relatively—that is, in their relation to each other—the sun stands still and the earth revolves around it.

SATAN

Lucifer and Babylon. Isa. 14:12-14.

Please explain the reference to Tyrus in the Garden of
Eden, and Lucifer in heaven, still being Babylon. Ezekiel
28:11-19 and Isaiah 14:12-14.

The first "king of Babylon" was and is Lucifer. Isa. 14:4, 12.
His spirit of selfishness in heaven as Lucifer is the spirit of Babylon,
strife and confusion, the same spirit which has controlled Babylon
ever since. The earthly king, or prince, of Babylon worked the will
of Satan, or Lucifer, the king. Isaiah 14:4-20 is a prophecy of what
will come upon Satan and all his children in the end, typified by
the destruction of ancient Babylon. Tyre was a city noted for its
pride and wickedness. The *prince* of Tyre, its earthly king, had
lifted up himself as God. Ezek. 28:2. In thus arrogating to himself such authority and wisdom, he was actuated by Satan, the
king of Tyre, described in his beginning and end in verses 11-19.
The garden of God is in the city of God, in heaven, where Lucifer
dwelt before his sin.

Creation and Satan. Gen. 1:2.

Was this earth made and in the condition of Genesis
1:2 any time before creation week? When was Satan cast
out into the earth?

Candidly, this is a question over which there is considerable
difference of opinion among even the best of Bible scholars. Some
hold there was absolutely nothing here until the first day of creation week, nothing but emptiness. Others believe that the matter
from which the earth was made was here in a formless state long
before creation week began. On this latter view it may be interesting to observe the following:

Genesis 1:1 seems to be cut off from the six days which follow by the passage which intervenes. It is not said, "In six days the Lord *created* heaven and earth;" but, "In six days the Lord *made* heaven and earth." The first verse of Genesis carries us back to the beginning, whenever that was, as the time when God began His creation. "In the beginning God created the heavens and the earth." The book of John begins in the same way. "In the beginning was the Word, and the Word was with God, and the Word was God. The same was in the beginning with God. All things were made by Him; and without Him was not anything made that was made." This may pertain to the very material out of which the heavens and the earth were made,—the finishing of many things and the calling into existence of our own solar system with others. Then we read that "the earth was without form, and void; and darkness was upon the face of the deep." See the Revised Version, "The earth was waste and void." It was in a chaotic condition. Out of that chaotic condition the creative and formative power of God brought the earth into the condition it was at the close of the six days' work.

Before that six days' work angels existed; for we read in Job 38:4-7: "Where wast thou when I laid the foundations of the earth? declare, if thou hast understanding. . . . When the morning stars sang together, and all the sons of God shouted for joy?" By reference to Isaiah 14:12-14 we learn that Satan before he fell was named Lucifer, the Daystar, the Son of the Morning, one of the morning stars. By reference to Revelation 22:16 we learn that the Son of God was one of the morning stars; in fact, Jesus declares: "I am the Root and the Offspring of David, and *the* Bright and Morning Star." When the foundation of the earth was laid, there was perfect harmony in heaven. The morning stars sang together; the very thought implying that there was to come a time when they would not, or, rather, the text was written at a time when that harmony did not exist. All the sons of God, all the heads of different worlds, sang together when this world was brought into existence. And yet shortly, seemingly, that harmony was dispelled. Lucifer was lifted up because of his beauty, and corrupted his wisdom by reason of his brightness, we learn in Ezekiel 28, where the fallen angel is spoken of under the figure of the king of Tyre. In his pride he fell.

He was cast out of heaven, where God dwells; came to this earth, the newest creation in God's universe, determined to overthrow those whom God had placed here. This he accomplished. Man yielded to his persuasion, and Satan became prince of the world; and so when the sons of God came to present themselves before the Lord, Satan came also among them, as stated in Job 1 and 2; and this position he seemed to occupy until Christ Jesus the Lord came. Then it was that Jesus met the tempter in the very fullness of his power; then, too, it was that He conquered; and then, too, was fulfilled Revelation 12:7-9. That war in heaven continued from the time that man fell until the time that Christ died upon the cross; for Michael, which means, "who is like God," is none other than Christ; and that casting down was the utter casting down, so that his appearance among the rulers, or heads, of worlds could no longer be recognized in heaven.

Can Satan Cure Sickness? 2 Thess. 2:8-10.

In Matthew 12:26 Jesus said Satan could not cast out Satan. Does it not say in some other place in the Bible that in the last days Satan shall work with all power and signs and lying wonders, curing sickness? A friend told me that sin led to sickness and death. If this is so, Satan could not cure sickness. Please explain.

Satan had not been able to cast out Satan, and yet it would seem as though he could command his own demons. The Bible represents the devil as the head of a company of evil angels called demons. These demons are at his command. They may affect an individual and cause functional difficulties and troubles, and Satan may be able for a time to relieve the individual so as to seem to cure the disease. There are two classes of disease: *functional,* in which the action of the organs is disturbed; and *organic,* in which some part or organ of the body is seriously affected, as of tuberculosis or cancer. Many times the first class is cured by the removal of the cause, the latter by miraculous power or by natural forces.

It would seem very reasonable to believe that where Satan caused the difficulties, as he does many times, he could in some instances, at least, remove them, so as to seem to cure. It is in 2 Thessalonians 2:8-10 where we are told that he will work "with all power and signs and lying wonders, and with all deceivableness of unrighteousness." Notice the falsehood that is implied in all of this. All true healing of sickness and all ultimate healing include both body and soul. The devil would be glad to have us turn our whole attention to the healing of the body, which is important. But infinitely more important is the healing of the soul from the effect of sin; because sin is the cause primarily of all trouble, for sickness would not have come had it not been for sin. But that does not mean that everyone who is sick is necessarily a sinner. There are many who have inherited sickness; some have it because of fruits of evil sowing, of which they have repented, although the fruits are not yet passed away.

Is the Devil a Separate Entity or a Principle?

Is there a personal devil? Do the terms "devil" and "Satan" refer to an evil principle or to an entity?

There is but one devil, in the Greek *ho Diabolos, the devil.* When the word occurs in the plural in the common version it is from "demon." At the head of all the demons, or evil spirits, is the devil.

He is called "that old serpent," "the devil, and Satan, which deceiveth the whole world." Rev. 12:9.

"Satan" means adversary, and the devil is *the* adversary of God. He is also called "Abaddon" and "Apollyon," meaning "destroyer." Rev. 9:11.

He is everywhere represented as a personal, intelligent, planning, scheming, plotting, morally responsible personality. See Matt. 4:1-11; Luke 10:18; Jude 9; 1 John 3:8; John 8:44; 1 Peter 5:8; Job 1 and 2.

He is called "dragon," and "serpent," because in that form he first tempted man. Gen. 3:3, 4. He is called "prince of this world" and "god of this world," because earthly kingdoms have yielded to him, and all mankind have been deceived by him, and the majority have followed and served him. John 12:31; 14:30; 2 Cor. 4:4; Rev. 12:9. He is therefore called "king of Babylon," and "king of Tyre." Isa. 14:4; Ezek. 28:12.

He was once an angel of light, one of the day, or morning, stars, named Lucifer (light bringer), and was the very highest of all God's creation. Isa. 14:12-14; Ezek. 28:12-15.

From this high position he fell because of pride, and became an accuser, an adversary, a liar, deceiver, murderer. He will finally be destroyed forever with sin, and God's universe will be clean. Ezek. 28:16-19; Heb. 2:14.

What Is the Unclean Spirit of Luke 11:24-26?

The scripture reads as follows: "The unclean spirit when he is gone out of the man, passeth through waterless places, seeking rest, and finding none, he saith, I will turn back unto my house whence I came out. And when he is come, he findeth it swept and garnished ["empty," also Matt. 12:44]. Then goeth he, and taketh to him seven other spirits more evil than himself; and they enter in and dwell there: and the last state of that man becometh worse than the first."

The parable was no doubt spoken in regard to the Jewish people. They had, as a people, been cleansed from their wickedness through the goodness of God; but instead of being filled with the fruits of righteousness by faith, their house had been left empty. They had swept and garnished it by their own high professions and formalities and their outward works of humility and righteousness; they were like whited sepulchers, which appear beautiful outwardly, but not having invited the Lord to take up His dwelling with them, they had left themselves where the evil spirit could return with sevenfold power, as it did in their rejection of Jesus Christ. It was true of them in the time of our Saviour. Under the powerful influence and preaching of John, many, no doubt, turned for a while from their sins; but instead of receiving Christ, whom John preached, the heart was left empty, and Satan came in and took the place which should have been occupied by Christ, and the nation went on from bad to worse, till it crucified its Lord.

It is just as true as regards individuals. The unclean spirit is cast out. God in mercy expels him to save the man, that the man may be free. The man asks for cleansing, and God cleanses, cleanses that the man may serve Him. The house is left empty, swept, garnished. The unclean spirit is cast out, that the Spirit of God may come in. The man is released from the bondage of Satan, that he may freely serve God. But this must be voluntary also. The man refuses, thinks to do nothing and yet go free. The evil spirit goes forth seeking rest and nourishment, but finds none; and he returns to his house,—the man who was cleansed,—and, finding the house empty, enters and again takes possession. He controls the man, and, to make possession sure, lets in others. Surely the last state of that man is worse than the first.

If Christ has cleansed us from one sin, set us free from one evil habit, it is that the good may take its place; and if we refuse to use the strength to do the good that Christ would put in the place of evil, sooner or later the evil will return leading a troop of others worse than the original, and we will be doomed to a worse bondage than ever before. We cannot remain neutral; it will avail nought to say, "We will do nought against Christ." The Master declares, "He that is not with Me is against Me; and he that gathereth not with Me scattereth." Luke 11:23. And then follows the above scripture. Surely the lesson is important. Who shall rule, Christ or Satan?

RELIGIOUS LIBERTY

Religious Liberty. John 12:47, 48.

The above scripture presents one of the grandest, noblest utterances ever spoken by any teacher in the world. Jesus said: "If any man hear My words, and believe not, I judge him not: for I came not to judge the world, but to save the world. He that rejecteth Me, and receiveth not My words, hath One that judgeth him: the word that I have spoken, the same shall judge him in the last day." In other words, man's right to absolutely free choice is here recognized. Our Lord would force no one to believe, no one to confess, no one to act contrary to his own convictions. Jesus presents in His teaching and in His life evidence sufficient to base faith upon, but the soul is left free. He will not judge; He will not condemn. Neither must His followers. All the condemnation which the sinner will need will be to face in the last great day the living words of Christ,—the words which would have saved if believed,—which he rejected. Would that those who seek to compel religious belief or practice could learn Christ's words and His Spirit.

"The Higher Powers." Rom. 13:1.

> Please explain Romans 13:1. Some persons claim that it refers to all officers from king or president down to the humblest overseer.

In a general way the application of the passage is as broad as above stated. "Let every soul be subject unto the higher powers," to every power in the sphere in which God has placed us. If we belong to an organization, we should acquiesce in all required of us *wherein* those in charge have jurisdiction. But the officer has no right to compel the observance of a civil law, for that is outside of his jurisdiction. He has no right to say that we must have family prayers, for that is outside of his jurisdiction. His authority lies exclusively within the field to which he is appointed. So in regard to magistrates and other civil officers.

God has ordained government, because the worst government in the world is better than anarchy. All civil government falls, in a general sense, within the scope of this scripture. But all civil governments are ordained for things *exclusively* civil. They have no right to command or to enforce religious ordinances, institutions, or observances, neither to prohibit religion; and if they do any of these things contrary to the conscience and belief of any soul within the territory they govern, that soul has a right to say, as did Peter, "We ought to obey God rather than men." For any civil power to attempt to control or to regulate religion, is to put itself in the place of God, and it thereby becomes a blasphemer. "The powers that be are ordained of God" to do the work for which they are ordained. God has not delegated to them His power or authority.

Section XIV

CHRISTIAN EXPERIENCE

Helpless in Sin. Rom. 7:15-25.

> Kindly explain Romans 7:15-25. We do not understand
> its meaning.

In general, the passage reveals the state of a sinner's mind whom
the Spirit of God by the law has convicted of sin. He sees that he
has transgressed a holy and good law. He longs to do differently,
but finds himself in bondage to sin, his master. His mind admires
and reverences the law of God. He hates sin. And yet he commits
sin. His mind is in bondage to the flesh. The Spirit reveals to him
the holiness of God's law without. In the beginning that same law
was written in man; but the sinner finds that good law perverted
in himself, and tending to sin and death, warring against the good
law of God unperverted by sin, and which his mind delights in.
But he cannot do it, for sin binds him. In his agony he exclaims,
"Who shall deliver me from the body of this death?" Jesus Christ
is there revealed, and the sinner finds deliverance from sin in his
Saviour. Finding deliverance, he serves the law in which his mind
delights; he is free, therefore, in Christ from the dominance of
the flesh.

Unconfessed Sin. 1 John 1:9.

> Would one sin unconfessed have the same effect as one
> commandment trespassed, in shutting one away from sal-
> vation? Give a few instances of what kind of sin needs
> to be confessed publicly, what kind to our neighbor, and
> what kind in the family circle.

The unconfessed sin is cherished, or else pride of heart is so
cherished that it leads us to keep the sin rather than confess it. God's
means of taking sin from His children is through confession. "If
we confess our sins, He is faithful and just to forgive us our sins,
and to cleanse us from all unrighteousness." 1 John 1:9. David

said, "I acknowledged my sin unto Thee, and mine iniquity did I not hide: I said, I will confess my transgressions unto Jehovah; and Thou forgavest the iniquity of my sin." Ps. 32:5. All sin is transgression of God's law, the transgression of some one or more commandments of that law. Therefore, to commit sin and retain the sin instead of putting it away by confession, is just the same as the transgression of one of the commandments of His law.

Wisdom as well as thoroughness should be used in the confession of sin. The confession should be made as broad as the sin if possible. If the sin, the wrong, is against God alone, we should confess it to God. For instance, if one has cherished hatred in his heart against a neighbor, if he has coveted that which belongs to another, and yet has not offended humanity in thus doing, it would be sufficient to go to God and tell Him of this and pour out the heart before Him. If one's sin has been an open sin before the public, if he has been an open Sabbathbreaker or a user of profane language, or a thief, so that it has become common knowledge, he should make that confession before the public. He should take such a stand that the public before whom he had committed these sins would know that he had turned from these sins and was obedient to God.

If he has sinned directly against his neighbor in his language or in his treatment of that neighbor,—a sin known to his neighbor, —he should certainly confess to his neighbor his sin. So in regard to family matters. There is a homely illustration that the plaster should be made large enough to cover the sore; and so the confession should be made large enough to cover the sin. Satan would be glad to have souls confess, before the public, secret sins that lie between them and God only. This the Lord does not demand.

"Be Perfect." Matt. 5:48.

> Kindly explain Matthew 5:48: "Ye therefore shall be perfect, as your heavenly Father is perfect."

God never sets before His children a low standard. It would be absolute cruelty to us for Him to do this. He sets before us always that which is perfect; and His admonition is, "Ye therefore shall be perfect, as your heavenly Father is perfect." That does not mean perfect in wisdom as God is perfect; for we are finite. It does not mean perfect in knowledge as He is perfect, or perfect in power as He is perfect; because His sphere of being is infinitely above us. But it does mean that we should love Him perfectly with all the heart and mind and soul and strength. This is what God desires; "for the eyes of the Lord run to and fro throughout the whole earth, to show Himself strong in the behalf of them whose heart is perfect toward Him." 2 Chron. 16:9. Therefore we can be perfect in our sphere by His grace, even as God is perfect in His sphere. The one who has perfect love will certainly desire to render perfect service.

Repeated Forgiveness. Isa. 55:7.

If a person sins and God forgives him, and then he does the same thing over and over, knowing it is wrong, is there any forgiveness for him?

There is forgiveness for a person just as long as there is sincere repentance. The danger is not that we shall so sin that God will not forgive us, but that we shall by sinning place ourselves where there is no more conscience for sin. God's mercy is unlimited in its exercise in the number of times as well as in quantity. Matthew 18:21-35; Luke 17:3, 4; Isaiah 1:18; Micah 7:18, 19, are all passages which point out God's wondrous mercy, unlimited in quantity and extent to all those who trust Him. But constant sinning against light hardens the heart and benumbs the conscience. There may be sorrow exercised to the very end because of the *consequences* of sin; but to him who continues to sin, the conscience becomes at last benumbed, so that while it mourns over the results of sinning, it still loves the sin, and is not offended at its presence. Like Esau, the sinner finds no place of true repentance, though he seeks it carefully with tears.

The fact that one is continually sinning ought to lead to thorough self-examination and humility. But to him who is truly repentant, who seeks forgiveness of God, there is hope. "Him

that cometh to Me," says the Saviour of men, "I will in *nowise*
cast out." He has no pleasure in the death of the wicked, but that
the wicked turn from his evil way and live. Ezek. 33:11. He will
abundantly pardon all those who forsake their way and return to
the Lord. Isa. 55:7. "Whosoever will" may come.

"Sanctification" and "Regeneration."

> I am told that regeneration is one step; that sanctifica-
> tion is a degree beyond to which we must attain, or be
> lost. Will you please explain these terms?

The two words express different things. "Regeneration" means
to be begotten again, born again. It is wholly of God. It is a new
creation wrought by His power in the person who yields to Him.
It makes a man a new creature. "Sanctification" means a separation *from* sin *unto* God. It is a setting apart to His service. It is
both instantaneous and progressive. When man gives himself
wholly to God, when he separates from the world unto God, he
is a sanctified, or separated, man, in which man acts his part by
yielding, and God His part by accepting and cleansing. The development of that setting apart comes every day as God's truth is
presented, enrolled, revealed, by the Spirit. So Jesus prayed, "Sanctify them through Thy truth: Thy word is truth." Yielding to
that word, following it, receiving and appropriating it, is constant
separation *from* the world *unto* God. It is a lifework in the development of character. Regeneration gives the new life; sanctification
maintains it.

Backsliding and the Prodigal Son. Heb. 6:4-6.

> Kindly explain the parable of the prodigal son. In
> Hebrews 6:4-6 it seems impossible for the backslider to
> return; but the prodigal son seems to have returned, and
> was received by his father.

Hebrews 6:4-6 does not imply that individuals cannot return,
but that they *will* not return. It says that it is impossible "to renew
them;" that is, no outward inducement of friends will bring them

back to God. The desire to return is gone. The parable of the prodigal son is too plain to need explanation. Any soul, it matters not who he may be, that longs to return to his Father's house, may return and find welcome, just the same as the younger son, who had wasted his substance, found welcome with his earthly father. Every desire which the backslider has to come back to his Father's house is but the echo of the pleading voice of the Spirit of God. Every longing for the good which is to be found alone in Christ is born of the love by which God calls the backslider to return. And God is as much more willing to receive us than the earthly father was to receive his son, as heaven is higher than the earth. Isa. 55:7-9. Read the description of backslidden Judah and Israel in Jeremiah 2 and 3, and then read Jeremiah 3:22, "Return, ye backsliding children, and I will heal your backslidings." And again, Jeremiah 4:1, "If thou wilt return, O Israel, saith the Lord, return unto Me." In fact, the record of all God's dealings with His people shows that He "delighteth in mercy," and that there is nothing He longs for so much as to have the backslider and the sinner come to Him. He says, "Say unto them, As I live, saith the Lord God, I have no pleasure in the death of the wicked; but that the wicked turn from his way and live: turn ye, turn ye from your evil ways; for why will ye die, O house of Israel?" Ezek. 33:11. If we will but come as did the prodigal, saying, "Father, I have sinned against heaven, and in Thy sight, and am no more worthy to be called Thy son," yet with simple faith in God's goodness, the Lord will receive us.

Will God Leave Him? Deut. 31:6.

> If a person humbly and honestly seeks God for wisdom and guidance to do a certain thing, truly desiring to do nothing to injure the cause of God, will God leave him to himself, or turn him over to the adversary?

Many questions similar to the above are asked to which no definite answer can be given by man, because man does not know all the facts having a bearing on the case. This we may say with assurance: God will leave no one to himself or to Satan who fully trusts in Him. God's "ways are ways of pleasantness," and all His "paths are peace." But the Lord may not have wanted the person to do the certain thing. Sometimes we wish a certain thing done, and we persuade ourselves that we are the one to do it, though we are not, and then we ask God for wisdom to do it. We may have started on a wrong principle in the first place. On this we may settle: God does nothing wrong; He does all things right; He will always keep His word. If we fail, it is our fault, not His. In our blindness we may not see our fault; it may be farther back than we wish to look; but if there be fault, it is with us, not God. Yet, after all, what we may call failures or mistakes may in God's wisdom be success. It is ever safe to trust God. See Isa. 45:19; Rom. 9:33.

If in our human wisdom we have made mistakes, let us confess the mistakes to God and to those directly affected by them, and then leave them with Him. He will take care of all results. If some will hold hard feelings over mistakes we have made but have tried to rectify, we cannot help that. God will see that His cause does not suffer by our repented-of and forsaken mistakes.

"Doth Not Commit Sin." 1 John 5:18.

"Whosoever is born of God doth not commit sin; for His seed remaineth in him: and he cannot sin, because he is born of God." Does John mean that if a person is born of God he cannot sin; and if he does sin, is it a proof that he never was born of God? Is it always true that the one who is born again "keepeth himself, and that wicked one toucheth him not"? 1 John 5:18.

It is the *purpose* which God regards, the *principle* that actuates and moves the soul. He who is born of God has the one purpose. He may fall, he may sin; but just as long as he holds unswervingly to that purpose, God counts him His. "The eyes of the Lord run to and fro throughout the whole earth, to show Himself strong in the behalf of them *whose heart is perfect toward Him.*" 2 Chron. 16:9. Understand "cannot" in the sense of "will not," as in the oft-quoted expression, "Look you, what I will not, that I cannot do;" or as in Luke 14:20, "I have married a wife, and therefore I cannot come,"—not that it was a physical impossibility, but that there was no desire. And so he that is born of God does not commit sin; that is not his purpose, his business. He cannot, because he will not. The Syriac has it, "doth not practice sin;" that is not his lifework. There is always danger of poor mortals' sinning, and yet the power of God is able to keep one from sin. "My little children, these things write I unto you, that ye sin not [or that ye may not sin]. And if any man sin, we have an advocate with the Father, Jesus Christ the righteous." 1 John 2:1.

Forgiveness. Col. 3:13.

> If persons that I have always thought to be my friends pass me by without speaking, and talk to injure me without a cause, am I bound to forgive them and feel as friendly as before, unless they ask forgiveness? Christ does not forgive unless we ask; need we unless we are asked?

We should hold the spirit of forgiveness toward all. This does not mean that we should go to him who has wronged us and say, "We forgive you," for that would be by implication charging him with wrong. But we should show that we are friendly and ready to forgive. Christ was anxious to forgive us a long time before we asked Him; and therefore as soon as we came to that place where we saw our need of His pardon, and by asking showed that we saw our need,—the only place where the forgiveness could do us good,—Christ there and then freely granted what He was anxious to do all the time. "Even as Christ forgave you, so also do ye." Col. 3:13. "And when ye stand praying, forgive, if ye have aught against any: that your Father also which is in heaven may forgive you your trespasses." Mark 11:25. But to forgive thus we must hold the spirit of forgiveness toward all, whether they ask pardon or not.

But this is the very thing which it is difficult for us to do. Shall we offer two suggestions which may be of help? 1. We can easier forgive others when we think that they by endeavoring to injure us are injuring themselves far more. They can only injure our reputation, or that which is to us extraneous, but can never injure our character without our consent; but they do injure that which to every soul should be of superlative value,—their own character. Knowing this, our pity should be aroused. 2. If we, in the language of the poet, would—

> "Remember thy follies, thy sins, and thy crimes;
> How vast is that infinite debt!
> Yet Mercy hath seven by seventy times
> Been swift to forgive and forget"—

we could more easily forgive.

He loved us, and therefore forgave, even praying God to forgive His tormentors. Can we not do the same?

Willful Sin. Heb. 10:26.

What is a willful sin? See Heb. 10:26. When the still small voice speaks to one who is walking in the light and says to him in time of temptation, "Do not do that now, wait awhile, for it will be a hindrance or a detriment to your spiritual understanding," nevertheless that one yields to the overpowering influence of the wicked one simply for the sake of gratifying baser passions of the mind, and commits the sin regardless of consequences, and this is followed by a troubled conscience, not because of the act itself, but because of not having a greater regard for the impulse of the Holy Spirit, is there hope for such a one, or has the poor mortal committed the unpardonable sin—sold his birthright?

As to whether it is a willful sin or not depends. The sin mentioned in Hebrews 10:26 is a grievous, God-defying sin. It means not only that, but continuance in sin. Compare the passage in Hebrews 6:4-8. The ground blessed of God that *continues* to produce thorns and thistles is at last rejected utterly. So the heart that *continually* shuts God out and *continually* yields to the influences of the flesh, sooner or later yields all. From the illustration used in the 28th verse of the chapter under consideration, it would seem that the willful sin is one that willfully sets at nought God's commandments. The men that set at nought Moses' law died without compassion. Of how much sorer punishment should he be worthy who had *trodden underfoot* the Son of God, and had counted the blood of the covenant wherewith he was sanctified, an *unholy thing,* and had done *despite* unto the Spirit of grace? That is, the Son of God is counted no more than common things; the blood of the covenant no more than common blood; and the Spirit of grace no more than an impulse. One who does this, by the very act of doing it, puts himself in that place where he is unable to discern the Spirit of God; unable to hear God's voice speaking to him.

The danger to the sinner is not that he will come to that place where *God* will not forgive, but that he will come to that place where there can be no sincere repentance. The very fact that there is true sorrow for sin is always an evidence that one has not passed beyond the limits of God's grace; that there is hope for him. Hope vanishes when the sinner reaches that place where he has no true sorrow for sin. He may be sorry because of the effects of sin. He may be sorry that he is found out. But he whose case is hopeless never has a truly grieved heart because he has sinned against God, who is so good, so kind, so merciful. Sometimes when one has sinned grievously, he is uncertain as to his condition for some time; he does not know whether his sorrow is real or not; whether his repentance is sincere or otherwise. God permits this in order that the soul may be thoroughly tested. The only way for that one to do is still to trust God; to take Him at His word. Read Isaiah 50:10: Let him trust in the name of Jehovah, and rely upon his God."

The unpardonable sin is the unrepentable sin. There is no limit to the infinite mercy of God. That does not mean that it is not dangerous to yield to sin. The danger is even greater than it would otherwise be. The human heart so easily gets accustomed to doing what is wrong that unconsciously it becomes hardened against the appeals of the Spirit of God. Therefore let this troubled soul say, "I will still have faith in God, I will learn the cause of my defeat, and I will yield myself anew to God, being more careful, more watchful, more zealous lest my feet slip."

The Christian Life.

It must be joy to serve God with gladness, knowing that one's life is cleansed from sin. But how such a condition can be obtained I cannot understand.

What if you cannot understand? Must you wait for that? You sow the seed in the ground; do you understand how soil and sunshine and moisture are transmuted into wheat and corn? Yet it is done. Do you wish to know the doctrine, the teachings, of Christ in yourself? Here is God's answer through His Son: "If any man willeth to do His will, *he shall know* of the teaching." John 7:17. You can do that. You may choose God's way, the self-denial, the humility of Christ, the giving up of all things to God, to be what He will make you, to do what He commands you to do. If you do that, believing Him to be in you all He has promised, you shall know the joy, the peace, the blessing, of life. Prove John 7:17, and believe Jesus Christ to be the way, the truth, the life, in you, *your* wisdom, righteousness, sanctification, redemption. John 14:6; 1 Cor. 1:30. Believe, simply believe.

THE CHURCH; ITS ORDINANCES

The First Church and Its Name. Acts 7:38.

What was the name of the first church? Did the church of which Christ was the cornerstone in Zion have any name?

We do not know as God gave His church any definite name. "Congregation of the Lord" it is often called in the Old Testament. Deut. 23:3. We can go back to the beginning, and read, "Then began men to call themselves by the name of the Lord." Gen. 4:26, margin. In Genesis 6:2 they are called "the sons of God;" in Exodus 19:6, "a kingdom of priests," a "holy nation." In the New Testament this congregation, this nation, is called "the church in the wilderness." Acts 7:38.

The word "church" comes from *ekklesia,* meaning something "called out." Sometimes it is "the church of God," sometimes "the church of Christ," sometimes only "the church." In Ephesians 1:23 and elsewhere these called-out ones are called the body of Christ; and in chapter 2:19, 20, "the household of God," on which both prophets and apostles builded, Jesus Christ being the chief cornerstone. All these refer to "the church of the living God, the pillar and ground of the truth." 2 Tim. 3:15. Twice the term "Christian" is used. Acts 11:26; 26:28. One epistle is addressed, for instance, to "the church of the Thessalonians;" another, "to the saints and faithful brethren in Christ which are at Colosse;" another, "to all the saints in Christ Jesus which are at Philippi;" another, "to the saints which are at Ephesus;" another, to "the churches of Galatia;" another, "unto the church of God which is at Corinth;" another, "to all that be in Rome, beloved of God, called to be saints;" sometimes, "the church that is in their [or his] house."

From these and other passages, it is evident that the "church" dates from the time that souls responded to God's call to come

out from the world, and that God has given that church no definite,
specific name. The true church of the living God centers in that
body of believers which has the twofold witness of the Scriptures,
and God's law translated through Christ Jesus into the life.

Belonging to a Church.

> Must we belong to the church called "The Church of
> Christ," in order that we may be saved? I ask this in
> view of the fact that it says, "Neither is there salvation in
> any other: for there is none other name under heaven
> given among men, whereby we must be saved."

We are not saved by any correlation or combination of letters,
whatever those letters may spell. "Name" in the Bible does not
mean a mere word. It stands for character, and in this case stands
for the personal character of our Lord Jesus Christ. There are
many instances of this given in the Bible. Therefore when the
child of God is baptized into the name of the Father, and into the
name of the Son, and into the name of the Holy Spirit, it does
not mean the mere pronouncing over them of these words; it
means they are baptized into the very character of the Father,
of the Son, and of the Holy Spirit—the Father for righteousness
in the place of our sins; the Son for self-emptying, self-denial,
self-abnegation, that God may fill us; and the Holy Spirit for
service. The Lord is not dependent upon any combination of men
to save men. He does not save because we go through a certain
particular form; He saves because the heart is yielded to Him,
and He can come into that heart and make it His own living
temple. "The eyes of the Lord run to and fro throughout the
whole earth, to show Himself strong in the behalf of them whose
heart is perfect toward Him." 2 Chron. 16:9. "By grace are ye
saved through faith; and that not of yourselves: it is the gift of
God." Eph. 2:8.

Simply calling ourselves Christians does not make us so, and
to unite with a church that is called Christian does not make us
Christians; and there are thousands and thousands of Christians

who are not called denominationally by the name "Christian."
We need not worry about that at all. The Lord saves us when
we give ourselves to Him, and accept of all that He gives us in
Jesus Christ by faith. Then, of course, we will walk in His commandments. We will be baptized, we will obey because we have
the spirit and the life of obedience; but that may lead us a long
way from those churches which arrogate to themselves the name
"Christian," while they do not always follow the Master. The
apostle Paul has stated the condition of salvation very clearly in
1 Corinthians 5:1-5, and we find it stated over and over again in
many places; but never do we find it, "You shall take such and
such a name in order to be saved."

"Rock" and "Stone." Matt. 16:17-19.

Will you please explain Matthew 16:17-19, which reads
as follows? "And Jesus answered and said unto him,
Blessed art thou, Simon Bar-Jonah: for flesh and blood
hath not revealed it unto thee, but My Father who is in
heaven. And I also say unto thee, that thou art Peter, and
upon this rock I will build My church; and the gates of
Hades shall not prevail against it. I will give unto thee
the keys of the kingdom of heaven: and whatsoever thou
shalt bind on earth shall be bound in heaven; and whatsoever thou shalt loose on earth shall be loosed in heaven."

In brief: Peter had just confessed Jesus as the Christ, the Son
of the living God. Jesus declared that that knowledge did not
come through Peter or any other man, but that it was revealed of
God. Then the Master proceeds to say, "Thou art Peter [Greek,
petros, a stone], and upon this rock [Greek, *petra*] I will build
My church; and the gates of Hades shall not prevail against it."
Upon that great truth of divine unfoldment, the revelation and
life from above, the confession of that truth in Jesus Christ, would
He build His church. It would not be a body of the flesh, as of
literal Jews, but a spiritual body, born of God, having hold of the
life beyond. John 1:12, 13; 3:3-5. Peter, believing, was a true,
living stone (1 Peter 2:5) of that foundation Rock, Christ Jesus

(1 Cor. 3:11). The gates of Hades are the power, or authority, which sin and death hold over men. That power is forever broken in Christ Jesus. "Keys" are instruments which open doors. God chose Peter first to preach salvation by the gospel keys to both Jews and Gentiles. See Acts 2:14; 15:7-14; 10. But that this did not give the primacy to Peter is shown by the fact that James presided at the first apostolic council at Jerusalem (Acts 15:13-21); and the further fact that Peter was in no respect above Paul (Gal. 2:1-11; 2 Cor. 11:5). The binding and loosing was the binding and loosing force of the message Peter and all the servants of God bore, according as it was rejected or accepted. To accept it was salvation and freedom; to reject it was bondage and destruction. The Bible illustration of this is found in Jeremiah's commission. Compare Jer. 1:9, 10 with 18:7-10. The binding and loosing, the building and overthrowing, depended on the acceptance or rejection of the message. And so it was with Peter and all the apostles. John 20:23. Every true minister who preaches God's true gospel bears the same power; and he who does not preach that true gospel, has not that power, whatever be his profession.

Disfellowshiping a Member. 1 Cor. 5:11-13.

Can a church disfellowship one without first laboring with him when such a one is willing to be labored with? And is such a one still a member of the church of God?

The business of a church is the business of her Lord,—to save life, not destroy it. It is the duty of the church of Christ to do all in her power to heal the spiritually sick, restore the spiritually lame, bind up the wounds made by Satan's fiery darts; to strengthen the bruised reed, to fan the smoking flax into a flame. She has no right to disfellowship a member until she has exhausted every resource of her power to save him. When the church does that, and fails to help the wandering one, it is manifest to all that he leaves the church, not the church him. The action of the church is its recognition of this.

Whether a man is a member of the church of God depends

on his relation to Christ Jesus. If he has been baptized into Christ, he is a member of Christ's body. If a church passes wrong judgment upon him, that does not affect his connection with Christ. In spite of all wrong judgment of men, he may be "holden up: for God is able to make him stand." Rom. 14:4. On the other hand, let the lost sheep come back to the fold. If he has sinned, let him confess and forsake his sin without any regard to what others have done or may do. If he does this truly, faithfully, wholeheartedly, condemning no others, accusing no others, excusing not himself, we know that God will receive him; and surely that church must be in a sad condition which will not gladly welcome the wanderer home.

Baptism in History.

What is the earliest practical date of baptism known among men since the days of Christ and His apostles, and by whom was baptism first practiced among those of Protestant faith?

We do not question the statement often made that baptism has been practiced by believers in Christ from His day till the present time. Like the Sabbath, it was perverted by the rapidly apostatizing church. In Schaff-Herzog Encyclopedia, article, "Baptism," it is said that "there is not a dissenting voice in all the literature of the Christian church for twelve hundred years" that "immersion was the act of baptism." "Historians, and those who treat of the early liturgies, unite in the same testimony." "The Oriental churches, Greek, Russian, Armenian, Coptic, and others, have always practiced immersion, and allow nothing else for baptism." "The Western churches also preserved the baptism of the New Testament for thirteen hundred years, and then gradually introduced pouring or sprinkling." "Luther sought, against the tendency of the times, to restore immersion." "Calvin was the first to assert that immersion was of no importance," and he is thus quoted: "Whether the person who is baptized be wholly immersed, and whether thrice or once, or whether water be only poured or sprinkled upon him, is of no importance; churches ought to be left at liberty in this respect to act according to the difference of countries. The very word 'baptize,' however, signifies to immerse; and it is certain that immersion was the practice of the ancient church."—*Institutes, book 4, chapter 15, section 19.*

Even in the Catholic Church, "the Council of Ravenna (1311) was the first to allow a choice between sprinkling and immersion."

The Baptists, who revived the true mode, appeared first in Switzerland in 1523. They were found in the years 1525-1530 with large churches, fully organized, in Southern Germany, Tyol, and in Middle Germany. "In all these places persecution made their lives bitter." From these and other facts it is most probable that they existed long prior to these dates, and were composed in most cases of the descendants of those who refused to depart in the fourteenth century from Bible baptism.

An important item will be found in the *Review and Herald* of Sept. 9, 1937, quoting from the Edinburgh Encyclopedia, of more than a century ago, telling of the Presbyterians' uncertainty as to the mode of baptism. In 1643 they settled the matter for their church by the close vote of 25 for sprinkling as against 24 for immersion.

Further material may be found in the section on Baptism of the "Source Book for Bible Students," and in the *Signs of the Times* of March 16, 1937.

How Often Celebrate the Lord's Supper?

If the Passover was a memorial yearly feast *forever* (Ex. 12:6, 14), and the Lord's Supper is a memorial of Christ's death (Luke 22:19), and He is "our Passover" (1 Cor. 5:7, 8), do the words "as oft" in 1 Corinthians 11:24, 25 mean any oftener than the Jews had been in the habit of observing their Passover? Is there any scriptural authority for observing it any oftener, or quarterly?

The Passover marked the beginning of the Jewish sacred year. It was a memorial of their deliverance from Egypt as well as a type of Christ. But every other feast or fast of the year likewise pointed forward to Christ or His work. They came yearly, and definite times were appointed for their national observance, that there might be order. In meeting these types Christ wrought His work once for all. He did not continue the old Passover as the memorial of His death, but instituted an ordinance to commemorate the event, without any respect to the time. In fact, no time is mentioned in connection with its institution. The directions given by Paul to Gentile Christians made no reference to any definite time; or does he even allude to the time, but to the rite itself in 1 Corinthians 5:7. "As oft" certainly does not refer to definite or regular time. An instance of its use is found in Revelation 11:6, "as often as they will." In meant, in connection with the Lord's Supper, either daily, weekly, quarterly, yearly, or whatever time was agreed upon. Some students believe that Acts 2:46 refers to a daily observance of the Lord's Supper; others declare that Acts 20:7 shows a weekly observance. We believe that it is safe to say that there was no stated time.

Feet Washing. John 13:3-17.

> Please explain John 13 concerning feet washing. The Saviour, after washing the disciples' feet, said: "If I then, your Lord and Master, have washed your feet; ye also ought to wash one another's feet. For I have given you an example, that ye should do as I have done to you." Was that to be observed by the disciples only in their time, or does it mean for all followers of Christ unto this present day?

Why was the ordinance given? What was its object? Does the need exist now?

There was strife among the disciples, Luke tells us, as to which should be the greatest. Some wanted to rule, and have the others serve them. Jesus the Master became an example of the lowliest of servants.

The object of the ordinance was to teach them that in love's kingdom the greatest did the most and best service, and the lowliest, too, if called for. "I am among you," said He on another occasion, "as he that serveth." He wanted to teach them their absolute equality as brethren, as sons of a common father, as servants of a common master, and each as servant to all.

Is it not needed now? Is there not the same old strife as to who should be the greatest? If Christ's instructions had been followed, we would never have had the orders and classes and castes in the church of Christ which now exist. Forever would Christ's words have been true, "One is your Master, even Christ; and all ye are brethren."

There is no reason in the world, then, except human pride, why our Lord's example should not be perpetuated; and the pride is not a reason, for it demands the continuance of the ordinance.

Note that it was not a mere act of hospitality that Jesus performed, for Peter knew what that meant; but he did not know this act of our Lord. Verse 7. The real knowledge of its meaning would come only through spiritual enlightenment. It was necessary for Peter to take part in this, and so learn the lowly spirit of true service or he would separate from his Lord. Verse 8.

Finally, there is no limitation of duration or place in the words of Christ: "If I then, the Lord and the Teacher, have washed your feet, ye also *ought* [are obligated] to wash one another's feet. For I have given you an *example*, that *ye also should do as I have done to you*. . . . If ye know these things, blessed are ye if ye *do* them." Verses 14-17. What would not the Sundaykeeper give for such evidence as this for Sunday observance! He would ask no more. He would deem it all-sufficient. Is it not sufficient for the perpetuation of feet washing, rightly called the "Ordinance of Humility"?

Secret Fraternal Organizations. John 18:20.

What is your stand regarding secret fraternal organizations? Please give reasons both from a spiritual and a worldly viewpoint.

From a worldly viewpoint wholly, there may be benefit in some of the secret organizations; but from the true Christian viewpoint there can be none, for the reason that in the church of the Lord Jesus Christ, according to 1 Corinthians 12, are found all the gifts and blessings that are necessary for His children. As expressed in the last verses of Ephesians 1, that church is "the fullness of Him that filleth all in all." Why should Christians turn from God's great reservoir which He has placed in this earth, and which is connected with the great Living Fountain, to the corrupted pools of this world?

Secondly, Jesus said, "I spake openly to the world; . . . and in secret have I said nothing." John 18:20. He had no blessing, no truth, no secrets, but that He was willing that the whole world should share and receive benefit of. He told His disciples to tell in the light and from the house tops the things they had learned in private. Matt. 10:27. They were not held for money or emoluments of any kind. The mysteries of the gospel of the Lord Jesus Christ were always to them who would submit themselves to Him. Not so with the fraternal organizations; they endeavor to hold the very best things which they may possess, many of which are utterly worthless even, to the members alone.

Thirdly, the admonition to the church of Christ is, "As we have opportunity, let us work that which is good toward all men, and especially toward them that are of the household of the faith." Gal. 6:10. Fraternal organizations carry out that in part; they have regard for their own household, but wherever tests come, all those without must suffer. Then too, there are the oaths; the extrajudicial oaths and vows that men are called to take upon themselves regarding that of which they know nothing, but which is in many cases to be afterward revealed. This is utterly out of harmony with the gospel. From a worldly viewpoint, it is questionable indeed, honeycombed as society now is with fraternal organizations, whether there is as much benefit in a fraternal organization as there is in money which is carefully saved and properly invested.

Fourthly, that there are sincere believers in Christ who are members of secret orders we would not for a moment deny; but to us it seems that they have an erroneous idea of true benevolence as exercised in these secret orders, and they also have a very low conception of the breadth, scope, work, and spirit which ought to be in and actuate the church of Christ. To turn from the church of Christ, from true union with Christ, to any lodge or organization, is like turning from the cool-flowing, life-giving waters of the mountain to the brackish waters stored in the broken cisterns of men.

Bread for Communion Service.

> 1. Should sponge cake be used at the Lord's Supper?
> 2. What kind of bread is used?
> 3. What kind of wine should be used.

1. No, sponge cake should not be used.

2. Different kinds of bread are used, some of which ought not to be used. Only *unleavened* bread should be used. There should be no leaven or fermentation connected with the Lord's Supper.

3. Unfermented wine alone should be used, the pure juice of the grape. This can be made and preserved in the fruit season the same as other fruit juices and fruit in general. Unfermented wine is usually procurable at any grocery or drug store. Where this cannot be procured, clean, good raisins may be boiled and the juice strained out.

The Gift of Tongues. 1 Corinthians 14.

> Please explain the subject of the gift of tongues, as found in 1 Corinthians 14. What does it mean by saying, "In the Spirit he speaketh mysteries"?

Among the gifts of God recorded in the twelfth chapter of 1 Corinthians are mentioned "divers kinds of tongues" and "the interpretation of tongues." A "tongue" that is a gift of the Spirit of God is an intelligible thing. It speaks intelligently, whether the individuals who are listening may understand it or not. The individual who is talking knows what he says, and is saying something in some language known to earth.

A very clear illustration of the Spirit's gift of tongues is recorded in the second chapter of Acts. There were in Jerusalem, on the day of Pentecost,—doubtless most of them having been drawn there to attend the Jewish feast,—people of all nationalities, and the holy city was stirred because of the events connected with the crucifixion of Christ. The story of the cross must be told, and must be understood by all these various nationalities; and when the Spirit was poured out on the day of Pentecost, the text says: "They were all amazed and marveled, saying one to another, Behold, are not all these which speak Galileans? And how hear we every man in our own tongue, wherein we were born? Parthians, and Medes, and Elamites, and the dwellers in Mesopotamia, and in Judea, and Cappadocia, in Pontus, and Asia, Phrygia, and Pamphylia, in Egypt, and in the parts of Libya about Cyrene, and strangers of Rome, Jews and proselytes, Cretes and Arabians, we do hear them speak in our tongues the wonderful works of God. And they were all amazed, and were in doubt, saying one to another, What meaneth this?" Acts 2:7-12.

Now that gift of tongues on that occasion, which is an illustration of God's plan, shows intelligence. It shows a need for that particular gift at that particular time, and it shows the people listening to the gospel, and understanding "the wonderful works of God" as they were presented.

There are people who claim to have the gift of tongues, but there is no intelligence connected with it. It is an unintelligible jargon. It is one of the deceptive counterfeits that Satan is foisting upon the world, with which to delude and destroy people. In the twelfth chapter of 1 Corinthians, note that after enumerating the various gifts, the apostle says, "But all these worketh that one and the selfsame Spirit, dividing to every man severally as He will." These gifts are bestowed upon individuals who will appropriately and intelligently use them, and as the need arises for such gifts. Otherwise they would not be given. They are not to be seized by individuals, and exercised upon their own authority or in harmony with their own whims.

Study closely all that God's word says in regard to God's gifts, and you will not be led astray. God is seeking continually to reveal the mysteries of His truth; and He asks us to base our faith upon mysteries that have actually been revealed, and not upon some mysterious something that no one can understand. God's people will ever be studying into the unfolding mysteries of His great truth; but their faith is based upon what they understand, and not upon something that is ever bewildering. There is something divinely dignified in the gifts of God, and they carry convincing power to intelligent people.

Darkness and Light.

I understand that the gospel as brought to view by Christ and His apostles in the first centuries and recorded in the Bible was covered up during the Dark Ages, and began again to be revealed at the commencement of the Reformation. What was the first light brought out, and when, and by whom? Was it justification by faith? And did later Reformers take up the same and carry it on through with them, or did they reject it?

No, it is not true that the gospel was wholly hidden during the Dark Ages. There were faithful followers of God who kept it alive in their own hearts through all that darkened time. There were those, like the Waldenses and others, out in the wilderness and among the mountains, who were loyal to God, and who had His word. There were those even in monks' cells, in the convents, among the priests of Rome, who had access to the Bible, and were faithful to it as far as they saw it. Of course, a mighty impulse was given to this in the time of the Reformation. Previous to that time, men had been stirred to study the Bible. Wycliffe's translation had been made, and portions of the Bible were translated by others. When printing was invented, that gave a great impetus to the spread of the gospel. Then followed other translations.

It is quite impossible to say just when or by whom or what was the first phase of the gospel developed, when there was more or less of it developed all the way. There were numberless men in the Roman Catholic Church who stood for the truth of God. Some of them went down to martyrdom. Others remained. The great message of the Reformation in Germany especially was justification by faith.

The great mistake made by many of the Protestant sects was that of trying to crystallize what they believed into a creed. It is impossible for human words to express the infinite truth of God;

and just as soon as men tried to define what God's word taught, they limited the word, and limited the faith of those who would accept the creed. Of course, there were always those within the creed-bound church who believed out beyond the creed, and whose faith ignored man's framing of God's truth, who saw greater light in the word of God, and consequently rebelled against the creed, separated themselves from the creed-bound body, gathered around them other followers, and sometimes made the same mistake over again — formed another creed.

That has been one of the great hindrances to Protestantism. If the word of God had been allowed to "have free course, and be glorified," and men had rallied around that, — the word and the word alone, — union would have come instead of the discord we see at the present time. Man's hope of preventing discord and divisions has resulted in only greater confusion.

There is very little difference among the creeds of Protestants, and it is growing less and less all the time. Of course, the Baptists have one phase of truth to which they hold, some of them tenaciously and loyally; namely, baptism. Some of the "modernists" among them are yielding even that. There are books on religions which will give the various creeds of churches. It is impossible even to indicate them here.

Questions on Healing.

> How are we to be healed? by medicine, or by chiropractic, osteopathic, and other worldly doctoring? Did Christ use medicine or drugs of any kind? He taught His disciples to heal through fasting and prayer. Now if we can be healed by prayer, what is the use of sending for a doctor or building sanitariums and hospitals?

On this question of healing, many persons seem to think that the infinite God should stand as their orderly servant, and whenever anything is the matter with them, they should order Him to heal them at once, and expect Him to do so. The Bible teaches divine healing. It plainly says that "the prayer of faith shall save the sick." But when Christ was here Himself, having anointed the eyes of a blind man with clay, He told him to go wash in the Pool of Siloam; and he went and washed, and returned seeing. And when Naaman the leper came to Elisha to be cured of his disease, Elisha told him to go and bathe in the river Jordan.

Luke, one of the apostles of Christ, according to Colossians 4:14, was also "the beloved physician." Then they had a doctor right among the early disciples (though Luke was not numbered among the twelve), and he was commended by the apostle Paul. If a man has a broken limb, the sensible thing for him to do is to go to a reputable surgeon and have it properly set; or if he has any other ailment that the science of the physician can remedy, he should avail himself of his services; and it is the privilege of the afflicted one at the same time to pray earnestly for the blessing of God upon the remedies that the skill of the physician provides.

To be sure, there are many quacks and impostors among medical men, the same as there are in all other professions; but the true physician is working in harmony with God, the Author of nature. When an individual is out of reach of a physician, or when his case is beyond the skill of the physician, the cases are numerous where God has directly interposed, and healed the individual.

God gives us the privilege of coming to Him, and availing ourselves of divine power to heal our diseases. He "healeth all thy diseases," and the word is full of promises of that character. But God also gives us common sense, and He expects us to use that in connection with divine healing.

Judas.

> Please explain about Judas. Could he help sinning, when it was according to the Scripture? And will he be lost for doing so, or did he repent?

God's foreknowledge does not mean God's foreordination. God's foreordination only takes in the characters of the holy. He marks out those, predestinates those, and calls men to those characters; and so He called Judas, so He gave Judas the greatest opportunity in the world of developing a character under the instruction of the holiest teacher that earth could ever know. But Judas rejected all these things, and cherished the thought of selfishness, which molded the character that he had. It was Christ's own compassion which led Him to give Judas the opportunity; and when he killed himself out of despair and remorse, in that death he went "to his own place." Acts 1:25. It is for this reason that Jesus calls him "the son of perdition,"—that is, the son of utter destruction.

That Judas might have done differently is shown in the very fact of his acknowledging his wrong after the deed was wrought. He evidently thought that Christ would release Himself, that Christ by His mighty power would not suffer Himself to be taken; and so he used the power of Christ to trade on, in order that he might get gain from it. Yet he had opportunity to repent of all his plans, right up to the very time, almost, of their consummation. It is often true that men who do the greatest sins against God are forced by the Spirit of God, insincere though they are, to confess at the very last, in order that God's cause may be vindicated. See Matt. 27:3-10.

Woman's Appearance in Public.

> Will you kindly comment on 1 Corinthians 11:5, 6, 10, 13, and also on 1 Corinthians 14:34, 35?

If we could place ourselves in Corinth in the time of the apostle, we should see much reason for his instruction which does not exist now. Corinth was one of the wickedest cities, if not the wickedest, in the apostle's day. Its position and commerce brought to it every form of idolatry and corruption, and licentious men and wanton women from all the world. In the language of that time, to "Corinthianize" was to play the wanton. There were idolatrous women, priestesses, devoted religiously to lives of abandon. They appeared in public with disheveled hair and frantic actions. The best classes of women, Jewish, Roman, and Greek, appeared in public veiled.

It is a fact that God's Spirit rested upon women in all ages, and they prophesied, talked, witnessed, sang, for Him. See Ex. 15:20, 21; Judges 4:4, 5; 5:1; 2 Kings 22:14-20; Joel 2:28, 29; Luke 2:36-38; Acts 18:26; 21:9. It was therefore perfectly right for women to speak in a proper way in public.

What the apostle taught was that the women in the Corinthian church should not go uncovered, like the shameless women of the world, or do anything that would not show just regard for the Lord's order. Some of them seem to have failed in this respect, and disorder was rampant. Different countries and different customs would have demanded different instruction. We may be sure that if the apostle were talking to unwise women living in a city or country where the shameless ones and wantons wore veils, and respectable women went unveiled, save in native and becoming modesty, he would give different instruction.

The basis of all his instruction is found just before in his letter (there were no chapters or divisions in it till modern times): "Whatsoever ye do, do all to the glory of God." 1 Cor. 10:31. In all things, Christian women should by their modesty and deportment commend the gospel of Christ.

Regarding 1 Corinthians 14:34, 35 there is help in the suggestion that the apostle is answering an objector who has uttered verses 34, 35. The apostle answers this objection: "What? came the word of God out from *you?* or came it unto *you only?*" Surely he would not forbid women to speak when he had just before given instruction as to how they should appear in public.

MISCELLANEOUS

Election.

> Will you kindly explain the following texts of Scripture? Do not these scriptures plainly set forth the fact that the destiny of every soul was fixed before they were born into the world, even before the foundation of the world? Rom. 9:18-23; 8:28-30.

The whole question of election is not difficult to understand if we will remember certain principles. But first let us say this: That the destiny of every soul is not fixed is shown clearly by 2 Peter 1:10, "Wherefore, brethren, give the more diligence to make your calling and election sure." If a person's case were irrevocably fixed, how could he consistently be exhorted to make it sure? How could we understand such scriptures as Hebrews 3:14, "We are become partakers of Christ, if we hold fast the beginning of our confidence firm unto the end," and Matthew 24:13, "He that endureth to the end, the same shall be saved"?

The important thing which God regards is character. That is more precious to Him than all else. The names written in the Lamb's book of life from before the foundation of the world (Rev. 13:8) are names of characters. To those various characters, God calls the children of this earth. To one of those characters, God called Cain. Character stands written in the book of life from the beginning. Cain failed, however, and someone else was called in to take his place. This is quite evident from Revelation 3:11, "Hold fast that which thou hast, that no one take thy crown." Certainly God would not thus warn us unless there were danger.

In the light of these principles, all the texts may be harmonized; as, for instance, Romans 9:18-23. In this scripture is set forth God's sovereign power, His right to do, His long-suffering and kindness. It does not mean that Pharaoh was born for the purpose of destruc-

tion, but God brought him to the throne in order that He might
show His power and glory through him. Pharaoh had the privilege
of having the Lord's power and glory shown by his being obedient
to God and helpful to God's people, just as Nebuchadnezzar did.
He would not do it, and therefore he went down under the mighty
hand of God. Yet equally the glory and power of God were shown.

Romans 8:28-30 simply shows this,—that God is able to carry
through to the very end all those who will yield to Him and submit to His plans and ways. Looked upon in the right way, election
is a very comforting matter indeed; looked upon in the wrong
way, it is discouraging.

Cruelty of David. 2 Sam. 12:29-31.

> Explain why David was so cruel. 2 Sam. 12:29-31.
> Has any church a right to do likewise?

The American Revised Version, on verse 31, reads as follows:
"And he brought forth the people that were therein, and put them
under saws, and under harrows of iron, and under axes of iron,
and made them pass through the brick kiln: and thus did he
unto all the cities of the children of Ammon." Some commentators
believe that while this was very cruel, yet it was almost justified by
the cruelty and wickedness of the Ammonites. But we cannot
justify ourselves by any mistakes that anyone has made in the
past. David did wrong when he caused the death of Uriah the
Hittite, but that does not excuse us; and he did a very wrong
thing when he committed adultery with Bath-sheba, but that is
no excuse for us.

There are others who contend that the translation above is not
a right translation, that, instead of putting them "under saws,"
it should be translated "*to* the saw." So Young translates, "And
the people who are in it he hath brought out, and setteth to the
saw, and to cutting instruments of iron, and to axes of iron," etc.
That is, he set them to laboring at that kind of work—made them
servants, so to speak. Spurrell renders, "And he brought forth the

people who were therein, and set them to serve with saws, and
with harrows of iron, and with axes of iron, and caused them to
pass under service in the brickkiln." Boothroyd renders, "And
he brought forth the people that were therein, and put them to
saws, and to harrows of iron, and under axes of iron," etc., and
then defends at some length this rendering, and utterly repudiates
the idea of representing David as sawing and harrowing and
chopping and burning the Ammonites. He contends that here,
as in 1 Chronicles 20:3, the words imply that David put them *to*
the saw, and sentenced them to other hard works of slavery; and
he refers to the Latin translation as a justification of this.

The "Companion Bible," in a note on verse 31, tells us that
"under" is "equivalent to 'with,' especially to 'work with.' The
Hebrew letter 'beth,' prefixed as a preposition, is equivalent to 'in,'
'within,' 'with.' When the preposition 'under' is equivalent to
'beneath,' then it is either a part of a verb, or one of four distinct
words. . . . 'Beth,' when translated 'under,' is only in the sense
of 'within,' as 'under (or within the shelter of) the wing,' or 'under
(or within) the earth.' Otherwise, used with a tool, or weapon, or
instrument, it always means 'with.' See 'with an ax' (Deut. 19:5;
Jer. 10:3); 'with axes' (Jer. 46:22; Ezek. 26:9; Ps. 74:6); 'with
nails and with hammers' (Jer. 10:4)," etc. On "pass through the
brickkiln," he says: " 'Pass through,' equivalent to 'pass by,' or
'before,' the Hebrew *abar,* as in Ezekiel 37:2; 46:21; Deuteronomy
2:30; Exodus 33:19; 1 Samuel 16:8, 9, 10, etc. 'Brickkiln,' equivalent to brickwork; hence, brick pavement or paved area (Revised
Version, margin). Not brickkiln; no brickkilns in Palestine. All
bricks there are sun-dried. Only once spoken of as burnt—as
being a strange thing (Gen. 11:3 and margin). Hebrew *malben*
occurs only here, Jeremiah 43:9, and Nahum 3:14, the former at
'entry' of royal palace, the latter said to be 'fortified.' Both out of
the question, and quite incongruous for a brickkiln. The very
paved area of Jeremiah 43:9 was discovered at Tahpanhes by
Flinders Petrie in 1886, where Nebuchadnezzar did exactly what
David did here and in chapter 8:2 and in 1 Chronicles 20:3. 'Thus
did he,' that is, as in 2 Samuel 8:2, with Moab, so here; he caused

the captives to pass by before him, he seated on a pavement of brickwork, or paved area, where he appointed them to the various departments of labor for which they were suited. Compare Jer. 43:9-11. These were the 'strangers' (that is, foreigners) and the 'abundance of workmen' referred to in 1 Chronicles 22:2, 15." This will certainly show that David was not cruel, but rather kind, to a nation that had been so wicked as had the Ammonites. But even if David had been so, that certainly would be no excuse for any church to do likewise. David was engaged in regular war between nations; but religious persecutions have almost invariably been for conscience' sake, against an utterly inoffending class, who were simply doing what they believed God wanted them to do in the way of teaching and believing. And God has not committed that judgment to man. See John 12:47, 48.

Salvation of Children.

1. Does the Bible teach that all children of godly parents under the age of accountability, or the age of deciding for themselves, will be saved?

2. If so, are they included in the 144,000 of the last generation?

3. Is it possible for a mother alone to meet outside influences and train her children aright without Sabbath school or church privileges?

1. The Bible does not deal, in its conditions, with those not responsible; but the affirmative to the first question, it seems to us, is self-evident. See Deut. 30:19; 1 Cor. 7:14. If children have not sinned against God, surely He will not hold them responsible. Jesus saves all from Adam's sin irrespective of character. Children have no sins of their own to condemn them. Will not the blood of Christ avail for them? We may safely leave all these things with God.

2. In the opinion of the writer, no. The 144,000 will have had an especial experience which children could not have. These children and others may stand with this representative company,

but not be numbered with them. In other Bible numberings, women and children are not included in the numbers, yet they stand with those numbered.

3. No, it is not possible for a mother alone to train her children for God, whatever the surroundings; but united with God, she has all power. It takes more than mortal power to save and mold the souls of children. First of all, let the mother give her children to God; then let her with Him train them for Him, prayerfully, perseveringly, hopefully.

Then if she does not have public Sabbath school and church privileges, she may have both within her home, at which she may be assured of heavenly attendants.

"The Kingdom of Heaven Suffereth Violence."

> Please explain Matthew 11:12: "From the days of John the Baptist until now the kingdom of heaven suffereth violence, and the violent take it by force."

The teaching is clear that when John came and began to preach his tremendous gospel of repentance, there was mighty earnestness manifested by those who heard. Men were strenuous in their effort to make things right and enter the kingdom. Some evidently were feeling that unless such effort was put forth, they would not be saved. "The kingdom of heaven suffereth violence," or, as the margin reads, "is gotten by force,"—not that men were slain, or that this violence was put forth against men. It was not manifested in strife. Those who accepted the Lord Jesus had calmer, sweeter rest in place of strife.

Gifts and Invitation Without Repentance.

> What is meant by Romans 11:29: "The gifts and calling of God are without repentance"?

Simply this: God is never sorry for doing any good thing. He calls every sinner to come to Him. He bestows His gifts upon the good and the bad. Some of these gifts are slighted, neglected, rejected, even by His own children; but God is not sorry that He gave them. Men repent of their gifts many times. We hear a man saying he is sorry he did something for such a one, or that he did something else for another one, because they have never been even grateful for it. You hear women regretting that they ever invited, or "called," someone who slighted their invitation. But that is not the true spirit of giving, after all. The soul who gives rightly, who has the true spirit of giving, is more blessed than the receiver, however he regards it; for it is the Master Himself who said, "It is more blessed to give than to receive."

"Voice" and "Sound." Acts 9:7; 22:9.

> Compare Acts 9:7 with Acts 22:9. Both passages relate to the same event, namely, the conversion of Saul. In the latter, Saul is relating the events leading to his conversion as mentioned in Acts 9:7, and says, "They heard not the voice;" while the passage in Acts 9:7 reads, "Hearing a voice."

This is one of the apparently contradictory passages of the Bible which are not contradictory at all if we but take into consideration the widely diversified use of words. "Voice" is used simply of the sound, and also of what it utters. The men who journeyed with Paul heard the sound, but did not understand anything the voice said. The margin of the Revised Version renders "sound" instead of "voice" in Acts 9:7. The "voice" was to them a mere "sound." In Acts 22:9, Paul is speaking of what the voice said. Those who were with him "beheld indeed the light, but they heard not the voice;" that is, they did not understand it, they did not grasp the words. Paul heard not only the sound, but he heard what the voice said. The "sound" was to Paul a clear "voice."

This is well illustrated by John 12:28, 29: "There came therefore a voice out of heaven, saying, I have both glorified it, and will glorify it again. The multitude therefore, that stood by, and heard it, said that it had thundered: others said, An angel hath spoken to Him." Some of them heard only an indistinct sound, like thunder; others knew that words were spoken. Jesus Himself

heard the very words that were said. Looking upon them in
this way, we see there is no contradiction between the two accounts
of Saul's experience. Rotherham also renders "sound" in the
margin of Acts 9:7. Boothroyd renders Acts 9:7, "And the men
who journeyed with him remained silent, hearing a sound, but
seeing no man;" and Acts 22:9, "And those that were with me
saw indeed the light, and were afraid, but they heard not the
words of Him that spoke to me."

"Caught Away Philip." Acts 8:39.

> Will you please give the correct rendering of the
> original word or words, "caught away Philip"? Acts
> 8:39.

This expression is rendered by various commentators, "The
angel of the Lord snatched away Philip." "The Critical and Ex-
planatory Commentary" remarks: "To deny the miraculous nature
of Philip's disappearance is vain. It stands out on the face of the
words, as just a repetition of what we read of the ancient prophets,
in 1 Kings 18:12; 2 Kings 2:16. And the same word (as Bengel
remarks) is employed to express a similar idea in 2 Corinthians
12:2, 4; 1 Thessalonians 4:17. . . . Philip was found at Azotus
—'found himself,' 'made his appearance,' an expression confirming the miraculous manner of his transportation." "The Bible
Commentary" says: "The work of conversion having been completed by baptism, this miraculous withdrawal of the evangelist
confirmed the Ethiopian's assurance of the divine mission of
his teacher. . . . The Alexandrian MS. subjoins, 'And the Spirit
of the Lord fell upon the eunuch, but the angel of the Lord
snatched away Philip.'"

Sin and Crime.

> What is the difference between sin and crime? Is not
> a criminal a sinner?

There is a vast difference between sin and crime. A crime
may or may not be sinful, and a sin may or may not be criminal.

"*Sin* is the transgression of the law," says the inspired word; that is, it is the transgression of God's law, and pertains not alone to outward deed or act, but to the spirit, thought, motive, intent, of the sinner. "The law is spiritual," says the apostle, and therefore may be transgressed in the realm of thought and motive. Not only is he a murderer who *kills* his brother, but he is a murderer who *hates* his brother. See 1 John 3:15. Adultery includes cherished lust. See Matt. 5:27, 28. This is sin.

Crime is transgression of civil law. If there were no law in this country against murder, to kill would not be a crime; but it would be a grievous sin, even as hatred is, which the civil law cannot prohibit. God's law says, "Thou shalt not covet." To transgress it is sin; but civil law could not prevent coveting. Civil law cannot, therefore, make sin a crime; it can only regulate the outward act.

It was a crime for the three Hebrew young men to refuse to bow down to the golden image set up by Nebuchadnezzar (see Daniel 3), but it was not sin; in fact, for them to bow down would have been sin. It was not sin for Daniel to pray to God, but the law of Persia made it a crime. See Daniel 6. Jesus Christ died a criminal, so did Paul, so has the great host of martyrs; but they were not counted sinners in God's sight.

The Word "Worlds." Heb. 1:1, 2.

Does not Hebrews 1:1, 2 show that there are other worlds?

The Greek word from which "worlds" comes in Hebrews 1:1, 2 and 11:3 is *aiōn,* meaning "age." If you will trace the word by means of a concordance, you will find it could be rendered thus in every instance of its occurrence in the New Testament. It is found in Matthew 13:39, "The harvest is the end of the world," or "age," and Matthew 28:20, "Lo, I am with you alway, even unto the end of the world"—"age." Of course, we know that the end of the world, or earth, does not come in either of these cases. What is meant is that we come to that period of earth's history where a great change takes place. And so it was through Christ that God constituted the ages, and by faith we understand that those ages have been marked out, or designated, or consituted. There is other very strong inferential proof which amounts almost to a demonstration that there are other worlds in the universe, but that fact is not stated in so many words. There is a wonderful amount of truth which will come to those who study the plan of God in the light of the ages.

Do All Have a "Chance" for Eternal Life?

Is it not taught that millions of the race have died without God and without hope in the world? that they have never heard the gospel, or heard of the name of Jesus? How can their condemnation be just, if they have never had a chance for eternal life?

Not one single intelligent soul has lived upon this earth since time began but has had sufficient to save him if he would but grasp it. The nineteenth psalm and the tenth chapter of Romans are clear proof of this, as well as the first chapter of Romans. Millions have died without hope and without God; but it was because they put God far away, and would not cherish the hope. The invisible things of God are seen in the visible.

The fact that God is a God of infinite power and wisdom, as revealed in His works, to the logical, thoughtful mind, demonstrates that He is a God of power and of love. Jesus Christ is the true light that "lighteth every man that cometh into the world." To every soul there comes some ray of light. This is shown in the experience of missionaries who have found heathen in the darkest lands living up to all the light they had. It is not knowledge that saves; it is love and loyalty. "The eyes of Jehovah run to and fro throughout the whole earth, to show Himself strong in the behalf of them whose heart is perfect toward Him." They may be heathen who are guilty of many sins of ignorance; but if their heart is perfect toward the little light they have, that light is sufficient to save.

One ray of light followed leads to the center of light. One ray of light from the throne of God followed will lead to God and His salvation. Our English name of Jesus may not be known. The thought is not the name, but the character. That man who has truly grasped the government of God, who sees the bearing of the law of God in the gospel of Jesus Christ, who knows the love of God, knows that the Lord will and has left all without excuse. The idiots, the irresponsible, will die; but the responsible ones will have to give an account of the light which they have had; and every Christian ought to do all in his power to let the light, more light, shine.

The Wicked; the "Narrow Way."

1. What will become of all earth's billions of ignorant wicked?

2. Why did God create the "narrow way" (difficult way) so obscure that few find it; and of the few who do, but a small proportion run to "the end of the race" for the prize?

1. Those who are "willingly ignorant," who are satisfied with themselves, will perish with that which they have chosen. Prov. 1:24-33. Those who receive the light, and follow the light, with all the heart, even though it is but the faintest ray, will have a part in "the inheritance of the saints in light." Col. 1:12. God gives light enough to every man to lead him to salvation. He "lighteth every man that cometh into the world." John 1:9. It is not the amount of light that saves, it is how man uses or treats that light.

2. God has not created the "narrow way" obscure to those who wish to know. Here is an infallible test: *"If any* man *will do His will,* he shall *know* of the doctrine." John 7:17. "The secret of the Lord is with them that fear Him; and He will show them His covenant." Ps. 25:14. "The meek will He guide in judgment: and the meek will He teach His way." Verse 9. But man cannot walk this way in his own strength; and the majority, in their pride, will not accept God's power. If they would but do

it, there is no such thing as fail; for "there is nothing too hard" for God. Jer. 32:17. All rests in the choice, the submission, the trust, of the sinner. To the true follower of Christ, the narrow way is the delightful way.

"Man Proposes; God Disposes."

Exodus 10:29 says that Moses said to Pharaoh, "Thou hast spoken well; I will see thy face again no more;" and Exodus 12:31 says that Pharaoh called for Moses and Aaron by night, and they came to him. Is not this a plain contradiction?

No; Moses meant that he would not call upon Pharaoh or seek an interview with him again. Again and again Moses had gone to Pharaoh himself to ask him to let God's people go. Pharaoh dismissed him abruptly, and told him not to come again, and Moses said that he would not. That is all that is implied in his words. Moses simply meant that so far as he was concerned, he would not again seek the face of Pharaoh. Moses was not giving a prophecy of the future; he was simply stating his purpose as God's servant. There is a possibility, of course, of his being mistaken; but so far as his own will was concerned, and his own choice, he would not see Pharaoh again. When he did see the king again, it was because he was especially sent for by the king. The king sought Moses, and not Moses the king. When Moses said, "I will see thy face again no more," God's work for Pharaoh in those respects was over.

"Sabaoth." James 5:4.

Why is "sabaoth" spelled in this way in James 5:4? Does it mean the same as "Sabbath"?

No; this is a different word from "Sabbath." "Sabaoth" is a Hebraism, and means *hosts*. The expression here conveys the thought that the Lord of all the hosts in heaven and earth is the guardian and avenger of the poor who are oppressed by the grasping rich.

15

The Third Heaven. 2 Cor. 12:2.

What is the third heaven spoken of in 2 Corinthians
12:2? I had always supposed that there was but one
heaven. What are the other two?

2 Corinthians 12:2-4 makes clear that the third heaven is the
place where God dwells. The apostle was caught up to the third
heaven; and giving further explanation of it, he says that he
was caught up to Paradise, and heard words which it is not
possible (margin) for a man to utter. In Revelation 2:7, we are
told the tree of life is in the midst of the Paradise of God; and
in the twenty-second chapter of Revelation, we are told that the
river of life proceeds from the throne of God, and that on either
side of the river is the tree of life. Putting these texts together,
we learn that Paradise is where the tree of life is, and that the tree
of life is on either side of the river of life, which proceeds from
the throne of God. So it would seem very plain, from these scriptures, that the third heaven, or the Paradise of God, is the place
where God Himself dwells.

There have been a great many speculations concerning the
heavens. The Jews had a list of seven heavens; the Mohammedans
also have the same. The Scriptures, as shown in the foregoing,
are quite clear in telling that the third heaven is where the throne
of God is, but they make no mention of anything beyond that.
Nor do they make mention of a first and a second heaven, and
therefore they do not specifically tell what God regards the first
and the second heaven to be. But in the first chapter of Genesis,
it is stated that "in the beginning God created the heaven and the
earth," also that He made the firmament. It has been usually
considered, by Bible students, that passages of this character refer
to the first and the second heaven, or to the atmosphere that
surrounds this earth, as the first heaven, and then the planets of
our system, and possibly the nearer stars, as forming the second
heaven, while the third heaven is the place in His great universe
where God Himself dwells. This distinction, however, cannot
be based upon definite Scripture statements which say in just

so many words what the first and the second heaven are; but we do have the foregoing clear Scripture teaching as to what the third heaven is. What God has so clearly revealed is the thing that we should accept and dwell upon, and there may not be particular value in speculating upon what He has not revealed.

Men have brought endless and useless discussions and strifes into the Christian world by trying to teach doctrines which could not be found plainly revealed in the Sacred Book.

Jacob and Esau.

> I cannot understand why God should love Jacob better than Esau, for Jacob and his mother were deceitful, and told a lie. Why should God bless him more than Esau?

We do not know how many lies Esau told. The Lord does not tell us that. It has been Satan's special object to get God's people to commit sin. This has ever been true; and the devil must have planned pre-eminently to destroy Jacob, the one through whom the promised Seed should come.

But it is worth while to know that in the great choice which the two brothers made—an eternal choice, a choice involving eternal character—unconverted though Jacob was, he stood for God's plan. The birthright was everything. Esau was willing to sell it for a mess of pottage. Jacob longed for it above everything else; and, being unconverted, he was willing to use any worldly means he could to secure it. We find, however, his humble and heartfelt repentance following. As he returned from Syria and met Esau, he could tell the Lord that he was unworthy of the least of all His mercies. In his wrestling with the Angel at the ford Jabbok, the heart of Jacob was emptied and yielded to God forever; and as a result, we find the change of his name, indicative of the change of character. No longer should his name be called Jacob, the supplanter, but Israel, the prevailer with God. See Gen. 32:22-30.

It is character, then, to which God refers in saying, "Jacob have I loved, but Esau have I hated." The passage is first found in

Malachi 1:2, 3. But we can readily see, by reading the context, that it has reference not to Jacob as an individual, but to Jacob as a people, and Esau as a people. The reason why God loved the one was because the one sought Him and followed Him. The other not only turned away from God, but turned their hands against every man.

Neither does it mean, by "hate," that God cherished evil feelings against Esau. The Lord, through His own prophet, Isaiah, pleads, "Look unto Me, and be ye saved, all the ends of the earth." And Esau is included among those whom the Lord would save.

It is well for us to remember that these persons who stand out in the Old Testament are frequently taken for types of character, as for instance, Cain and Abel, Esau and Jacob, Ishmael and Isaac, Jezebel and Elijah. To remember this will help us to understand some of the references made to them in later scriptures.

What Is Usury?

> What is usury? Nowadays I understand that it is unlawful interest; but does not the Bible teach us, in Exodus 22:25; Psalm 15:5; Ezekiel 18:8, and parallel passages, that it is increase?

The word itself means compensation for use. When God gave His people the land of Canaan, all had sufficient. They were dependent for their existence upon the land, not upon loaning money. They were therefore forbidden to loan money to their poor brethren, and charge for the use of it. But when a person is dependent upon his money for his living, and has but a limited amount of it, it seems to us perfectly proper that those who borrow his money in order to get increase should pay the owner of the money a reasonable interest. Conditions now are vastly different from those in Palestine under the Lord's rule. Yet, according to God's word, a well-to-do or rich man should never charge a poor and worthy brother interest, nor should he charge anyone exorbitant interest. The same principle of just and generous dealings exists now as then.

Cain and His Wife. Gen. 4:16, 17.

> Will you please explain Genesis 4:16, 17? And who
> was Cain's wife?

Cain deserved to die, but the Lord reserved to Himself the
execution of that punishment. Therefore God "appointed a sign
for Cain, lest any finding him should smite him." Verse 15,
A. R. V. Then Cain became a wanderer, for "the land of Nod"
means "the land of wandering." His wife was his own sister,
one of Adam's daughters. Many years may have elapsed between
verses 16 and 17.

"Accursed From Christ."

> Kindly explain what Paul meant in Romans 9:3.
> Did he really mean he wished that he did not know
> Christ, because his brethren did not know Him?

This scripture reads as follows: "I could wish that myself
were accursed from Christ for [or in behalf of] my brethren, my
kinsmen according to the flesh." Paul's longing for the salvation
of his brethren was so intense that he would be willing to lose
eternal life himself, if by so doing he could accomplish the salvation of his people — not that he was desirous of being cut off
himself from Christ, unless his brethren would be benefited thereby.
He felt his whole being swallowed up in the salvation of his
people. Moses manifested a similar spirit when, in his deep
remorse for the sin of the children of Israel, he said, "Yet now, if
Thou wilt forgive their sin —; and if not, blot me, I pray Thee,
out of Thy book which Thou hast written." Ex. 32:32.

The Garden of Eden. Gen. 2:8-10.

> Where was the Garden of Eden planted?

All that we know about it is that it was upon this earth. These
rivers mentioned in Genesis 2 would make it seem almost as
though the Garden of Eden were located in Asia; but the names
are there given because of their meaning and not as proper

names to indicate locality. The world at that time was different from what it is now, or has been since the Deluge. How much change took place, of course, we cannot say; but the apostle Peter tells us that men in speculating over these things willfully forget that "there were heavens from of old, and an earth compacted out of water and amidst water, by the word of God; by which means the world [*cosmos,* arrangement] that then was, being overflowed with water, perished." 2 Peter 3:5, 6. Now if the "arrangement," or the *"cosmos,"* that then was perished, we certainly have no right to endeavor to use the present cosmos, or arrangement, of the earth's surface as proof of where some locality was then.

Pharaoh's Free Will. Ex. 9:12.

How could Pharaoh let Israel go if God was hindering him?

But Pharaoh *did* let Israel go. Now if he could do it at last, he certainly could have done it at first. Only by withdrawing His Spirit does God harden anyone's heart; and He does not withdraw His Spirit until men reject Him. It was God's desire that Pharaoh, like Nebuchadnezzar and Cyrus, should be converted. The Lord brought that king to the throne that His power might be manifest and the glory of His name spread abroad. And if the king had yielded to God, this would have been the case. God would have used Egypt mightily, even as He did Babylon and Persia. Every request that Moses made of the king was reasonable (Ex. 4:23; 5:1; 8:1, etc.); and the plagues brought upon Egypt were to show Pharaoh and his people that the gods in which they trusted were nothing. Note also that it was not till all hope was gone that God "hardened Pharaoh's heart" by withdrawing His Spirit. In Exodus 4:21 the Lord declares there will come a time when He will harden the king's heart, but this does not take place till all hope is past. Ex. 9:12. Previous to that (Ex. 7:13, 22), "Pharaoh's heart was strong;" (Ex. 8:15, 32), "he made heavy his heart;" (Ex. 8:19), "Pharaoh's heart was strong;"

(Ex. 9:7), "was stubborn" (A. R. V.; margin, "heavy"). But when even the magicians could not stand before Moses, and the king was still stubborn against the Spirit of God, God withdrew His Spirit, left the king to himself, and thus fulfilled what He had said. Ex. 9:12.

Children of Ham. Gen. 10:6-20.

> Is there good authority for the statement that the Negroes are the descendants of Ham? If so, is it probable that it was the result of the curse pronounced upon Canaan by Noah? It does not seem possible that God would allow what seems so unjust a thing, especially when Canaan had nothing to do with it, and it was the result of Noah's drunkenness.

Yes, the Negroes are descendants of Ham, as you will learn by tracing the ethnological branches of the Hamitic branch of Noah's family. See Gen. 10:6-20. They spread abroad to the south, and inhabited Africa. God's curse upon Canaan was not an arbitrary one; it was the simple declaration of what would come upon Ham's descendants as the result of the father's weakness of character. Noah's drunkenness was doubtless accidental, through ignorance; but Ham's sin was a revelation of low character, which, transmitted to his children, would make them the weakest branch of his family. Yet from that curse there always has been and is redemption in Christ Jesus.

Origin of Races. Genesis 10.

> Will you be so kind as to give your opinion as to where the black and colored races sprang from?

The origin of the races which now people the world is given as definitely in Genesis 10 as in any other book or writing. The idea which you mention of the colored people's descending from Cain is erroneous, for the descendants of Cain were all swept away by the Flood, unless some of them had intermarried with the descendants of Seth, the line from which Noah sprang. Genesis

10 tells us that Noah had three sons, Shem, Ham, and Japheth. The children of the latter, Gomer, Magog, Madai, Javan, Tubal, Meshech, and Tiras, and their descendants, peopled the north; most of the European nations sprang from them. The sons of Shem — Elam, Asshur, Arphaxad, Lud, and Aram — peopled with their descendants the lands round about Palestine. From Asshur sprang the Assyrians, etc. The children of Israel descended from Shem through Arphaxad. The children of Ham peopled Canaan for a time, and Africa. They were Cush, Mizraim, Phut, and Canaan. From Mizraim sprang the Egyptians, from Canaan the Canaanites, from Cush the Ethiopians, etc. Many of the nations, races, and tribes of the world sprang from a mixture of the above.

Cruelty to Children. Num. 31:13-18; 2 Kings 10.

Please give some light on the following scriptures: Numbers 31:13-18; 2 Kings 10, the commands of Moses as they involved cruelty to children.

It would help us very much to understand these if we would take into account the conditions that existed when Moses gave these commands. Midian had planned to destroy a nation. They had done this under the teaching of Balaam, who sold himself for hire. The nation of Midian itself had gotten to that place where it was tending to evil, and only evil. Had it been allowed to continue, the children and all connected with it would have not only gone to destruction themselves, but would have brought others, doomed to destruction, into the world. And if they had been allowed to work their arts upon Israel unrebuked, both Israel and Midian would have gone to utter destruction. God in His wisdom saw that it was necessary to bring a check to that wickedness, and He did so summarily. Surely, it was mercy to those who were slain, to be slain at that time in their innocency, many of them, rather than to go on in unmitigated, high-handed wickedness, bringing others into the same conditions. It is better sometimes to cut off an arm or a leg than to lose a life.

Moses did not act on his own initiative. God directed him as to what to do, and certainly we can see wisdom in the directions given. We need not necessarily believe, however, that God was in all the work that the overzealous Jehu did, although the worshipers of Baal were doubtless worthy of all they received, for they, too, aimed at destruction. The very religion itself, Baal worship, would even put to death the innocent as a part of its religious service. Baal worship was destroying God's people, and all the other nations with which it was connected; and this summary punishment was brought to save nations from the sad consequences of the cruel and licentious Baal religion. It would have proved a great deal more effective in this case if Jehu himself had been faithful to God, and had not turned to the worship of the calves.

False Prophets Used by God.

How could the Lord speak through such men as Balaam, and the prophet in 1 Kings 13:11?

God uses the very best instruments He has at hand always. Balaam was once evidently a true prophet of God. Through his foretelling of events, temptation came to him. Kings and noted men were willing to pay him. They had seen that after he uttered curses, curses followed; and where he blessed, blessings followed. So Balak tempted him by offering him great riches; yet God guarded the prophet, covetous though he was, so that he spoke His truth. Balaam afterward sought to earn his ill-gotten gain by corrupting Israel, or giving advice to Balak as to how Israel might be corrupted through idolatrous women; but in the wars that followed, Balaam himself was slain.

The disobedient prophet was destroyed because he trusted a brother prophet. The Lord does not declare that His children are infallible. Moses made his mistake. We even have the case of the Lord's using the wicked high priest of the Jews. See John 11:50. "It is expedient for you that one man should die for the people, and that the whole nation perish not," was what Caiaphas said. The verse following: "Now this he said not of himself: but being high priest that year, he prophesied that Jesus should die for the nation." God used him; and so He always uses the very best material that He has at hand. All that He has to use for the salvation of humanity among humanity, is imperfect humanity. It is only God who could thus use them.

Time of Egyptian Plagues. Ex. 7:15; 9:31; 10:15.

Is there any record to show the length of time that passed *between* the plagues that fell on the Egyptians, as recorded in Exodus?

This can be ascertained to some extent by the study of the text together with a knowledge of climatic and crop conditions of Egypt. When the plagues began, the Nile must have been high, as the land was soaked with water; the plague of flies, when the waters were abating; of storm and tempest upon the growing, early crops; of locusts upon those which revived from the hail and sprang up later. All the cattle of Egypt which were attacked died; that is, such as were in the field. It is reasonable to suppose that many Egyptians gathered their cattle in. And after this plague it is reasonable to suppose that they took of the Israelites' cattle. The plagues seem to have lasted nearly or quite a round of the seasons.

Seeing God Face to Face. Num. 14:14.

Please show the harmony between the statement made in Exodus 33:20, that no man should see God's face and live, and that in Numbers 14:14, which declares that the Lord is seen face to face.

The passage in Exodus 33:20 has reference to God and His ineffable glory. Moses pleads, "I beseech Thee, show me Thy glory;" and Jehovah answers, "I will make all My goodness pass before thee," but "thou canst not see My face: for there shall no man see Me, and live." That is, no man in his mortal, sinful condition could look upon His face and live. It was for this very reason that God manifested Himself in His Son. That Son took upon Himself the form of a servant, and, while the character of God was in Him, yet the glory of that character was veiled in the position which He assumed,—in the ancient times, in the form of an angel; after His incarnation, in the form of a man. Jacob looked upon Him as an angel (Gen. 32:30), and so also did others; but as the all-glorious Deity no man could or can behold Him until he stands complete in God's image. And there is this distinction made between God the Father and God the Son. No man has beheld the Father; the Son alone reveals Him. Matt. 11:27. So when the Son comes in all the glory of the Father, the wicked will not be able to behold that glory, but will perish in its presence.

Taking an Oath. James 5:12.

Is it right to be sworn? See James 5:12 and Matt. 5:34.

These scriptures forbid *extrajudicial oaths*. There are many persons who seem to think their word will not be believed unless they connect with it some oath, such as "I hope to die;" or they swear by the earth, or by their head, or by some saint or prophet. All these things the Lord tells us are wrong. All extrajudicial oaths are out of place; but when authorities require us to take oath, it is proper for us so to do. Even so Jesus was sworn at the time of His trial. See Matt. 26:63. "I adjure Thee by the living God," was the form of the oath that was put to the Lord by the high priest. Before this Jesus answered nothing; but when the oath was put to Him by the priest, He replied. So we read in Hebrews 6 that the Lord swore by Himself. It is proper on right occasion for the Christian to take oath.

Jephthah's Daughter. Judges 11:31.

Did Jephthah offer his daughter up for a burnt offering?

We do not think he did. One writer says: "The original of Judges 11:31 when properly translated reads thus:

"'And it shall be, that whoever comes forth of the doors of my house to meet me, when I return in peace from the children of Ammon, shall surely be Jehovah's, and I will offer to Him a burnt offering.'

"The vow contains two parts: 1. That person who met him on his return should be Jehovah's, and be dedicated forever to His service, as Hannah devoted Samuel before he was born. 1 Sam. 1:11. 2. That Jephthah himself would offer a burnt offering to Jehovah. Human sacrifices were prohibited by the law (Deut. 12:30, 31); and the priests would not offer them. Such a vow would have been impious, and could not have been performed. It may safely be concluded that Jephthah's daughter was devoted to *perpetual virginity;* and with this idea agree the statements that 'she went to bewail her virginity;' that the women went four times in every year to mourn or talk with (not for) her; that Jephthah 'did with her according to his vow, and she knew no man.'"— *Appendix to Emphatic Diaglott.*

Child and Sinner of a Hundred Years.

> Will you please explain Isaiah 65:20: "The child shall die an hundred years old; but the sinner being an hundred years old shall be accursed"?

The text and the context clearly refer to the end of sin and the entering upon the eternal inheritance. Let us consider what is elsewhere revealed of some of the events of the great day of God.

The great day of God's wrath begins with the close of probation and the pouring out of the seven last plagues.

Under the pouring out of the seventh plague Christ comes, and all the living wicked that are left perish in the presence of His awful glory. See Revelation 14 to 19.

During one thousand years—the "many days" of Isaiah 24:22 —the earth is left desolate; the wicked are dead, and the saints are in heaven with Christ.

At the close of the one thousand years, the "many days," the wicked are raised from the dead, and vindicate God's infinite justice by yielding themselves once more to the deceptions of Satan. He organizes them again into armies, and attempts to take the city of God. Rev. 20:5-8; Isa. 54:15, 17. This is a "little season," as compared with the thousands of years of his existence. Many hold the opinion that this "little season" will be about one hundred years in length.

There will be among these wicked ones the young who have just passed the age of accountability, and have rejected God. There will also be the hardened sinner; and for that period of time they will, by yielding to Satan's control, demonstrate that God has justly rejected them.

Now in the light of these facts read Isaiah 65:17-21. Verses 17-19 present before us the glorious new earth and its capital city, in which sorrow and crying will never enter. See also Rev. 21:1-4.

The next verse gives the reason,—for before that, all the former conditions will have passed away, the premature old man, the abnormally old infant; for at the close of that little season the child of wickedness will die a hundred years old, and the sinner being a hundred years old shall be accursed. And when God's glory appears above that city, they shall all perish in His presence. Rev. 20:9. The age of each is expressed by that period, their resurrection life; their experience in sin by the terms "child" and "sinner."

We do not gather from the scripture that every responsibly wicked child shall live to be just one hundred years old; nor do we believe that the reference is to antediluvian children, some of whom were fathers at sixty-five (Gen. 5:15, 21); but these post-millennial years cover that wonderful period in which God's plan will receive final vindication in justice from all the universe, and every false theory will be determined at its true worth of utter emptiness and falsity. Man's presumptuous claim to inherent immortality, to deityship enthroned, to "divine immanence," to Christ within, whatever the character, will be laid bare, and Christ's words, "No man can come to Me, except the Father which sent Me draw him," and, "Without Me ye can do nothing," are proved forever true.

His word declares that by nature men are "alienated from the life of God," "having no hope," and "without God in the world;" that the only hope in the world is by living faith to grasp God's promises, God's life, and God's regeneration. Those who do this will be saved. Those who do not do this will remain condemned; and God will, in the period which follows the thousand years, demonstrate the truth of His word to all the universe in the negative as well as in the positive. In the negative He will show that the great mass of the wicked will in and of themselves have no desire whatever to worship Him or to do His will. Right in the sight of the glorious city of God, in the face of the fact that they live only by His power, they are deceived by the enemy still to fight against God. Having utterly rejected the law, the gospel, and the Spirit of God, they have no power to repent, no desire to return, no love for righteousness; they have placed themselves utterly outside of the plan of God. Their hearts are wholly carnal. Satan deceives them. He marshals them into armies,—a long and tedious task. He plans the mightiest campaign earth ever knew. He forges, through earth's mightiest artisans, the weapons of hell. But not a soul, whether of morally responsible youth or of mature age, during that period turns to God; and at the close comes the total destruction of sin and all demonstrably identified with it. God will demonstrate His truth in a positive way in the fulfillment of all the blessed promises that He has given to the redeemed. The wicked are forever cut off. Beyond lie the glorious new heavens and earth, which the righteous shall inherit; and from henceforth "there shall be no more curse."

Does God Cause Earthquakes? Ps. 104:32.

> Does God cause the earthquakes and volcanic erup-
> tions? Does God allow Satan to bring harm to His
> people?

To both questions, Yes, and No. All the power there is in the world is from God, and the Source of that power or energy designed that it should always be used for good. Satan and sin have perverted that power, so that God's living law perverted "worketh wrath;" but it always works to the destruction of sin. What God permits, He is often said to do. He permits power to be perverted by rebellion, that men may see that His way only is life and preservation; and in His wisdom He has so ordered things that sin will always work out destruction. He therefore does not cause earthquakes in the sense that they are a part of His plan. They are among the evils which sin has brought, but which God is using to His glory. Yes, He allows Satan to bring temporal and seeming harm to His children. Satan brought it to Job, he brought it to Christ. Are we better than our Master? The harm would be permanent were not our God the living God, and to every soul who trusts Him God will turn all the evil to good. For "we know that to them that love God God worketh all things with them for good." Rom. 8:28, A. R. V.

SCRIPTURAL INDEX

Not all the following texts are explained by any means. Some are used as proof texts, some as illustrations, some as parallel passages to those quoted. The reference is to the *page* in the book.

16

TOPICAL INDEX